Praise for
My Grandfather's Blessings
by Rachel Naomi Remen, M.D.
A Finalist for the Books for a Better Life Award

"Through a series of unpretentious, affecting vignettes, the author of the bestseller *Kitchen Table Wisdom* encourages readers to recognize and celebrate the unexpected blessings in their own lives. . . . She gently illustrates her advice through simple yet powerful stories. . . . [An] exceptional book."

—*Publishers Weekly* (starred review)

"*My Grandfather's Blessings* is a lovely, warm, inspiring book for the soul. From the moment you begin reading the first story, you know that once again, Rachel has succeeded in transmitting truths that bring tranquility to the human spirit."

—Caroline Myss,
bestselling author of *Anatomy of the Spirit*
and *Why People Don't Heal and How They Can*

"This book is a wonder and a gift to the world—which it is sure to bless. *My Grandfather's Blessings* is so full of wisdom, light, and life-changing insight that I found myself reading it slowly, savoring each story, and taking notes so that I could remember that each of us can bless life and thus repair the world just by being ourselves. Let Rachel Remen's stories show you how."

—Christiane Northrup, M.D.,
bestselling author of *Women's Bodies, Women's Wisdom*

"Rachel is a true genius of the heart, mind, and soul. This is one of the most extraordinarily moving books I have ever read, one of the few that really can transform your life. I am a better person for having read it." —Dr. Dean Ornish

"Rachel Remen is both a physician-healer and a masterful storyteller. The stories she tells in *My Grandfather's Blessings* are simple and profound, with healing lessons for all of us."

—Andrew T. Weil, M.D.,
author of *Eight Weeks to Optimum Health*

continued on next page . . .

"Rachel Naomi Remen provides us with stories to savor, stories that remind us of the goodness and wisdom that exist in us all. It is a wonderful book, a pleasure, and a blessing to read."

—Jean Shinoda Bolen, M.D.,
author of *The Millionth Circle*

"A book of great charm and rare wisdom. I felt blessed by these stories."

—Sam Keen,
bestselling author of *Fire in the Belly*

"A triumph of the heart. This book actually heals and inspires as you read. It is a treasure house of great love."

—Jack Kornfield,
bestselling author of *A Path with Heart*

"Yes! It *is* true that serving others, out of love, is both the natural response of the heart and the source of its greatest happiness. People will carry this book around with them, keep it next to their beds, memorize the stories, tell them to folks they meet, and Rachel's grandfather's blessings will continue to nurture, inspire, and sustain in ever-widening circles of blessing."

—Sylvia Boorstein,
author of *It's Easier Than You Think*

"*My Grandfather's Blessings* is an enduring legacy of the heart. The stories are like pearls strung on a thread of light, and as you read them you will slowly recognize them as your own. Never has a book touched me this deeply. It will be a lifelong source of wisdom and blessing as I read it time and again, sharing the stories with my children and grandchildren. This is the best book I have ever read. You will want to give it to everyone you know."

—Joan Borysenko, Ph.D.,
author of *A Woman's Book of Life* and *A Woman's Journey to God*

"This book is a treasure of present moments seized and savored. Rachel's wise and loving voice weaves her grandfather's stories and her own into one seamless story that is, mysteriously, really about each of us. Its resonances can soothe and buoy us in even the darkest of moments. Listen deeply as these magical stories of the ordinary enter your heart and heal you and bless you as they celebrate what is deepest and most beautiful in our lives, and so easily missed."

—Jon Kabat-Zinn, Ph.D.,
coauthor of *Everyday Blessings*
and author of *Wherever You Go, There You Are*
and *Full Catastrophe Living*

"Some books are to be read, others to be saved, and a very few are to be treasured as is *My Grandfather's Blessings*. This book is a reminder of the generation-to-generation transmission of wisdom that used to be commonplace. The stories and parables are true gems."

—Barbara Montgomery Dossey, R.N., M.S.,
author of *Florence Nightingale* and coauthor of *Holistic Nursing*

Praise for Rachel Naomi Remen's *Kitchen Table Wisdom*

"A heartfelt call for change as well as a display of compassionate and courageous thinking."

—*Publishers Weekly*

"Dr. Rachel Naomi Remen is a pioneer in the medicine of the future. With the elegance of simplicity, she shows how physicians can become healers by no longer remaining mere technicians of the human body, but by becoming alchemists of the soul."

—Deepak Chopra, M.D.,
author of *Ageless Body, Timeless Mind*

"Read these gorgeous, from-the-soul stories at the risk of burying cynicism, finding hope, learning a good deal more about life and living—and having a damned good time."

—Norman Lear

"Rachel Remen is one of the most important women of our time. She is an extraordinary combination of wounded patient and highly skilled physician, an intuitively compassionate healer, who is also a gifted author and dynamic speaker. She has had a life-changing impact on me."

—Naomi Judd

"Rachel Remen and her work are pure inspiration. Let her stories heal your heart and soul."

—Christiane Northrup, M.D.,
bestselling author of *Women's Bodies, Women's Wisdom*

"I loved *Kitchen Table Wisdom*. . . . When you read this collection of stories, you will find yourself pausing to remember holy pieces of yourself, when you were awed by the Great Mystery, and glimpsed humanity's relationship to divinity, or felt a deep soul connection with another."

—Jean Shinoda Bolen, M.D.,
author of *Crossing to Avalon*

"A delightfully rich merger of heart-felt love and compassion combined with that quality of mature thought that encourages people to seek the deeper meaning behind the natural dilemmas that make up a human lifetime. . . . Reading this book will only make you feel better, even about the more challenging areas of your life."

—Caroline Myss,
bestselling author of *Anatomy of the Spirit*

"Readers will find themselves again and again knocking on Dr. Remen's kitchen door. . . . Enter. Be welcome. Make yourself at home. This is your kitchen, your table. Come share in this extraordinary outpouring of human wisdom Dr. Remen reveals to us in the mirror of her own boundless heart. Don't let an opportunity like this go by."

—Jon Kabat-Zinn, Ph.D.,
author of *Wherever You Go, There You Are*

ALSO BY RACHEL NAOMI REMEN, M.D.

Kitchen Table Wisdom

Wounded Healers (editor)

The Human Patient

MY
GRANDFATHER'S
BLESSINGS

MY GRANDFATHER'S BLESSINGS

Stories of Strength,
Refuge, and Belonging

RACHEL NAOMI REMEN, M.D.

RIVERHEAD BOOKS
NEW YORK

RIVERHEAD BOOKS
Published by The Berkley Publishing Group
A division of Penguin Putnam Inc.
375 Hudson Street
New York, New York 10014

Book design by Amanda Dewey
Cover design © Tom McKeveny
Front cover photograph © Eiji Yanagi/Photonica

First Riverhead hardcover edition: April 2000
First Riverhead trade paperback edition: April 2001
Riverhead trade paperback ISBN: 1-57322-856-7

The Penguin Putnam Inc. World Wide Web site address is
http://www.penguinputnam.com

The Library of Congress has catalogued
the Riverhead hardcover edition as follows:

Remen, Rachel Naomi.
My grandfather's blessings : stories of strength, refuge,
and belonging / by Rachel Naomi Remen.
p. cm.
ISBN 1-57322-150-3
1. Jewish way of life. 2. Remen, Rachel Naomi—Religion.
3. Ethics, Jewish. 4. Exempla, Jewish. I. Title.
BM723.R46 2000 99-058061
296.7'2—dc21

PRINTED IN THE UNITED STATES OF AMERICA

10 9 8 7 6 5 4 3 2 1

TO

Rachel and Meyer Ziskind
Gruna and Nathan Remen
Sarah (Gladys) and Isidore (Ray) Remen
for the blessing of life,

AND

Esther Newberg
Susan Petersen Kennedy
Amy Beth Hertz
for the chance to bless the life in others.

For Everyone Who Has Been Given
More Blessings Than They Have Received

CONTENTS

IV. The Web of Blessings

V. Befriending Life

INTRODUCTION

OFTEN, WHEN HE came to visit, my grandfather would bring me a present. These were never the sorts of things that other people brought, dolls and books and stuffed animals. My dolls and stuffed animals have been gone for more than half a century, but many of my grandfather's gifts are with me still.

Once he brought me a little paper cup. I looked inside it expecting something special. It was full of dirt. I was not allowed to play with dirt. Disappointed, I told him this. He smiled at me fondly. Turning, he picked up the little teapot from my dolls' tea set and took me to the kitchen where he filled it with water. Back in the nursery, he put the little cup on the windowsill and handed me the teapot. "If you promise to put some water in the cup every day, something may happen," he told me.

At the time, I was four years old and my nursery was on the sixth floor of an apartment building in Manhattan. This whole thing made no sense to me at all. I looked at him dubiously. He nodded with encouragement. "Every day, Neshume-le," he told me.

And so I promised. At first, curious to see what would happen, I did not mind doing this. But as the days went by and nothing changed, it got harder and harder to remember to put water in the cup. After a week, I asked my grandfather if it was time to stop yet. Shaking his head no, he said, "Every day, Neshume-le." The second week was even harder, and I became resentful of my promise to put water in the cup. When my grandfather came again, I tried to give it back to him but he refused to take it, saying simply, "Every day, Neshume-le." By the third week, I began to forget to put water in the cup. Often I would remember only after I had been put to bed and would have to get out of bed and water it in the dark. But I did not miss a single day. And one morning, there were two little green leaves that had not been there the night before.

I was completely astonished. Day by day they got bigger. I could not wait to tell my grandfather, certain that he would be as surprised as I was. But of course he was not. Carefully he explained to me that life is everywhere, hidden in the most ordinary and unlikely places. I was delighted. "And all it needs is water, Grandpa?" I asked him. Gently he touched me on the top of my head. "No, Neshume-le," he said. "All it needs is your faithfulness."

This was perhaps my first lesson in the power of service, but I did not understand it in this way then. My grandfather would not have used these words. He would have said that we need to remember to bless the life around us and the life within us. He would have said when we remember we can bless life, we can repair the world.

My grandfather was a scholar of the Kabbalah, the mystical teachings of Judaism. My parents and my aunts and uncles took a dim view of this study, some seeing it as an embarrassment, a paternal idiosyncrasy, and others as something highly suspect, a sort of dabbling in magic. When he died, the old handwritten leather-covered books he had studied daily simply disappeared. I never discovered what had happened to them.

According to the Kabbalah, at some point in the beginning of things, the Holy was broken up into countless sparks, which were scattered throughout the universe. There is a god spark in everyone and in everything, a sort of diaspora of goodness. God's immanent presence among us is encountered daily in the most simple, humble, and ordinary ways. The Kabbalah teaches that the Holy may speak to you from its many hidden places at any time. The world may whisper in your ear, or the spark of God in you may whisper in your heart. My grandfather showed me how to listen.

One is encouraged to acknowledge such unexpected meetings with the Holy by saying a blessing. There are hundreds of such blessings, each one attesting to a moment of awakening in which one remembers the holy nature of the world. In such moments heaven and earth meet and greet and recognize one another.

There is a blessing that is said whenever one encounters something new and of significance in one's experience. My mother was present at the moment when I met my grandfather. Soon after I was born, she took him to the hospital to see me for the first time in my incubator. She told me that he had stood regarding me in silence through the viewing room window for a long time. I had been very premature. Concerned that he was anxious or even repelled that I was so small and frail, she was about to reassure him when he whispered something under his breath. She had not quite heard and she asked him to repeat it for her. He had turned to her with a smile and said in Hebrew, "Blessed are Thou, O Lord Our God, King of the Universe, who has kept us alive and sustained us, who has brought us whole to this moment." It is a blessing of gratitude for the gift of life, and it was also the beginning of our relationship.

My grandfather was a man of many blessings. These blessings were prescribed generations ago by the great teaching rabbis, and each is considered to be a moment of mindfulness—an acknowledgment that holiness has been met in the midst of ordinary life. Not only are there blessings to be said over food; there are blessings to be said when you wash your hands, when you see the sun rise or set, when something is lost or when it is found, when something begins or ends. Even the humblest of bodily functions has its own blessing. My grandfather was an Orthodox rabbi and he said them all, tipping his black fedora to the Holy many times each day as he dealt with the smallest details of daily life.

I was the child of two dedicated socialists, who viewed all religion as the "opiate of the masses." Although such blessings were never said in my own family, saying them with my grandfather felt quite natural to me. At one time I knew many of them by heart, but I have long since forgotten them. What I have remembered is the importance of blessing life.

When I was young, I seemed to be caught between two very different views of life: my grandfather and his sense of the holy nature of the world and my highly academic, research-oriented uncles, aunts, and cousins. All my grandfather's children were doctors and nurses, and many of their children are as well. As I grew older and time created a greater distance between us, my grandfather seemed to become an island of mysticism in a vast sea of science. Desperate to be successful and make a contribution to society, I gradually put him in the back of my memory with the other things of my childhood. He had died when I was seven. It would be many years before I would make the connection between his ways and the work of medicine. Sometimes if you stay the course long enough, divergent paths reveal themselves to have the same destination. My grandfather blessed life, and his children served life. But, in the end, it has turned out that these may be one and the same thing.

As a young doctor, I thought that serving life was a thing of drama and action and split-second judgment calls. A question of going sleepless and riding in ambulances and outwitting the angel of death. A role open only to those who have prepared themselves for years. Service was larger than ordinary life, and those who served were larger than life also. But I know now that this is only the least part of the nature of service. That service is small and quiet and everywhere. That far more often we serve by who we are and not what we know. And everyone serves whether they know it or not.

We bless the life around us far more than we realize. Many simple, ordinary things that we do can affect those around us in profound ways: the unexpected phone call, the brief touch, the willingness to listen generously, the warm smile or wink of recognition. We can even bless total strangers and be blessed by them. Big messages come in small packages. All it may take to restore someone's trust in life may be returning a lost earring or a dropped glove.

Blessings come in forms as simple as the greeting commonly used in India. On meeting even a total stranger, one bows and says *NAMASTE:* I see the divine spark within you. Here we are too often fooled by someone's appearance, their age or illness or anger or meanness or just too busy to recognize that there is in everyone a place of goodness and integrity, no matter how deeply buried. We are too hurried or distracted to stop and bear witness to it. When we recognize the spark of God in others, we blow on it with our attention and strengthen it, no matter how deeply it has been buried or for how long. When we bless someone, we touch the unborn goodness in them and wish it well.

Everything unborn in us and in the world needs blessing. My grandfather believed that the Holy has made all things. "It is up to us to strengthen them and feed them and free them whenever possible to find and fulfill His purposes for them, Neshume-le," he told me. Blessings strengthen life and feed life just as water does.

A woman once told me that she did not feel the need to reach out to those around her because she prayed every day. Surely, this was enough. But a prayer is about our relationship to God; a blessing is about our relationship to the spark of God in one another.

God may not need our attention as badly as the person next to us on the bus or behind us on line in the supermarket. Everyone in the world matters, and so do their blessings. When we bless others, we offer them refuge from an indifferent world.

The capacity to bless life is in everybody. The power of our blessing is not diminished by illness or age. On the contrary, our blessings become even more powerful as we grow older. They have survived the buffeting of our experience. We may have traveled a long, hard road to the place where we can remember once again who we are. That we have traveled and remembered gives hope to those we bless. Perhaps in time they too can remember this place beyond competition and struggle, this place where we belong to one another.

A blessing is not something that one person gives another. A blessing is a moment of meeting, a certain kind of relationship in which both people involved remember and acknowledge their true nature and worth, and strengthen what is whole in one another. By making a place for wholeness within our relationships, we offer others the opportunity to be whole without shame and become a place of refuge from everything in them and around them that is not genuine. We enable people to remember who they are.

I first learned to do this from people who were dying, people who had moved into a more authentic relationship with those around them because only that which is genuine still had meaning for them. These people had let go of the ways in which they had changed themselves to win approval, and so they made it safe for others to remove their masks as well. Their unwavering acceptance allowed me to remember something almost forgotten. In their presence I realized that many of the ways I had changed myself had made me smaller and in some ways weaker. Parts of myself that I had judged and hidden for years were welcomed and even needed by those who were dying. I felt the life in me blessed by such people; felt it expand to become its real size and shape and power, unashamed. It was a long time before I realized that you do not have to be dying in order to bless others in this way.

Those who bless and serve life find a place of belonging and strength, a refuge from living in ways that are meaningless and empty and lonely. Blessing life moves us closer to each other and closer to our authentic selves. When people are blessed they discover that their lives matter, that there is something in them worthy of blessing. And when you bless others, you may discover this same thing is true about yourself.

We do not serve the weak or the broken. What we serve is the wholeness in each other and the wholeness in life. The part in you that I serve is the same part that is strengthened in me when I serve. Unlike helping and fixing and rescuing, service is mutual. There are many ways to serve and strengthen the life around us: through friendship or parenthood or work, by kindness, by compassion, by generosity or acceptance. Through our philanthropy, our example, our encouragement, our active participation, our belief. No matter how we do this, our service will bless us.

When we offer our blessings generously, the light in the world is strengthened, around us and in us. The Kabbalah speaks of our collective human task as Tikkun Olam; we sustain and restore the world.

As a child I had loved the story of Noah and the Ark the best of all my grandfather's stories. He had given me a coloring book that had pictures of all the animals, two by two, and Noah and his wife, looking much like Mr. and Mrs. Santa Claus but dressed in a different way. We spent hours coloring in this book together which is how, at almost four, I had learned the names of many animals. We had also discussed the story at length, and wondered about the surprising possibility that even God sometimes makes mistakes and has to send a flood and start all over again.

The last picture in the book was a beautiful rainbow. "This represents a promise between God and man, Neshume-le," my grandfather told me. After the flood, God promises Noah and all of us that it will never happen again.

But I was not so easily fooled. This whole thing had started because people had been wicked. "Even if we are very naughty, Grandpa?" I asked. My grandfather had laughed then. "That is what it says here in this story." He looked thoughtful. "But there are other stories," he told me. Delighted, I asked him to tell me another one.

The story he told me is very old and dates from the time of the prophet Isaiah. It is the legend of the Lamed-Vov. In this story, God tells us that He will allow the world to continue as long as at any given time there is a minimum of thirty-six good people in the human race. People who are capable of responding to the suffering that is a part of the human condition. These thirty-six are called the Lamed-Vov. If at any time, there are fewer than thirty-six such people alive, the world will come to an end.

"Do you know who these people are, Grandpa?" I asked, certain that he would say "Yes." But he shook his head. "No, Neshume-le," he told me. "Only God knows who the Lamed-Vovniks are. Even the Lamed-Vovniks themselves do not know for sure the role they have in the continuation of the world, and no one else knows it either. They respond to suffering, not in order to save the world but simply because the suffering of others touches them and matters to them."

It turned out that Lamed-Vovniks could be tailors or college professors, millionaires or paupers, powerful leaders or powerless victims. These things were not important. What mattered was only their capacity to feel the collective suffering of the human race and to respond to the suffering around them. "And because no one knows who they are, Neshume-le, anyone you meet might be one of the thirty-six for whom God preserves the world," my grandfather said. "It is important to treat everyone as if this might be so."

I sat and thought about this story for a long time. It was a different story than the story of Noah's Ark. The rainbow meant that there would be a happily-ever-after, just as in the stories my father read to me at bedtime. But Grandpa's story made no such promises. God asked something of people in return for the gift of life, and He was asking it still.

Suddenly, I realized that I had no idea what it was. If so much depended on it, it must be something very hard, something that required a great sacrifice. What if the Lamed-Vovniks could not do it? What then? "How do the Lamed-Vovniks respond to the suffering, Grandpa?" I asked, suddenly anxious. "What do they have to do?" My grandfather smiled at me very tenderly. "Ah, Neshume-le," he told me. "They do not need to *do* anything. They respond to all suffering with compassion. Without compassion, the world cannot continue. Our compassion blesses and sustains the world."

Recovering a greater compassion may require us to confront the core values of our culture. We are a culture that values mastery and control, that cultivates self-sufficiency, competence, independence. But in the shadow of these values lies a profound rejection of our human wholeness. As individuals and as a culture we have developed a sort of contempt for anything in ourselves and in others that has needs, and is capable of suffering. It is not a gentle world.

As life becomes colder and somehow harder, we struggle to create places of safety for ourselves and those we love through our learning, our skills, our income. We build places of security in our homes and our offices and even our cars. These places separate us from one another. Places that separate people can never be safe enough. Perhaps our only refuge is in the goodness in each other.

In a highly technological world we may forget our own goodness and place value instead on our skills and our expertise. But it is not our expertise that will restore the world. The future may depend less on our expertise than on our faithfulness to life.

Remembering how to bless each other is more important now than ever before. The solution to the destructiveness in this world is not more technical knowledge. Repairing the world may require us to find a deep connection to the life around us, to substitute the capacity to befriend life for our relentless pursuit of greater and greater expertise. It has been said that it has taken us thousands of years to recognize and defend the value of a single human life. What remains is to understand that the value of any human life is limited unless there is something in it that stands for the benefit of others and the benefit of life itself. A woman who lives in Pinson, Texas, sent me a quotation from Exodus that I think my grandfather would have loved: "Build altars in the places where I have reminded you who I am, and I will come and bless you there." The blessing we will receive when we have remembered how to bless life again may be nothing less than life itself.

I have learned a great deal about blessing and serving life from the people that I see in my office, perhaps because cancer forces people so deeply into their own vulnerability that they have touched the place of knowing that we hold such vulnerability in common. Once this is seen, there is no way one cannot respond. I have seen so many people emerge from their encounter with great loss more effortlessly compassionate and altruistic than before that I have come to wonder if blessing life is not a final step in some natural process of healing from suffering. A blessing is a place of refuge, a connecting back to the place in us where we are coherent and whole. A remembering of who we are.

One of my patients, a civil rights lawyer who almost died of cancer, told me several years afterward that this experience had enabled him to discover an unexpected power. "I find something in others that I have found in myself. Something struggling to break through obstacles and live whole," he told me. "I can see its struggle and speak its language. So I can strengthen it"—he paused thoughtfully—"as others have strengthened it in me. My wife tells me that I have finally opened my heart. Perhaps so, but that's not exactly it." He falls silent. "If it didn't sound so odd to say, I guess I can bless the life in other people and be blessed by them. I do it in my work, but it goes beyond my work. It seems just now like the most important thing I can do."

A friend and colleague told me about the first hours after she discovered that her fifteen-year-old son had drowned. She had gone downstairs to get a cup of tea, and another woman, herself shaken by grief, had chided her, asking her how she could drink tea at a time like this. "Up until then, Rachel, I had been a person who was always afraid of doing things wrong, always hesitant and full of self-doubt over the smallest action. But when she spoke to me I suddenly knew that in this I could do nothing wrong: This had struck me to a place of such depth that everything I did or said or thought or felt in response was completely true. This was beyond rules, beyond judgments. This was all mine."

Her healing has taken time, more than eighteen years. She works now with groups of people who have cancer, helping them to move through their grief and losses in order to connect back to the place in them that is coherent and whole. Speaking of this she says, "For me, the loss of my son went from a singular event to something that is woven into the fabric of my being. It is always present to me, part of my work, part of my experience. Having experienced that deep a grief, that suffering, I am no longer afraid to go back there. I have been around it and with it and come through it and I know it very well. I have also somehow survived it. I think the people in my groups know this. They know that I am not afraid anymore. It gives us permission to go to that place of grief or suffering, to acknowledge our losses and their deep significance, if that is where we need to go. I think it brings a kind of safety to the room."

She pauses thoughtfully. "It is also very affirming to return to that place because it is a place that has enormous meaning for me. Sometimes it is as if I get to be with my son again, sometimes in those moments when there is that kind of grief in the room."

The thirty-seven years that I have been a physician have shown me that any of the stuff of our lives—our joys, our failures, our loves, our losses, even our sickness—can become the stuff of service. I have seen people use anything to bless life. There is such a simple greatness in us all that nothing need be wasted.

The power to repair the world is already in you. When someone blesses you, it reminds you a little—untying the knots of belief and fear and self-doubt that have separated you from your own goodness. Freeing you to bless and receive blessings from everything around you.

One afternoon when he was very sick, my grandfather spoke to me of death and told me that he was dying. "What does this mean, Grandpa?" I asked, worried and anxious. "I will be going somewhere else, my Neshume-le. Closer to God." I was struck dumb.

"Will I be able to visit you there?" I said, filled with distress. "No," he told me, "but I will watch over you and I will bless those who bless you." Almost fifty-five years have passed, and my life has been blessed by a great many people since then. Each of you has my grandfather's blessing.

I.

RECEIVING YOUR BLESSINGS

MOST OF US have been given many more blessings than we have received. We do not take time to be blessed or make the space for it. We may have filled our lives so full of other things that we have no room to receive our blessings. One of my patients once told me that she has an image of us all being circled by our blessings, sometimes for years, like airplanes in a holding pattern at an airport, stacked up with no place to land. Waiting for a moment of our time, our attention.

People with serious illness have often let go of a great deal; their illness has created an opening in their lives for the first time. They may discover ways to receive all the blessings they are given, even those that were given long ago. Such people have shown me how to receive my blessings.

Many years ago I cared for a woman called Mae Thomas. Mae had grown up in Georgia and while she had lived in Oakland, California, for many years, she had in some profound way never left the holy ground of her childhood. She had worked hard all her life, cleaning houses in order to raise seven children and more than a few grandchildren. By the time I met her, she had grown old and was riddled with cancer.

Mae celebrated life. Her laugh was a pure joy. It made you remember how to laugh yourself. All these years later, just thinking of her makes me smile. As she became sicker, I began to call her every few days to check in on her. She would always answer the phone in the same way. I would say "Mae, how ya doin'?" and she would chuckle and reply, "I'm blessed, Sister. I am blessed."

The night before she died, I called, and her family had brought the phone to her. "Mae," I said. "It's Rachel." I could hear her coughing and clearing her throat, looking to find breath enough to speak in a lung filled with cancer, willing herself past a fog of morphine to connect to my voice. Tears stung my eyes. "Mae," I said. "It's Rachel. How ya doin'?" There was a sound I could not identify, which slowly unwrapped itself into a deep chuckle. "I'm blessed, Rachel. I am blessed," she told me. Mae was one of those people. And so, perhaps, are we all.

Martin Buber reminds us that just to live is holy. Just to be is a blessing. If Buber is right, what keeps us from receiving life's blessings? It is not always so simple a thing as a lack of time. Often we may not recognize a blessing when it is given, or we may have ideas about life that keep us from experiencing what we already have. Sometimes we become frozen in the past or unaware of the potential in the present. We may even come to feel entitled to what has been given us by grace. Or we may become so caught up in what is missing in the world that we allow our hearts to break. There are many ways to feel empty in the midst of our blessings.

We can bless others only when we feel blessed ourselves. Blessing life may be more about learning how to celebrate life than learning how to fix life. It may require an appreciation of life as it is and an acceptance of much in life that we cannot understand. It may mean developing an eye for joy. It is not necessary to sit in judgment in order to move things forward, and our anger may not be the most potent tool for change. Most important, it requires the humility to know that we are not in this task of restoring the world alone.

Larry knew none of these things. He and his wife had been coming to see me as a couple for a few months. His wife came to their final appointment alone. "Where is Larry?" I asked her. "He got a call from Washington," she told me. "He was still on the phone when I left." "But didn't he promise to take Wednesdays off?" I asked. She looked at me and just smiled. "I'm leaving," she told me. "I thought if I could get him here, he might focus on me and the kids long enough for me to tell him."

My heart sank. I had met Larry ten years before when he was first diagnosed with non-Hodgkin's lymphoma. He was twenty-nine at the time, a young stockbroker with a promising future. Two words from a doctor had taken all that away. Larry and his wife had fought back. Deeply in love, they had supported each other through a year of brutal chemotherapy. Their children were small, and there was much to live for. But eight months after his chemotherapy was complete, the cancer returned. This time Larry had a bone marrow transplant. Back then one out of two people who underwent this procedure died. Larry took this chance because he loved life fiercely. And he was one of the lucky ones.

He emerged from this treatment a changed man. "There is more to life than making money," he had told me back then. Convinced that his life had been spared for a reason, he felt he had to use his time to make a difference. He left the world of business and began working in the new field of conservation.

Over the next ten years, conservation became a nationwide movement, and Larry became a man possessed. He began working a fifty-hour week. And then a sixty-hour week. Now he traveled almost constantly and, when he was at home, worked far into the night by fax and e-mail. He ate and slept irregularly. Months went by without his having a talk with his children, an evening with his wife, or any time for himself. He lived on the edge of burnout. But there was always something more to be done, another project, another cause. His wife and children had been lonely at first, but gradually they had built a life without him.

"Tell him that I would like to see him," I told his wife.

She nodded. "I'll tell him after I give him the news," she said.

Larry came in a few days later. He sat down wearily in the chair opposite. I was shocked at his appearance. "Carol said you wanted to talk with me."

"Yes," I said. "She told me she was leaving."

"Yes," he replied. "She told me, too."

He began to cry. "Ten years ago, I was losing my life," he told me. "I didn't lose it then, but I've lost it now."

"What was it like for you back then?" I asked him.

"Desperate," he said. "Life was slipping through my fingers. I felt that I was running out of time." He paused. "I still feel that way," he told me. "The world is dying. We may not have another chance."

We sat looking at each other in silence. My heart ached for this good man. "When was the last time that you ate with your family?" I asked him.

He shook his head. "I don't remember."

"Or the last time you went to sleep without setting an alarm clock?" He shook his head again. "Do you remember the last time that you played a game or read a story to your children?"

"I don't remember," he said softly.

"Larry, would you treat a spotted owl in this way?" He looked down at the floor and shook his head. I saw that he had begun to cry again.

"I don't think I can go on," he said.

I told him that I understood how important his work was. Silently he nodded. "Has serving life made you happy?"

He looked at me, confused. "How can serving life make you happy?" he asked me. "Service requires sacrifice."

But perhaps not. One of the fundamental principles of real service is taught many times a day aboard every airplane in the United

States. Larry, who flies more than a million miles every year, had heard it hundreds of times without recognizing its relevance to him. It is the part just before takeoff when the stewardess says, "If the cabin loses pressure, the oxygen masks will fall from above. Put your own mask on first before you try to help the person next to you." Service is based on the premise that all life is worthy of our support and commitment. For Larry, this was true of every life except his own.

If I wished to defeat those who wanted to use their lives to make a difference, this is exactly the way in which I would go about it. Few such people would be tempted from their purpose by fame, or power, or even by wealth. But I could confuse them and stop them in just the same way Larry found himself stopped. I could use their own dedication against them, driving them to work until they became so depleted and empty that they could no longer go on. I would make certain that they never discovered that blessing life is about filling yourself up so that your blessings overflow onto others.

BLESSING

On Friday afternoons when I would arrive at my grandfather's house after school, the tea would already be set on the kitchen table. My grandfather had his own way of serving tea. There were no teacups and saucers or bowls of granulated sugar or honey. Instead, he would pour the tea directly from the silver samovar into a drinking glass. There had to be a teaspoon in the glass first, otherwise the glass, being thin, might break.

My grandfather did not drink his tea in the same way that the parents of my friends did either. He would put a cube of sugar between his teeth and then drink the hot tea straight from his glass. So would I. I much preferred drinking tea this way to the way I had to drink tea at home.

After we had finished our tea my grandfather would set two candles on the table and light them. Then he would have a word with God in Hebrew. Sometimes he would speak out loud, but often he would close his eyes and be quiet. I knew then that he was talking to God in his heart. I would sit and wait patiently because the best part of the week was coming.

When Grandpa finished talking to God, he would turn to me and say, "Come, Neshume-le." Then I would stand in front of him and he would rest his hands lightly on the top of my head. He would begin by thanking God for me and for making him my grandpa. He would specifically mention my struggles during that week and tell God something about me that was true. Each week I would wait to find out what that was. If I had made mistakes during the week, he would mention my honesty in telling the truth. If I had failed, he would appreciate how hard I had tried. If I had taken even a short nap without my nightlight, he would celebrate my bravery in sleeping in the dark. Then he would give me his blessing and ask the long-ago women I knew from his many stories—Sarah, Rachel, Rebekah, and Leah—to watch over me.

These few moments were the only time in my week when I felt completely safe and at rest. My family of physicians and health professionals were always struggling to learn more and to be more. It seemed there was always more to know. It was never enough. If I brought home a 98 on a test from school, my father would ask, "And what happened to the other two points?" I pursued those two points relentlessly throughout my childhood. But my grandfather did not care about such things. For him, I was already enough. And somehow when I was with him, I knew with absolute certainty that this was so.

My grandfather died when I was seven years old. I had never lived in a world without him in it before, and it was hard for me. He had looked at me as no one else had and called me by a special name, "Neshume-le," which means "beloved little soul." There was no one left to call me this anymore. At first I was afraid that without him to see me and tell God who I was, I might disappear. But slowly over time I came to understand that in some mysterious way, I had learned to see myself through his eyes. And that once blessed, we are blessed forever.

Many years later when, in her extreme old age, my mother surprisingly began to light candles and talk to God herself, I told her about these blessings and what they had meant to me. She had smiled at me sadly. "I have blessed you every day of your life, Rachel," she told me. "I just never had the wisdom to do it out loud."

WRESTLING WITH THE ANGEL

SOMETIMES A WOUND is the place where we encounter life for the first time, where we come to know its power and its ways. Wounded, we may find a wisdom that will enable us to live better than any knowledge and glimpse a view of ourselves and of life that is both true and unexpected.

Almost the last story that my grandfather told me was about a man called Jacob who had been attacked in the night as he slept alone by the bank of a river. He had been traveling, and when he had stopped to make his meal and settle down to sleep, the place had seemed safe enough. But it was not so. He awakened to find himself gripped by muscular arms and pinned to the ground. It was so dark that he could not see his enemy, but he could feel his power. Gathering all his strength, he began to struggle to be free.

"Was it a nightmare, Grandpa?" I said hopefully. I often suffered from nightmares back then and had to sleep with a nightlight on. I moved closer to my grandfather and took his hand. "No, Neshume-le," he answered, "it was quite real but it happened a long time ago. Jacob could hear his attacker's breath, he could feel the cloth of his garments, he could even smell him. Jacob was a very strong man, but even using all of his strength he could not free himself and he could not pin his enemy down either. They were evenly matched and they rolled on the ground and struggled fiercely."

"How long did they struggle, Grandpa?" I asked with some anxiety.

"A long, long time, Neshume-le," he replied, "but the darkness does not last forever. Eventually it was dawn and as the light came, Jacob saw that he had been wrestling with an angel."

I was astonished. "A real angel, Grandpa?" I said. "With wings?"

"I don't know if he had wings, Neshume-le, but he was definitely an angel," he told me. "With the coming of the light, the angel let go of Jacob and tried to leave, but Jacob held him fast. 'Let me go,' the angel told Jacob, 'The Light has come.' But Jacob said, 'I will not let you go until you bless me.' The angel struggled hard, for he wanted badly to escape, but Jacob held him close. And so the angel gave him his blessing."

I was very relieved. "Did he leave then, Grandpa? Is that the end?" I asked. "Yes," my grandfather said, "but Jacob's leg was hurt in the struggle. Before the angel left, he touched him on the place where he was hurt." This was something I could understand; often my mother did this, too. "To help it get better, Grandpa?" I asked. But my grandfather shook his head. "I do not think so, Neshume-le. He touched it to remind Jacob of it. Jacob carried it all the rest of his life. It was his place of remembering."

I was very puzzled by this story. How could it be that one might confuse an angel with an enemy? But Grandfather said this was the sort of thing that happened all the time. "Even so," he told me, "it is not the most important part of the story. The most important part of the story is that everything has its blessing."

In the year before he died, my grandfather told me this story several times. Eight or nine years afterward, in the middle of the night, the disease I have lived with for more than forty-five years declared itself in the most dramatic way imaginable. I had a massive internal hemorrhage. There was no warning at all. I was in a coma and hospitalized for months. The darkness and the struggle lasted for many years afterward.

Looking back on it, I have wondered if my grandfather, old and close to the time of his death, had not left me with this story as a compass. It is a puzzling story, a story about the nature of blessings and the nature of enemies. How tempting to let the enemy go and flee. To put the struggle behind you as quickly as possible and get on with your life. Life might be easier then but far less genuine. Perhaps the wisdom lies in engaging the life you have been given as fully and courageously as possible and not letting go until you find the unknown blessing that is in everything.

THE SHELL GAME

THE CAPACITY FOR spiritual experience is so universal that every language has its name for it: the Atman, the Neshuma, the Ra, the Purusha, the Ruach, the Divine Spark. The Seneca called it the Orenda; the great Christian mystic Meister Eckhart called it the Godseed. We call this capacity the soul. The soul is the basis for the value of every human life, and the foundation of our experience of wholeness and integrity, despite physical change. It may also be the source of our healing.

It is only recently that illness and healing have been defined in terms of the body. At the beginnings of medicine, the shamans, or medicine men, defined illness not in terms of pathology but in terms of the soul. According to these ancients, illness was "soul loss," a loss of direction, purpose, meaning, mystery, and awe. Healing involved not only the recovery of the body but the recovery of the soul.

Listening to people with cancer as their physician and living with my own chronic illness have shown me a great deal about the power of illness to draw the soul and its issues closer. These experiences have shown me that the soul is not just a human capacity; in times of loss, illness, and crisis, it is a human need. At such times, spirit is strength.

The language of the soul is meaning. We may first discover the soul when life events awaken in us the need for meaning. In serious or chronic illness, even people who have never considered this dimension of experience before instinctively reach for a personal meaning in events that have disrupted their lives. Meaning helps us to see in the dark. It strengthens the will to live in us.

In the sixties when I went to medical school, the meaning of illness was seen as irrelevant. We did not know then that there is a healthy way to have a disease, a way to use this difficult experience to come to know more intimately who we are and what is important to us. Our focus was on cure and not healing. Science and its expertise cures, but often it is meaning that heals us. Such healing is highly individual. The same disease means something different to every person touched by it. Over time, meaning heals many things that are beyond cure.

Finding meaning does not require us to live differently; it requires us to see our lives differently. Many of us already live far more meaningful lives than we know. When we go beyond the superficial to the essential, things that are familiar and even commonplace are revealed in new ways. Meaning may change the way we see ourselves and the world. People who have felt themselves to be victims may be surprised to realize they are heroes.

Through illness, people may come to know themselves for the first time and recognize not only who they genuinely are but also what really matters to them. As a physician, I have accompanied many people as they have discovered in themselves an unexpected strength, a courage beyond what they would have thought possible, an unsuspected sense of compassion or a capacity for love deeper than they had ever dreamed. I have watched people abandon values that they have never questioned before and find the courage to live in new ways. Often these ways are more soul-infused.

When I first became ill with Crohn's disease more than forty-five years ago, I felt profoundly diminished, different, and even ashamed. I had not known then that what challenges the body can evolve and strengthen the soul. I had focused on the curing of my disease and despaired when this was not possible. It took years for me to recognize the movement toward wholeness that was happening in me while my attention was elsewhere.

THE SPICE OF LIFE

IN 1944, WHEN I was almost seven, I found one of my uncle Frank's books on reproductive physiology. My uncle was a physician, a general practitioner, and the book was a standard medical textbook. The words were far too difficult for me, but the pictures were clear enough for even a six-year-old to understand. What they showed was surprising. I tore several of the pages out of the book and took them to school to show my friends. We were in the first grade.

As a result of this, my mother was called to school by the principal in the middle of her workday and I was made to wait alone on a bench outside his office until she arrived. Something like this had never happened before and I felt bad. My mother was a nurse and her job was helping sick people. I could not understand why she had to stop helping people and come to school right away.

Soon after she arrived, this became quite clear. The principal was very angry with me. Bringing us both into his office, he told my mother what I had done and demanded that I apologize to the children who had seen the pictures and that she write a letter of apology to their parents. He also demanded that I be punished.

I was frightened by his tone of voice, but my mother was not intimidated in the least. She asked the principal to explain exactly what I had done wrong. His voice shaking, he commanded me to tell her what I had told my classmates. She listened carefully to my very simple description of sexual intercourse and looked at the pictures I had shown the other children. Then she looked at the principal. "I don't understand the problem," she told him in a very even tone of voice. "It's true, isn't it?" Afterward my mother had asked me to apologize to my uncle for tearing the pages out of his book. Hearing the whole story, he had laughed.

Despite my family's lack of concern, I had felt shamed by the incident in a way that I could not easily talk about. If I had not done anything wrong, why had the principal been so angry? My whole family seemed to know about it. I suspected that even my grandfather had been told, and I was certain that he had not heard of such things before either. For the first time, I was afraid to ask him questions, and I became deeply unhappy.

Several weeks after this incident at school, he and I had a discussion about the Sabbath, the day when God tells people to stop work. People are expected to shed all the pressures and worries and concerns of being a person, like clothing that is too tight, and go home to be with those they love and with God. "Every day we are required to support our lives, to earn food and shelter, to help each other. It is hard work, Neshume-le. And so God rewards us each week with the Sabbath. On the Sabbath, we rest," said my grandfather.

This was not how things were done in my home, and I wanted to know more. "When is it Sabbath, Grandpa?" I asked him. He told me that the Sabbath begins at sundown on Friday night and ends at sundown on Saturday night. I thought about this for a while. "Does it end with bedtime stories?" I asked him.

He laughed. "No, Neshume-le, it ends with blessings and prayers. And people light a special candle which is really three candles that have been braided into one." He reached out and lifted one of my own thick braids. I had never seen such a candle, and I wondered if people braided it the same way my mother braided my hair every morning. I was intrigued. "Why do they light this candle, Grandpa?" I asked him. "This has been done for such a long time that nobody alive remembers," he told me. "But I think it is to help us remember that we have thoughts and feelings and bodies and that all three can kindle and nourish the light of the soul."

I thought about this for awhile and about what he had said about the Sabbath. "Are people very sad when it is over and they have to go back to work?" I asked him. He smiled at me and asked me to bring him the little wooden box that always stood on his library table. It was shaped like a castle, perhaps eight inches high, a wonderfully carved thing with many tiny open windows and turrets and little wooden flags flying. It made you happy just to look at it. As I brought it to him, I noticed that it smelled faintly sweet.

He held it in his hands, and his face grew still. For a moment, it seemed to me that his thoughts were far away. I leaned against his chair and waited. After a while, he looked at me fondly. "This little box is filled with fresh spices," he told me, and he opened it. I could smell the delicious smell of cinnamon. "At the end of the Sabbath, a box of spices like this is passed from hand to hand and everyone breathes in the fragrances of the earth." I was puzzled. "Why, Grandpa?" I asked. His eyes twinkled, and he said that perhaps it was to help people not be sad, to remind them that while the Sabbath is beautiful and peaceful and holy, the things of the world are beautiful and holy too.

"This world is not all work, Neshume-le," he told me. "God has made life joyful. There are joys like dancing and eating and seeing and hearing that we can only experience here on earth. And there is the special joy that people give to one another with their bodies." I looked at him suddenly, feeling a flush of shame. He continued on. I was glad that he had not noticed.

"You know, when you hug your friends, how your hearts meet?

How sweet that moment is? Well, there is something even sweeter. When grown-ups hug in a special way, their souls can meet." Once again he looked over the top of my head, seeing something faraway. "That joy is one of God's greatest blessings, Neshume-le," he told me softly. Although he never said another word about it, something gray and heavy in my heart simply melted away. Not only did my grandfather know about the things in Uncle Frank's book but God knew about them, too. So it must be all right.

About a year later, my grandfather died. I was in his study shortly afterward and noticed that the little wooden castle was no longer on the library table. In the distress that surrounded his death, I forgot to ask about it, and then I simply forgot it.

The mystery of the spice box was solved many years later by my mother after she, too, had grown old. She was reminiscing about her childhood, speaking to me about her mother, my grandmother Rachel. She told me that Rachel had been a very beautiful woman and that my grandfather had been deeply in love with her for all of their marriage. "But he never spoke of her," I said.

"No, he didn't," my mother replied. "He was a very private man."

Her parents had lived their married life according to the laws of Orthodox Judaism. For two weeks of every month, a married couple sleeps together in the same large bed. For two weeks after the beginning of the wife's menses, she sleeps alone in a small bed at the foot of her marriage bed. At the end of this time of separation, she goes with other women to the Mikvah, the ceremonial baths, to renew herself by bathing in the living waters and saying prayers. That night she will again sleep in her husband's arms.

When she returned home from the baths to resume the physical side of her marriage, my grandmother faced a common problem. Orthodox law forbade her husband to look directly at her, and both her religion and Victorian modesty made speaking of sexuality simply out of the question. My mother's eyes met mine. "So women of her generation found their own ways to tell their husbands they would once again be together," she said.

The evening after she returned from the Mikvah, my grandmother Rachel would go to the study where my grandfather was as usual deeply engrossed in the study of the Talmud or the Kabbalah. Without saying a word to him, she would take the spice box from its customary place on the shelf and place it on the library table next to his hand. I could imagine my grandfather as a young man, never lifting his eyes from the holy book and smiling. "When he had finished studying, he would come upstairs to their bedroom bringing the spice box with him," my mother said tenderly. "We children always knew."

Deeply touched, I looked at my mother. "Did it look like a little castle, Mom?" I asked her. She smiled and nodded. I told her that I remembered seeing it on the library table when I was small and asked her what had become of it. She gave me the sort of look that only women exchange. "It's with your grandfather," she told me. "He wanted us to bury him with it."

My grandmother had died young, long before I was born. She had left the spice box with him for almost twenty-five years. But he had finished studying now and come upstairs. Their separation was over and once again he would sleep in her arms.

LOT'S WIFE

ENID WAS AN older woman whose husband had died unexpectedly two years before she came to see me. Withdrawn and distant, she had not cried or spoken of his death to anyone in all that time. She no longer cooked or looked after her garden or her house. Most of the time she sat in her bathrobe in the living room, looking out the window at nothing at all. She had been given antidepressants by her doctor but they had not made much difference, and after a while she had simply stopped taking them. "They won't bring him back," she had said. She had been brought to see me by one of her daughters who told me, "I lost both my parents the day my father died."

At first Enid and I sat and looked at each other in silence. She was a lovely woman in her early seventies, but she seemed as lifeless as the chair she sat on, as if she were only the wrapper that had once enclosed a life. She seemed so fragile that I wondered if she would have the strength to stay the full hour.

I opened the conversation by asking her why she had come. "My husband has died," she replied, turning her head away from me to look out my window. "My daughters would like me to talk about it, but I do not think that I care to." When I gently asked her to say more about this she said simply, "Talking seems a waste of time. No one could possibly understand."

I nodded in agreement. "Yes, of course," I said. "You have lost your life. Only your husband could understand what you have lost.

Only he knew what your life together was like." At this she turned back to look at me. Her eyes were gray, like her hair. There was no light in them. I nodded again. "If he were here, Enid, what would you tell him?" I asked her.

She considered me for a long moment. Then she closed her eyes and began to speak to her husband aloud, telling him what life was like without him. She told him about going to their special places alone, walking their dogs alone, sleeping in their bed alone. She told him about needing to learn to do the little things he had always taken care of, things she had never known about. She reminded him of times that only he would remember, old memories that no one else had shared. And then for the first time since he died, she began to cry. She cried for a long time.

When her tears stopped, I asked her if there was anything she had not said. Hesitantly she told me how angry she was with him for abandoning her to grow old alone. She felt as if he had broken a promise to her. She missed him terribly and all that he had brought into her life.

"He was a teacher of love for me," she told me. The child of rigid and suspicious people, she had been amazed at her husband's selflessness, his readiness to extend his hand to others, even to strangers. She told me story after story of his generosity, his kindness, her eyes looking beyond me to the past. "Herbert always went the extra mile," she said. "So many people loved him."

I was deeply touched by Herbert and by the woman he had loved. "Enid," I asked her, "if Herbert were here, what would he say to you about the way you have lived the last two years of your life?" She looked startled. "Why, he would say 'Enid, why have you built a monument of pain in memory of me? My whole life was about love.' " She paused. Then for the first time I saw the hint of a smile. "Perhaps there are other ways to remember him," she said.

Afterward she told me that she had felt that if she let go of her pain, she would betray Herbert's memory and diminish the value of his life. She now saw that she had indeed betrayed him by holding on to her pain and closing her heart. She never came back to see me again. Herbert had told her everything that she needed to hear.

Every great loss demands that we choose life again. We need to grieve in order to do this. The pain we have not grieved over will always stand between us and life. When we don't grieve, a part of us becomes caught in the past like Lot's wife who, because she looked back, was turned into a pillar of salt.

Grieving is not about forgetting. Grieving allows us to heal, to remember with love rather than pain. It is a sorting process. One by one you let go of the things that are gone and you mourn for them. One by one you take hold of the things that have become a part of who you are and build again.

About a year after this meeting, Enid sent me a clipping from the local paper about a group of widows she had organized to help elderly people with the tasks they could not do for themselves in their homes. There was no note with the clipping, just a tiny one-breath poem she had written and signed: "Grief. / I pull up anchor, / and catch the wind."

HAVING WHAT YOU HAVE

THE MIDDLE DRAWER of my mother's dresser was filled with silk stockings, dozens of pairs in many exquisite colors, each wrapped in its original package from the store. They had never been worn. I used to love to pull a chair up to the open drawer and touch them, counting the packages and admiring the beautiful colors. Once I asked my mother why she never wore them. She told me that they were too good to wear, if she wore them they would get torn or otherwise damaged and they could not be replaced. It was wartime, and all the silk in the United States had been diverted into making parachutes. She was saving them, she said, for a special time.

Each year in August we would go away to a little rented cottage on Long Island to escape the hottest part of the summer, leaving our apartment in Manhattan empty. One year when we came home we found that the apartment had been burglarized and ransacked. I remember walking through the rooms behind my parents, shocked to find many of our family's things missing and others broken and thrown all over the floor. But the most shocking thing was in the bedroom. My mother's dresser drawers hung open. The middle one was completely empty.

This was my first serious lesson about loss. At the time, I was always being scolded by my teachers for not taking better care of my things. But my mother had taken very good care of her stockings. She had never even used them. I puzzled about this for a long time.

This happening had a profound effect on us all. My father bought more locks for our doors, and every place we ever lived afterward had at least three locks on every outside door. But this did not seem to answer my questions. Eventually I began to use everything I owned.

An elderly patient who had outlived his entire family once told me that all we get to keep are our memories. Perhaps the only way we get to keep anything may be to use it up. More than fifty years later, I still think about those stockings with regret. Perhaps we are all given many more blessings than we receive.

LETTING GO

A WOMAN WHOM I have never actually met sent me a letter about a story I had told during a talk that had touched her very personally. It was the story of a man who could not take care of himself because he saw taking his medication as tantamount to surrendering to the authority of his cancer. He had seen his cancer as a black hole that was constantly trying to pull him in. It took all his strength to resist this pull. When he imagined himself letting go and being drawn into this hole, in its darkness he found a profound healing.

As soon as she heard this, she realized that there was just such a hole in the middle of her own life. This surprised her greatly, but it was unquestionably true. Many of her behaviors and ways that had seemed merely eccentric now made a new kind of sense. Her own cancer had been successfully treated almost a decade ago. She had thought it a part of her past. But she realized now that this was not entirely the case.

For many years she had not bought a really *good* pair of shoes, the kind that last, as if perhaps she might not get to wear them out and they would be wasted. She made vacation plans with her family a year in advance but always bought her clothes at the very last minute as if it was not until then that she could be sure that she might actually take the trip. And she had put off having expensive dental work done many times for no good reason at all. She had never really looked at any of this before.

Now that she had noticed it, she felt a sort of undertow, a pull to the past that had kept her from fully living her life. "Enough is enough," she thought and so, closing her eyes in the middle of the lecture, she imagined the hole and allowed it to pull her in.

At first she experienced being in endless darkness. It seemed to her that she was falling, but before she could become frightened she realized that this was not true. In this total darkness there was no "up" or "down," and she was simply floating in a vast, softly dark space. Tentatively at first, she did a cartwheel to her right. And then another. And then one or two to the left. Something new began to grow in her, and she allowed it to send her into a series of somersaults head over heels. She felt a sudden rush of freedom and began to laugh softly to herself. As she continued to dance weightless in the darkness, this sense of freedom grew until she kicked down hard with both her feet. It seemed to her, this sent her upward, faster and faster, a great joy growing in her until suddenly she was gone, exploding into a million bright sparks of joy that fell, like a rain, into the hearts of people everywhere. Slowly she opened her eyes. She felt totally at peace.

"I do not know what all this means," she wrote, "but things seem a little different. Perhaps it is just fanciful. All I can say is this week I bought a pair of Italian shoes. They were very expensive. I have them on now. I just wanted you to know."

OWNING

LONG AGO, THE little son of my friends and I became quite good friends ourselves. A lot of the time we played with his two tiny cars, running them from windowsill to windowsill, parking them and racing them and telling each other all the while what we imagined we passed "on the road." Sometimes I would have the one with the chipped wheel. Sometimes he would have it. It was great fun, and I loved this little boy dearly.

At that time these little Hot Wheels cars were avidly collected by most six-year-old boys. Kenny dreamed of them and I yearned to buy him more, but I could not think of a way to do this without embarrassing my friends. Kenny's father was an artist and a lay preacher, and his mother was a housewife who brought beauty to everything she touched. They lived very richly indeed but they had little money.

Then one of the major gas companies began a Hot Wheels giveaway: a car with every fill-up. I was delighted. Quickly I persuaded the entire clinic staff to buy this brand of gas for a month, and organized all twenty of us with checklists, so that we would not get two fire engines or Porsches or Volkswagens. In a month we accumulated all the Hot Wheels cars then made, and I gave them to Kenny in a big box. They filled every windowsill in the living room, and then he stopped playing with them. Puzzled, I asked him why he did not like his cars anymore. He looked away and in a quivery voice he said, "I don't know how to love this many cars,

Rachel." I was stunned. Ever since, I have been careful to be sure not to have more Hot Wheels than I can love.

Many people have too many Hot Wheels to love. It can make you feel empty. A woman who found a new life after having cancer once told me that before she became sick she had always felt empty. "That's why I needed to have more and more things. I kept accumulating more and more goods, more and more books and magazines and newspapers, more and more people, which only made everything worse because the more I accumulated the less I experienced. 'Have everything, experience nothing.' You could have put that right on my front door. And all the time I thought I was empty because I did not have enough."

The change had started with a bathrobe, one of the few things she had taken with her to the hospital for her cancer surgery. Every morning, she would put it on, really enjoying how soft it was, its beautiful color, the way it moved around her when she moved. Then she would walk in the hall. "One morning as I was putting it on I had an overwhelming sense of gratitude," she told me. She looked at me, slightly embarrassed. "I know this sounds funny, but I felt so lucky just to have it. But the odd part, Rachel, is that it wasn't new," she told me. "I had owned it and worn it now and then for quite a few years. Possibly because it was one of the five bathrobes in my closet, I had never really seen it before."

When she finished chemotherapy, this woman held a huge garage sale and sold more than half of what she owned. She laughs and says that her friends thought she had gone "chemo-crazy," but doing this had enhanced her life. "I had no idea what was in my closets or what was in my drawers or on my bookshelves. I did not really know half the people whose home numbers were in my phone book either, Rachel. Many of them never even sent me a card. I have fewer things now and know fewer people, but I am not empty. Having and experiencing are very different. Having was never having enough."

We sat together for a few minutes, watching the sun making shadows on the office rug. Then she looked up. "Perhaps we only *really* have as much as we can love," she said.

KEEPING IT TOGETHER

As a part of a research study, I once asked seventy-three physicians to rank order the same list of twenty-one life-values twice, first according to what was most important to them in their work, and then according to what was most important to them personally. The list included values such as admiration, control, wisdom, competence, love, power, compassion, happiness, fame, success, and kindness.

None of those who responded made two identical lists, and often the two lists were strikingly different. Kindness, for example, might be number two on someone's list of personal values and number fifteen on their list of desirable work values. Competence might be someone's number-one professional value and come in dead last on their personal list. Many people were dismayed to discover that they lived in one way and believed in quite another. The task had made them aware of this difference for the first time. In discussing these outcomes, a surprising number of physicians said that they did not think that it was possible to live by the values that were personally important to them. As one man put it, "Life diminishes you." But, of course, only with your permission.

What is true of these doctors is, I think, true of us all. The experience of sacrificing integrity to expediency is one that many people have daily. Countless people with cancer have told me that they have not spoken their truth to others for years out of fear of rejection or some other form of loss or because they find themselves living or working among people who see things differently than they do. They have become invisible in order to survive or maintain the status quo. But when we do not live coherently with ourselves, something begins to erode in us. We may survive, but we will never be whole or fully alive.

Perhaps losing integrity with yourself is the greatest stress of all, far more hurtful to us than competition, time pressure, or lack of respect. Our vitality is rooted in our integrity. When we do not live in one piece, our life force becomes divided. Becoming separated from our authentic values may weaken us. This may be why, when people's lives are challenged by significant illness and they instinctively begin to gather their strength, their values are often among the first things that change.

It has been surprising to see how often people do not realize that their deepest values are as personal as their fingerprints. Not knowing this, many of us have sacrificed certain things in order to have other things that we have been told are more important. Some of the things we have let go of in order to be seen as successful may be far more important to us personally in the end than some of the things we have held on to or even fought for. Sometimes it takes a wake-up call like cancer to bring us back to ourselves. The crisis of illness may shake us free of the life that we have created and allow us to begin a return to the life that is our own. Often what then turns out to be important is not a surprise at all. One patient, a CEO diagnosed with cancer, told me, "I always knew what mattered. I just never felt entitled to live by it before."

When Harry discovered he had colon cancer, he was the administrator of a large insurance company. The first in a family of farmers to attend college, he had excelled academically almost from the start. He was known in the industry as a driving, politically sophisticated, and ambitious man whose career was his whole life. His cancer had been caught early, and his prognosis was excellent. Everyone had expected him to be back in his office as soon as his scars had healed. But two days after he returned to work, Harry resigned. It had taken everyone by surprise.

His company had suspected that he had received a better offer, but this was not the case. Harry did not work for about a year. Then he bought a vineyard and moved his family to it. He has been growing grapes and making wine for the past five years.

"From the moment that I awoke from that surgery, Rachel," he told me, "I knew beyond a doubt that I was living someone else's life. There had been so much pressure to succeed from my family; they were so proud that I had escaped from the hard life that we had led for generations. I got caught up in the challenge of it all at first, wondering if I could do it, and then I just kept pushing it. Somewhere in the process, I stopped listening to myself. My father was a farmer and my grandfather and my great-grandfather. My father had hated this work, but I am a different sort of man; I understand the land and it matters to me. I know this work as I know myself. I belong here in a way that I never belonged anywhere else."

We sat on the deck of his home, looking over a vast green sea of grapevines gently moving in the wind. Pink roses grew along his fence lines. Double indemnity and corporate life were another world. As if reading my thoughts, he turned to me with a rueful smile: "My favorite saying used to be 'My way or the highway.' I was so proud to be living personally and professionally on my own terms. It was hard to see that I had sold myself out so completely that I had not even noticed."

Integrity is an ongoing process, a dynamic happening over time that requires our ongoing attention. A medical colleague describing his own experience of staying true to himself told me that he thinks of his life as an orchestra. Reclaiming his integrity reminds him of that moment before the concert when the concertmaster asks the oboist to sound an A. "At first there is chaos and noise as all the parts of the orchestra try to align themselves with that note. But as each instrument moves closer and closer to it, the noise diminishes and when they all finally sound it together, there is a moment of rest, of homecoming.

"That is how it feels to me," he told me. "I am always tuning my orchestra. Somewhere deep inside there is a sound that is mine alone, and I struggle daily to hear it and tune my life to it. Sometimes there are people and situations that help me to hear my note more clearly; other times, people and situations make it harder for me to hear. A lot depends on my commitment to listening and my intention to stay coherent with this note. It is only when my life is tuned to my note that I can play life's mysterious and holy music without tainting it with my own discordance, my own bitterness, resentment, agendas, and fears."

Deep inside, our integrity sings to us whether we are listening or not. It is a note that only we can hear. Eventually, when life makes us ready to listen, it will help us to find our way home.

AT THE END OF THE DAY

In 1998 Commonweal, the center at which I work, installed a labyrinth exactly like the one that has been in the cathedral at Chartres since 1300. The labyrinth is a walking meditation in the form of a circular pattern that lies on the floor of a room as large as a gymnasium. A narrow path weaves back and forth within this large circle, and a person, walking very slowly, follows this path as it doubles and redoubles back upon itself until eventually it reaches the center of the circle. The distance from start to center and back is about a third of a mile.

Walking the labyrinth is deceptive. At the beginning one seems to be heading directly for the center when one is actually farthest away from it, and moments before reaching it one is walking near the outermost edge of the circle. Among other things, walking the labyrinth causes you to confront the world of illusion, the difference between our hard-edged perception of how the world works and how the world works. It can be a humbling experience. It often creates in people a willingness to look past the familiar evidence of their eyes and a greater ability to hope for that which is unseen.

Many insights can be gained in this walking meditation. The first time I stood in the center, I had an odd thought. Lying around me was the path I had walked from the beginning with all its complexity, frustrations, and many turnings. It was complete, and I suddenly realized that, despite my experience to the contrary, I had always been heading for the center. Perhaps this was true of my life as well. Could events that seemed meaningless, or even wasteful, be taking me to a destination as surely as the twisting and turning path I had just followed? Perhaps my path only seemed random because I was still on it. At the end, from the center, would I someday see my life as complete and whole and recognize a hidden direction and pattern that redeemed loss and failure and pain and utterly changed their meaning and value?

Perhaps this is the perspective that death will afford us, that moment when we stand squarely in the mystery that is at the heart of our life. Many people have told me that death has been associated with a greater clarity for them. Some of these are people who themselves are near to death. Others are husbands and wives, children and friends who have found, after someone's death, that something familiar yet previously unrecognized has been seen clearly for the first time. Often it is only as a life becomes complete that the pattern which upholds it, its underlying meaning, can become visible.

The son of a patient of mine came to see me in the weeks after his father's death. Their relationship had been a troubled one, the son being an adventurous and radically innovative artist and the father a conservative and careful businessman, whose opinionated ways had angered his son from adolescence. In reflecting on his father, he spoke of these differences:

> I keep thinking of the aggravating things he used to say—"Look before you leap," "Fools rush in where angels fear to tread"—and how cautious he was about any sort of risk. As I was growing up, it seemed to me that every step I took forward had to be tested against his skepticism. I recently sold a huge show to a major museum and after my presentation to the board, one of the trustees came up and said, "How could

we have refused you? You had anticipated and solved every one of our objections. Your thinking about the risk of it was so seamless that we had to go along." In that moment, I saw my dad in a completely different way. Because of him, I have become expert at putting solid foundations under my dreams.

I am a builder of new ideas and new forms. I had not realized that Dad was a builder, too, because what he built was foundations: foundations of values, foundations of financial security. He was rigid, but a good foundation has to be rigid. Like a compass, he always pointed due north. His "north" was security and caution. I had thought that his pointing meant that this was the direction I needed to take, that he wanted me to take. I think I was mistaken. What it meant was that this was due north and I could orient my own direction from the constancy of it. He never failed me.

I was talking about this to my mother, who suggested I read Gibran's poem from *The Prophet,* the one on children. The last paragraph broke me up. He talks about not being able to follow your children or even understand them because they belong to the future that you can never visit, not even in your dreams. Then he compares parents to the bow and children to the arrows. He says to the parents, "Let your bending in the archer's hand be for joy. For as He loves the arrow that flies, so too He loves the bow that is stable." "The bow that is stable." I cried when I read that. That was my old man. He was the foundation under my dreams.

He fell silent for a few moments. Then he smiled at me. "I guess I didn't really get it until he was gone."

REMEMBERING

SOMETIMES WE LIVE in ways that are too small, and in places that focus and develop only a part of who we are. When we do, the life in us may become squeezed into a shape that is not our own. We may not even realize that this is so. Despite this, something deep in us that holds our integrity inviolate will find ways to remind us of the breadth and depth of the life in us and assert its wholeness.

In 1962, when I was one of few women in my medical training program, the feminine was something, by and large, collectively denied not only by my male colleagues but by my female colleagues as well. I and no one around me saw being a woman as a strength, and I did everything possible to make my gender difference invisible.

In the first year of my training, I was randomly assigned to a house staff team with several star players, all men. I greatly admired the skills and competence of my fellows and was delighted to be a part of this team. Once when we had struggled through a long night in an inner-city emergency room, dealing with seizures, beatings, and one heart-stopping automobile accident involving three small children, my senior resident turned to me as we were walking, exhausted, toward the elevators that would take us to the doctors' quarters. Shamefacedly, he confessed that he had not wanted me on his rotation but that now that I was here he was glad that I had been assigned to him. "You are as good as anyone on the team," he told me. "Working with you is just like working with any of the other guys."

Although I was careful to appear unmoved by his words, inwardly I was overwhelmed. It was a treasured moment in my professional life. It would be a long time before I stopped seeing it as a compliment. For the next ten years or more, there was little in my professional experience that spoke to me of my wholeness or honored it in any way. And as I had not realized I had lost it, I did nothing to defend it.

When I was thirty-one years old, I received a powerful reinforcement of the way I was living; I was appointed Associate Director of the Pediatric Clinics at Stanford, my first position of real authority within the medical system. I now had an office of my own with my name on the door and a tiny budget to buy a few items of professional furniture. Thrilled, I had gone shopping for a lamp and a chair.

In a lamp store I had found a little porcelain statue of a slender Asian woman spilling water from a flask onto the ground. The minute I saw it, I knew that I had to have it for my office. It matched my new rug perfectly. But my budget had no leeway for such a thing, and I had left without it. That night I dreamed of the statue. In my dream the porcelain woman called out to me, begging me not to leave her behind. For some reason, this had a powerful effect on me, and I awoke feeling anxious and distressed. Even though it meant no movies or dinners out for the rest of the year, I went back and bought the little statue out of my own slender funds.

There was no free shelf space in my office, and so I stood the statue on my desk next to the phone. It was there for many years. Often I would hold it in my hand while I was working through some of the more complex decisions about the clinic and its large staff or returning the calls my patients had made to me. When I left the university, it was one of the only things I took with me. It was mine. Everything else in the office belonged to Stanford.

Shortly before I left, I had discovered that the little statue was an image of Kwan Yin, the goddess of compassion, sometimes described as the feminine aspect of the Buddha. Despite a lifelong effort to cast myself in another mold, something in me had recognized her instantly and had claimed her for my own. I had held her close to me long before my conscious mind knew who she was and that in a profound way she represented my healing.

Symbolism is the language of the unconscious mind, the deep wisdom that is part of how we are made. Sometimes the unconscious talks to itself and occasionally shares its wisdom aloud in the form of symbols. Many things we do without thinking are ways the unconscious reminds us of our larger nature. It may take many years before we can draw the sword from the stone personally and know who we are. Before that time, our integrity may reach out without our knowing to parts of ourselves that have been denied and disowned, to feed them and strengthen them until we can come back for them.

GETTING REAL

In 1972, Stanford's medical school pioneered in offering students a course on human sexuality. The first session of this course was several hours long and consisted of watching, nonstop, dozens and dozens of films on every sort of sexual practice. Some were funny, some were sad, a few were elegant, others crude, but all were graphic. By the end of the day, sexuality had become as banal as eating dinner. The idea, I suppose, was to desensitize future physicians, and help us to talk with patients about sexual issues in a way that was unembarrassed, professional, and personally neutral. Since then, physicians trained at medical schools throughout the country have told me that they have sat through such a day at the movies. Many medical schools take a similar approach even today.

When I think of what it must be like to need to speak of achingly intimate, fragile, and important things to someone who has stripped them of all meaning, I feel sad and diminished. I think that many of us could probably have served people in sexual anguish far better before this session than afterward. It took me many years to recover a sense of the power and mystery of sexuality. For a long while sex seemed absurd, if not ridiculous.

Whereas medical school taught me the banality of sex, American culture taught me that sex is only for the young and perfect, those without a hair on their bodies, a blemish on their skins, a wrinkle, or an extra ounce of fat. Many years ago, I had sat on the beach at Diamond Head in Hawaii, unwilling to take off my robe because six months before, a part of my intestine had been surgically removed and I now wore an ileostomy appliance. All around me powerful-appearing, handsome men sat in small groups, smoking cigars and presumably discussing the market with each other as slender young women many years their junior sunned themselves or played Frisbee in tiny swimsuits. Their bodies were uniformly Barbie Doll perfect, and, watching them, I had been on the verge of tears. Absorbed in their own conversations, the men paid little attention to these women.

About the middle of the afternoon, the curtain of one of the cabanas was pushed aside, and a middle-aged woman with a mane of black curly hair emerged. She was wearing a white suit meant for someone perhaps fifteen or twenty pounds thinner. Very slowly and deliberately and with the utmost confidence, she sauntered across the sand and entered the ocean. By the time she reached the water, all conversation on the beach had ceased and every male eye was on her. Many of the women were looking at her, too. It was my first lesson in the difference between perfection and sexuality.

Real sexuality heals. In its presence I could begin to reclaim my own sense of possibility and wholeness, and I am grateful to this woman for inhabiting her body in this way. Without knowing me at all, she helped me to begin to inhabit my own life. Now more than thirty years later I have seen hundreds of others, people with cancer, reclaim their wholeness by reclaiming their sexuality.

Clare was one of these. In her beige linen suit and white silk blouse, she appeared flawless, competent, and totally in control. In comparison to her elegance, my waiting room looked shabby. When I said her name, she rose and shook my hand. Without another word she followed me into my office and folded herself into a chair, crossing her long, beautifully shaped legs at the ankle.

I settled myself opposite and smiled at her. Without any warning whatsoever, she burst into tears. The contrast between her tears and her self-possession was so extreme that I was caught completely by surprise, and for a moment I was stunned. Then I reached forward and took her hand between my own as she sobbed. We sat like that for a long time, until she had cried enough. Turning a tear-stained face toward me, she commented, "How embarrassing. I have not cried in years."

"These are special times," I said. She nodded. "Would you tell me about it?" I asked her.

She had come because eight weeks before she had undergone surgery to remove her right breast. After much discussion, she and her doctor had made this decision together. She felt certain that it was the right choice, and she had healed nicely. "And how has this been for you?" I asked her. "I don't know," she told me.

She was in her late twenties, unmarried, and successful as a businesswoman. Until her surgery, she had worked out daily and had been very proud of her body. Men had always found her very attractive, and having a man in her life was important to her. She'd had many lovers, mostly colleagues she had met in the business world. "But that is over, now," she told me. "I could never allow anyone to see me disfigured like this." After the surgery, she had ended her relationship with the two men she was seeing. Both had accepted it gracefully and moved on.

No one at work and none of her friends even suspected that she had cancer, she told me. She had done it entirely alone. So obsessed had she been with secrecy that she told everyone that she was going on a vacation to Europe and had even made arrangements to have cards sent to them from abroad. Even her parents did not know. But she was here because the pressure of keeping this secret had become too much, and she needed a place to talk and to be herself. "I can't come very often," she told me. "People would begin to suspect."

"Come whenever you need to," I told her.

For the next few years, I saw her every three or four months. On the surface her life was much as it had been, except that she lived as a celibate, putting all her energy into her work. During one of her infrequent visits I had called this to her attention and asked her if she planned to be alone for the rest of her life. "Only for five years, Rachel," she told me. Seeing my look of surprise, she explained that her oncologist was very conservative. She had picked him because she, too, was conservative. Early on, they had discussed a breast reconstruction. He had encouraged her to put off having this surgery until the fifth anniversary of her diagnosis. "And this is so that any recurrence can be easily seen?" I asked. She nodded her head. "Yes," she said. "After five years the chances are I will be home free."

A little more than a year before this important anniversary, we had one of our sessions. During the hour, she told me that she had gone to an opening at an art gallery and had struck up a conversation with a painter who had asked her to join him for a cup of coffee. "He is a very attractive man, but obviously totally unsuitable as a lover," she told me. "So I said, 'yes.' "

"Because he is unsuitable?" I said, puzzled.

"I thought we could become friends," she had replied. Surprisingly, she had a very good time. "Will you see him again?" I asked her.

"Yes, I think so," she told me. "He is such good company."

Three months later when she returned for another session, Peter's name came up in our conversation over and over again. They had gone to the zoo. She had visited his studio and had been very impressed with his work. By now, she had met many of his friends who were artists and sculptors and found that she liked them very much. It had surprised her to discover that she fit in so well with these people and was even more comfortable with them than with people she knew from her own work. "Perhaps it's because you are creative yourself, Clare," I told her. "Business can be as much of an art form as paint or stone." She thought this over for several moments. She had never seen herself in this way before.

About two months later, she called to schedule an urgent visit. She came into the office looking somber. "It's the end," she told me. Thinking that perhaps she had suffered a recurrence, my heart jumped into my throat. But this was not what she had meant at all. "Peter left a message on my voice mail, inviting me away for the weekend. I will have to tell him now," she said. "It is over."

Relieved, I said, "Perhaps once he knows he might not feel that way about things."

"I doubt it," she replied. "He is exactly the wrong sort of man. Beauty is his whole life. He will be completely repulsed."

"When will you tell him?" I asked, my heart sinking.

"Tonight at dinner," she said.

"Call if you need to," I told her.

I found myself thinking of her all evening, but she did not call. As the weeks went by, I continued to wonder what had happened, but I resisted calling her to see how things went. As was her way, she came in again three months later. In response to my questioning look, she laughed. "I was wrong," she said. "He still wants to be friends."

It turned out that Peter wanted to be more than friends, but Clare had refused. Her body was too ugly, too maimed. "My fifth anniversary is less than six months away and I will have my reconstruction," she told me. "Perhaps then." She went on to tell me her plans. She had scheduled the date of her reconstructive surgery more than a year ago and interviewed several surgeons and some of their patients before deciding on the surgeon she would use. She had arranged vacation time at work. As her insurance did not cover this sort of surgery, she had begun saving the money for it right after her mastectomy and over the past five years had enough put away. It would be very expensive and difficult, but she hoped it would return her to wholeness. She looked down at her hands clasped in her lap for a few minutes. Then she looked up. "I hope it works, Rachel," she said. I was not sure, but I thought there were tears in her eyes.

I did not see her again until a few days before her fifth anniversary. She came in, looking excited and happy. I was delighted to celebrate this milestone with her, and I asked her about the upcoming surgery. She smiled and told me that she had canceled it. I looked at her in surprise. "How come?" I asked her. She returned my look for a long moment. Then slowly she unbuttoned her blouse and shrugged it off her shoulders. She was not wearing a bra, and her left breast was exquisite. But its beauty was overshadowed by the radical change in her body. Her mastectomy scar had been covered over with a mass of tiny, exquisite tattooed flowers. They looked real. In the most delicate of pastel shades, they climbed to the top of her right shoulder. As she turned away from me, I could see that they fell across it and down her back as if scattered by gravity or the wind. She stood, pulling her slacks down over her hips. Her body was beautiful. One little tattooed flower had come to rest in the small of her back, and another lay against her right buttock. Under it was a tiny initial "P." My mouth dropped open in shock, while at the same time I experienced a pang of envy. She was indescribably erotic. Men encountered women like her only in their dreams.

Shrugging back into her blouse and buttoning her slacks, she sat down again, laughing aloud at my look of astonishment. "Isn't it beautiful?" she said. "Peter painted it and we went to Amsterdam to have it done. Then we used the money I had saved for the surgery for a honeymoon. I am so happy, Rachel," she said, blushing slightly. "My husband has convinced me beyond the shadow of a doubt that anything of real beauty is one of a kind."

WHAT MATTERS

MOST YEARS, I give a lecture called "Meaning" to the second-year class at the UCSF medical school. About halfway through the hour, I suggest that the students reflect for a few minutes and find an image that symbolizes for them what the practice of medicine means to them personally. Then we spend the rest of the hour talking.

The deepest meaning often lies below the surface of the conscious mind, and some universal and archetypal concepts will emerge in the discussion of these symbols and images. One year toward the end of the hour, a student volunteered that he had done it wrong and hadn't gotten a symbol at all. Instead he had remembered a phrase of music that he had recognized as a part of Beethoven's Third Symphony. When I asked him what he made of this, he said that he was not sure. Perhaps it was about the ability to overcome physical limitations. Beethoven had written the Ninth Symphony with its extraordinary "Ode to Joy" when he was totally deaf. Maybe others could be helped to overcome their limitations in the same inspiring way.

Although this seemed reasonable enough, meaning lies beyond reason, and I suspected that there might be more to it than this. Deciding to pursue it a little, I asked him when he had last heard Beethoven's Third. He looked at me steadily and his eyes became sad. It had been played four weeks ago at the funeral of his friend who had died in a motorcycle accident. The class became very still.

"What have you learned from your friend's death?" I asked him. He paused. He missed his friend terribly, he told us. Several times in these past weeks, he had reached for the phone to call him and share something with him. Each time, he had remembered, and he had felt his loss anew. He had tried talking with others but it had not been the same. It never would be. He had not thought about it in so many words, but his friend's death had shown him that no one can be replaced. Every life is unique and precious. He sat for a moment in silence on the edge of tears. "I guess this is the bottom line for me," he told us. "If this was not so, none of this stuff we're learning would matter to me at all." We all sat together thinking this over. In the silence, many of us recognized that this was the bottom line for us, too.

When I was small, there was a week when the whole country knew that every human life is irreplaceable. It was many years ago, but, as I recall, a child somewhere in the Midwest fell down an abandoned well, and for a week rescue teams worked to bring her out. This was a time before television, and radios were playing everywhere—in the stores, in the buses, even at school. Strangers met in the street and asked each other, "Any news?" People of all religions prayed together.

As the rescue effort went on, no one asked if that was the child of a professor down there, the child of a cleaning woman, the child of a wealthy family. Was that child black, white, or yellow? Was that child good or naughty, smart or slow? In that week everyone knew that these things did not matter at all. That the importance of a child's life had nothing to do with those things. A person lost touched us all, diminished us all.

And without saying this aloud, we all knew that there was nothing personal in this. That not only was this human life of great value, but our own lives were of equal value. If we ourselves had been down that well, the thoughts and prayers of the whole country would have been with us, too.

If on the occasion of someone falling down a well we all knew this, then we knew it all along. This dramatic crisis had simply allowed us all to remember something true. Then the rescue was completed and we all forgot again. It is really surprising how easy it is to forget that every life matters, that we are each one of a kind and worthy of unconditional love.

TEACHERS EVERYWHERE

I CAN CLEARLY remember something that happened when I was in third grade. I was walking with my mother on a downtown street in New York City, pushing through crowds on our way to I no longer remember where. I had just been put into a special class at school because I had done well on an IQ test, and my new teacher had told us that being in her class meant that we were brighter than most of the people in the country. As we moved through the hurrying crowds, I remembered this and was filled with an eight-year-old's outrageous pride. I told my mother that my teacher had said that I was smarter than most of the people around us. She stopped walking immediately and knelt down so that we were at eye level with each other. As the crowd flowed past us on either side, she told me that every one of the people around us had a secret wisdom; each of them knew something more about how to live, about being happy, about loving than I did.

I looked up at the people passing by. They were all adults. "Is this because they are all grown-ups, Mama?" I asked her, taken aback. "No, darling. It will always be that way," she told me. "It is how things are." I looked again at the crowd moving around us. Suddenly I wanted to know them all, to learn from them, to be friends.

This lesson became lost among the many others of my childhood, but shortly after I became a physician I had a dream that was so powerful that I remembered it even though I did not understand it. In this dream, I am standing in the threshold of a door. I seem to have been standing there a long time. People are passing through the door. I cannot see where they are going or where they have come from, but somehow this does not seem to matter. I meet them one at a time in the doorway. As they pass through they stop and look into my face for a moment and hand me something, each one something different. They say, "Here, here is something for you to keep." And then they go on. I feel enormously grateful.

Perhaps we are all standing in such a doorway. Some people pass through it on their way to the rest of their lives, lives that we may never know or see. Others pass through it to their deaths and the Unknown. Everyone leaves something behind. When I awoke from that dream, I had a sense of the value of every life.

YOU HAVE TO BE PRESENT TO WIN

JUST AFTER SHE started working as a physician on the Indian reservation, Elizabeth was asked to see an elderly woman and her daughter. The older woman was far into her nineties, tiny and dry, her hair dressed in the traditional way. She had many significant physical problems that had never been adequately treated. For the past few years she had lived in the home of her daughter, who provided for her care. In Elizabeth's office it was the daughter who did most of the talking. The old woman simply watched and listened.

Elizabeth saw them together every other week for more than two years. During that time, she diagnosed and successfully treated many of the old woman's complex physical problems. She gave antibiotics for an infection of the urine, managed the old woman's diabetes and brought her blood sugar into the normal range, digitalized her and reversed her incipient heart failure, revised her diet in keeping with the limitations of a liver that was barely functioning. She ordered many lab tests. She also mobilized social services to help the daughter in caring for her mother and enabled her to find financial support from a government grant. Finally at ninety-six, the old woman had died. By this time her chart was more than an inch thick. Reading through it in order to write a summary, Elizabeth had been proud of the way she had handled this complex case.

Several months later, she received a call from a researcher at the University of Arizona. He was wondering if she had the time to talk to him. He was writing a book on the American Indian medicine traditions and was especially interested in the great medicine women who had received the lineage and kept alive the ancient ways of healing. Few were still living, and he had been able to locate the family of one of them. Unfortunately, the woman herself had recently died. Her family could not answer many of his questions and had told him to contact Elizabeth. They had told him that she too was a doctor. That she had taken care of their mother and met with her many times. She knew their mother well. She would have the answers he needed.

Elizabeth smiled ruefully. "I have never forgotten it," she said. "I think of her sitting there all those months, watching me shuffling my papers and tracking my lab data and knowing what she knew. I wonder what was going through her mind. I had been so busy with my numbers and tests. What I would give for even one hour with her now, to ask her any of my unanswered questions, to have her perspective on suffering or loss or illness or death. Or simply to ask for her blessing."

Sometimes I wonder if too great a scientific objectivity can make you blind. Elizabeth's story gives me pause. It makes me wonder how many opportunities I myself have missed, how many times wisdom has passed me by as I track lab data. Probably quite a few.

KNOWING THE HEART

IN THE FALL of my third year of medical school we began, under careful supervision, to see our own patients. The first patient assigned to me was an elderly widow with uncomplicated left-sided heart failure. She was the ideal patient for someone who did not yet know much about medicine, a textbook case of an easily treatable disease. I was able to make the diagnosis by myself simply by listening to her heart and hearing the third sound, or "gallop," that is found in failure. The studies I ordered confirmed that I had heard correctly; she had arteriosclerotic heart disease with significant left-sided hypertrophy. Together with the attending physician, I was able to work out a treatment plan; I would use a diuretic and Digoxin to bring her out of heart failure. I was thrilled.

Over the next few weeks on this treatment her third heart sound faded, her ankle swelling diminished, her shortness of breath disappeared, and her exercise tolerance curve began to improve. For some reason, these signs of improving cardiac function did not seem to excite her as profoundly as they excited me. I remember thinking that this was probably because she was so old that life did not matter to her as much as it mattered to me. Shortly before Christmas, I discharged her from the clinic on a maintenance Digoxin dose with instructions to return in six months. As I wrote her my first prescription, I felt like a real doctor.

In early March, looking over my clinic appointments for the day, I was horrified to see that she was back. She was the third patient on my schedule, and, as I moved through my other appointments, I went over her case anxiously in my mind. I was certain that I had done something wrong and that she was in heart failure again. Why else would she have come back so early? What could I have missed? I couldn't think of anything.

I found her sitting fully dressed in the examining room. In response to my look of surprise, she told me that she had not come to be examined. She had just wanted to bring me something. Reaching to the depths of her large purse, she drew out a twist of wax paper and placed it in my hand. I opened it and found four little purple flowers. I looked at her, mystified. "They are Grape Hyacinths," she said. She and her husband had planted them in their garden more than forty years before. Every spring they returned faithfully, the first evidence that life was stronger than winter.

When she had felt her own life withdraw and falter last fall, she had not thought of winter but of death. She had remembered the hyacinths and the other flowers in her garden that came back each spring, and thought she would never see them again. She had been very afraid. She had listened to my careful explanation of the drug I planned to give her and what it would do, but she had not really believed. I was so young, how could I really know? She smiled at me then, across a gap of almost sixty years. "Thank you, Doctor," she said. "Thank you for your help."

I had known but I had not really understood. My textbook of pharmacology had told me about actions of Digoxin, its contraindications and its dosage. I knew that even at eighty-four the failing heart would respond to it. The textbook had told me everything I needed to know except that the love of life is not a function of the strength of the heart muscle.

Twenty years later my own eighty-four-year-old mother, a far more outspoken woman, had looked her young cardiologist in the eye and told him that she expected him to fight to the mat for her. "I just want to be sure that you know that my life is precious to me, young man," she said. "As precious as yours is to you."

Recently during a physicians' seminar on listening, we all took out our stethoscopes and spent several minutes listening to our own hearts. We are all middle-aged people and for the first little while everyone anxiously diagnosed themselves, fearful of hearing a split S1, a third heart sound, or perhaps the murmur of an arteriosclerotic valve. But as time went on, we moved past all that and heard something steadfast in the midst of our lives that had been there always, even before we were fully human. Our lives and all other lives depended on it. It was a profound and ineffable encounter with the mysterious. Most of us were deeply moved. We had auscultated and diagnosed hearts for years, but none of us had ever experienced this before. In that moment we had glimpsed something beyond our habitual way of seeing and hearing and knew that what we work with every day is life itself. It was the sort of moment my grandfather would have blessed.

Afterward there was a silence. Then one of the cardiologists present began to speak about his work and to wonder aloud how one could be so close to something holy and not know it. It reminded him, he said, of a prayer that he had heard some time back. Somewhat embarrassed, he began to recite it aloud:

> Days pass and the years vanish and we walk sightless among miracles. Lord, fill our eyes with seeing and our minds with knowing. Let there be moments when your Presence, like lightning, illumines the darkness in which we walk. Help us to see, wherever we gaze, that the bush burns, unconsumed.

And we, clay touched by God, will reach out for holiness and exclaim in wonder, "How filled with awe is this place and we did not know it."

I had heard the final line many times before. It was one of my grandfather's favorites.

COUNTING YOUR CHICKENS

When she was eighty-four and newly widowed, my mother had come from New York City to live with me. Frail and very sick with a heart condition, her physical needs were complex and I had found her care overwhelming. Over and over she had sudden attacks of pulmonary edema, a sort of internal drowning from which I would rescue her by placing rotating tourniquets on her arms and legs and injecting her with morphine. On four occasions, she had a cardiac arrest in our living room. With the help of paramedics, I had resuscitated her each time and kept her going. In the last year of her life, these good people came to our house so often that I knew many of them by name.

It was clear that time was running out, and I became concerned not only for my mother's physical well-being but also for the state of her soul. She was not a religious woman, and what rituals she observed seemed more like superstition than spiritual practice. I had read somewhere about the importance of encouraging old people to reflect on their lives in order to die in peace. Without such remembering it would not be possible to receive and offer forgiveness, to uncover meaning and to complete a life well. I did not know much about such things then, but I believed what I had read and wanted the best for my mother. Yet every attempt I made to encourage her to reflect on her past and her relationships was rebuffed.

Some of my friends were involved in spiritual practices of various sorts, and one by one I had invited them over to talk with her about their spiritual paths. A few even attempted to interest her in their ways. She listened politely to their enthusiastic discussions of such things as tai chi, mindfulness meditation, yoga, and vipassana. But afterward she would tell me that meditation just wasn't for her. It was too quiet.

As she became sicker, I became more intent on my agenda. A nonmeditator myself, I even began to sit for fifteen minutes in the morning and invited her to sit with me. Surprisingly she agreed with enthusiasm, but every time I opened my eyes I would find my mother looking at me with great love. After a few weeks of this, I suggested that we abandon it but she refused, saying that she enjoyed having the chance to look at me for fifteen minutes every morning. Eventually I just gave up.

So I was overjoyed when one evening in the living room after dinner, my mother sighed and spontaneously closed her eyes for more than an hour. Once I had determined she was not asleep, I sat in silence with her all that time. When at last she opened her eyes and looked at me, I asked her what she had been doing. "Why, I was counting my chickens," she said with a smile.

Meeting my puzzled look with a laugh, she told me that it had suddenly occurred to her as she was eating dinner (it was chicken) that she had eaten a chicken once or twice a week for many years. She had begun to calculate this in her mind: two chickens a week, fifty-two weeks a year times eighty-four years turned out to be more than 8,500 chickens. It seemed to her to be a great number of chickens just to keep one old woman alive. She had closed her eyes then to try to imagine what 8,500 chickens might look like. It had taken some time, but she had finally gotten a picture of them in her mind. It had been overwhelming. "All that innocent life," said my mother.

She had begun to wonder whether she had been worth this sacrifice. And so she had begun to review her life, looking at as many of her important relationships as she could remember, examining her own heart and her own motivations. It had taken a long time, but at the end she had realized that, while she was certain that she had disappointed and even hurt people in the course of her life, she could not remember deliberately causing pain or harm to anyone, or resenting anyone else's good fortune or hating anyone or taking something that was not hers or even telling a significant lie. She smiled at me again. "I believe I have been worthy of my chickens, Rachel," she said.

Life has an elegance that far exceeds anything we might devise. Perhaps the wisdom lies in knowing when to sit back and wait for it to unfold. Too hasty an activism may lead to lesser outcomes and, more important, may cause us to trust ourselves rather than learning to trust life.

L'CHIAM!

MANY YEARS AGO my grandfather gave me a silver wine goblet so small that it holds no more than a thimbleful of wine. Exquisitely engraved into its bowl is a bow with long ribbon streamers. It was made in Russia long ago. He gave it to me during one of the many afternoons when we sat together at the kitchen table in my parents' home memorizing phrases from his old books and discussing the nature of life. I was quite young then, no more than five or six, and when I became restless, he would revive my attention by bringing out the sacramental Concord grape wine he kept in the back of the refrigerator. He would fill my little beribboned wineglass with Manischevitz and then put a splash of wine into his own, a big silver ceremonial cup, generations old. Then we would offer a toast together. At the time, the only other celebration I knew was singing "Happy Birthday" and blowing out the candles. I loved this even better.

My grandfather had taught me the toast we used. It was a single Hebrew word, *L'Chiam* (pronounced *le CHI yeem*), which he told me meant "To life!" He always said it with great enthusiasm. "Is it to a happy life, Grandpa?" I had asked him once. He had shaken his head no. "It is just 'To life!' Neshume-le," he told me.

At first, this did not make a lot of sense to me, and I struggled to understand his meaning. "Is it like a prayer?" I asked uncertainly.

"Ah no, Neshume-le," he told me. "We pray for the things we don't have. We already have life."

"But then why do we say this before we drink the wine?" He smiled at me fondly. "Grandpa!" I said, suddenly suspicious. "Did you make it up?" He chuckled and assured me that he had not. For thousands of years all over the world people have said this same word to each other before drinking wine together. It was a Jewish tradition.

I puzzled about this last for some time. "Is it written in the Bible, Grandpa?" I asked at last. "No, Neshume-le," he said, "it is written in people's hearts." Seeing the confusion on my face, he told me that *L'Chiam!* meant that no matter what difficulty life brings, no matter how hard or painful or unfair life is, life is holy and worthy of celebration. "Even the wine is sweet to remind us that life itself is a blessing."

It has been almost fifty-five years since I last heard my grandfather's voice, but I remember the joy with which he toasted Life and the twinkle in his eye as he said *L'Chiam!* It has always seemed remarkable to me that such a toast could be offered for generations by a people for whom life has not been easy. But perhaps it can only be said by such people, and only those who have lost and suffered can truly understand its power.

L'Chiam! is a way of living life. As I've grown older, it seems less and less about celebrating life and more about the wisdom of choosing life. In the many years that I have been counseling people with cancer, I have seen people choose life again and again, despite loss and pain and difficulty. The same immutable joy I saw in my grandfather's eyes is there in them all.

II.

BECOMING A BLESSING

WHETHER WE ARE aware of it or not, we will refine the quality of our humanity throughout the course of our lives. More and more, people seek spiritual techniques to help them do this. But joy and suffering will do this for you, too. Every lifetime offers countless opportunities to become more whole.

Life offers its wisdom generously. Everything teaches. Not everyone learns. Life asks of us the same thing we have been asked in every class: "Stay awake." "Pay attention." But paying attention is no simple matter. It requires us not to be distracted by expectations, past experiences, labels, and masks. It asks that we not jump to early conclusions and that we remain open to surprise. Wisdom comes most easily to those who have the courage to embrace life without judgment and are willing to not know, sometimes for a long time. It requires us to be more fully and simply alive than we have been taught to be. It may require us to suffer. But ultimately we will be more than we were when we began. There is the seed of a greater wholeness in everyone.

A while ago I had a chance to be part of a group gathered in the living room of one of my friends, a Tibetan Buddhist, when her teacher, Gelek Rinpoche, gave a dharma talk. Rinpoche is a round and delicious man filled to the brim with some sort of secret joy. It is infectious. This evening he spoke about "taking refuge in the Buddha," a phrase that I, a non-Buddhist, had never heard before but that had the Buddhists around me nodding in recognition. Taking refuge, said Rinpoche, does not mean going outside of oneself to find the Buddha, but rather going within, to that place in everyone which is a buddha seed, a Buddha in potential, that has the capacity to be a Buddha. He paused to let us reflect on this, and it seemed to me that his joy intensified momentarily like a banked fire finding a hidden pocket of sap deep inside a charcoaled log.

I had a sense of the part in me and in others that he was referring to. I had just never thought of taking refuge in it. Refuge from what? I wondered. I think now it is refuge from suffering.

The buddha seed is the part of everyone that has the capacity for wisdom. Wisdom is not something that we acquire; it is something that over time we may become. It involves a change in our basic nature, a deepening of our capacity for compassion, lovingkindness, forgiveness, harmlessness, and service. Life itself waters the buddha seed within us. Our capacity for wisdom naturally grows throughout our lives.

Knowing that a buddha seed is present in everyone changes the way you see things. We are all more than we seem. Many things do not wear their true nature on their sleeve. What you can see and touch about an acorn, its color, its weight, its hardness, length, and width will never hint at the secret of its potential. This secret is not directly measurable, but given the proper conditions over time it may become visible.

An acorn makes no sense unless we know that woven into the way it is made, there is something waiting to unfold that knows how to become an oak tree. An acorn is defined by this capacity. Something can be the size, shape, weight, texture, and color of an acorn, but without this hidden power to become an oak tree, it is not an acorn.

Our essential humanity is defined by the buddha seed in us, the capacity to grow in wisdom and the ways of wisdom. None of us are only the way we seem.

Every acorn yearns toward the full expression of its nature and uses all opportunity to realize its capacity to become an oak tree.

There is a natural yearning toward wholeness and wisdom in us all as well. This varies in strength from person to person. It may be quite conscious in some and deeply buried in others; it may form the focus of one life and lie on the periphery of another, but it is always there. Wholeness is a basic human need.

None of us are born wise. The grandfather I knew was an old man. By the time we met, life had burnished him and taught him many things. Before that, he had been young, a brilliant Old Testament scholar, proud of his intellect and his learning, the center of a congregation of devout Orthodox Jews who had accepted his teachings absolutely as the law. He had lived in a world that was black and white, with a clear sense of what was right and what was not. I do not think I would have loved him then. I am not sure that his own children did.

My mother once told me about something that had happened when she was a little girl. According to strict Orthodox law, it is forbidden to have graven images, not just in the synagogue but also in the home. This law extended to dolls, and my mother and her younger sister had never had one. One of the women in the little Russian town in which they lived had taken pity on the two little girls and given my mother a doll as a gift. The doll had a china head, blue eyes, and real yellow hair. It had meant the world to the two little sisters. But their father had discovered it. In a rage he had taken it and flung it across the room. When it hit the opposite wall, it had broken into a hundred pieces. My mother was over seventy when she told me this story. Even then, her eyes had filled with tears.

The story of how the family got its American name is also revealing. A few years before the first of the pogroms that swept through Poland and Russia in the early part of the twentieth century, my grandfather awoke one night from a dream that disturbed him deeply. Death had reached out a great black wing and extinguished the lights in all the synagogues in Eastern Europe. He knew most of them by name, and he had watched in horror as they were snuffed out, one by one. He could not get this dream from his mind and yet he did not understand it. When, a few weeks later, he dreamt it for the second time, he took it to be a message and a warning. Gathering up his family and his entire congregation, he had immigrated to America.

Like so many others, our family was renamed at Ellis Island in New York City. When at last they reached the immigration desk, the man behind it asked my grandfather for his name. My grandfather, sheltered by the respect and tradition that had surrounded him in Russia, had never been addressed in this tone of voice before, and he simply stared at this man. The clerk, thinking that perhaps he had not been understood, asked my grandfather for his name again, this time in Yiddish: *"Vos is dein Nommen?"* At that time, Yiddish was the language of the uneducated and of the women and the children. While he understood it well, my grandfather rarely spoke it and was usually spoken to in Hebrew, the language of God. Offended to the bone, he had simply turned his back. I can see him in my mind's eye, standing there, young and outraged, black overcoat, black hat, full black beard, his arms crossed in front of him and his back to the offending clerk. It is hard to believe that this is the same man who, forty years later, would tell his five-year-old granddaughter that it is as great a separation from God to take offense as to give offense.

Meanwhile my grandmother Rachel, herself a young woman, was trying to calm her six small children frightened by the unfamiliar world around them. She spoke to them soothingly in Yiddish, trying to still their crying and comfort them. *"Sha, sha,"* she told her little ones. *"Shay-neh Kinder. Zis-seh Kinder."* ("Hush, hush.

Beautiful children. Sweet children.") And so the clerk, getting no further response from my outraged grandfather, had simply said, "Ziskind . . . Next!" And my grandfather became Rabbi Ziskind (Sweetchild) for the rest of his life.

It is hard for me to put stories of my grandfather in his youth together with the old man who was the center of my world as a young child. But over time he had grown beyond them. By the time I knew him he had come to understand that the letter of the law was far less precious than its spirit, that the spirit of God lived in the soul and not the mind and that the heart of a little girl who spoke neither Yiddish nor Hebrew could speak to God directly, in His own language.

Everyone and everything is caught up in the process of manifesting its soul. This struggle of the personality to become transparent to the soul is a struggle to become free from illusion, to grow in wisdom. The process of growing in wisdom, of becoming more transparent to the soul is going on within us and all around us. This is not usually a graceful or a deliberate process. We stumble forward, often in the dark, using everything to become more of who we are. It is an effort worthy of our patience, our support, our compassion, and our attention.

According to those who have returned from a near-death experience, we are all here to grow in wisdom and learn how to love better. As we each do this in our own ways, we slowly become a blessing to those around us and a light in the world.

GETTING IT RIGHT

IN THE MISHNA Torah, Maimonides, the great doctor rabbi, describes the eight levels of "charity," or ways of giving to others. This was one of the many traditional teachings that my grandfather and I discussed and puzzled over. At the time, he was an Orthodox rabbi, a lifelong student of the Talmud, and I was five years old. When a text was as subtle and complex as this, he would simplify all of it but its most basic wisdom. Here is the way that he told it to me.

At the eighth and most basic level of giving to others, a man begrudgingly buys a coat for a shivering man who has asked him for help, gives it to him in the presence of witnesses, and waits to be thanked.

At the seventh level, a man does this same thing without waiting to be asked for help.

At the sixth level, a man does this same thing openheartedly without waiting to be asked for help.

At the fifth level, a man openheartedly gives a coat that he has bought to another but does so in private.

At the fourth level, a man openheartedly and privately gives his own coat to another, rather than a coat that he has bought.

At the third level, a man openheartedly gives his own coat to another who does not know who has given him this gift. But the man himself knows the person who is indebted to him.

At the second level, he openheartedly gives his own coat to another and has no idea who has received it. But the man who receives it knows to whom he is indebted.

And finally, on the first and purest level of giving to others, a man openheartedly gives his own coat away without knowing who will receive it, and he who receives it does not know who has given it to him. Then giving becomes a natural expression of the goodness in us, and we give as simply as flowers breathe out their perfume.

At the time, it was very important to me to be good and to do things right, and I listened to this description very carefully. "I will only do it the right way, Grandpa," I assured him. He began to laugh. "Ah, Neshume-le," he said to me tenderly. "Here we have a special sort of thing. Suppose we all gave to those around us as the first man does, begrudgingly offering a coat we have bought in the presence of witnesses to someone who has need and who asks us for help? If we all did this, would there be more suffering or less suffering in the world than there is now?"

I thought for a long time, the need to do it right battling in me with the simplicity of my grandfather's question. "Less suffering, Grandpa," I said finally in some confusion. "Ah yes," he said, beaming, "this is true. Some things have so much goodness in them that they are worth doing any way that you can."

Unquestionably there are ways of giving that may diminish others, stripping them of their dignity and self-worth. We can learn how to give without taking something away, and often we may learn as we go. But according to my grandfather, it is better to bless life badly than not to bless it at all.

THE GIFT

Every Christmas Eve when I was small my father and I would take the subway to downtown Manhattan and go shopping for presents for my mother, my aunt, my friends, my teacher, and other important persons in my life. These were special, even magical, times. Everything was decorated for Christmas. The windows of the stores up and down Fifth Avenue were magnificent, and some even had whole mechanical villages that moved or a mechanical Santa that waved. It was almost always cold, and the nighttime streets were crowded with smiling people carrying beautifully wrapped packages, the women in furs and men in overcoats with velvet collars. Thinking back on it now after more than fifty years, it seems to me that I could see the joy in people shining in the streets. Christmas music poured out of every open doorway. In my memory, it is always lightly snowing, and everyone had snowflakes on their coats and in their hair.

We would start at Rockefeller Plaza and stare in awe at the enormous, beautifully decorated tree, debating whether this year's decorations were more beautiful than last. They always were. We would watch the skaters for a while. And then we would move slowly down Fifth Avenue, stopping in every store, thinking of the people I loved, one at a time, looking at many, many things until I found just the right one for each one of them. At some point during the evening, my father would hand me his big gold pocket watch and tell me that when it chimed I was to come and meet him right where we were standing, and then I would go off alone in whatever store we were in to find his present. While I was gone, my father would do a little shopping of his own.

I got to stay up late, far later than my usual bedtime, and it was often close to midnight when we got home, our arms filled with boxes, each of which had been specially wrapped at the store. My mother always had cocoa waiting, and we would show her the beautiful boxes and tell her about the wonderful things we had found for everyone—but not, of course, what we had found for her.

It was a chance to think about each one of my beloved people, who they were and what might make them glad. I remember the indescribable feeling of finding each present and the joy of recognizing it as just the very thing. There was such pleasure in choosing the paper and the ribbon and watching it wrapped in a way that was as special as the person it was for. I loved finding these presents. It made me feel very lucky.

In thinking back, I realize that I never actually saw many of these presents opened. They would be mailed away or left under other people's Christmas trees. Somehow this never mattered. The important moment wasn't in the opening, or in the thanking. The important thing was the blessing of having someone to love.

BEING USED

MY MEDICAL TRAINING taught me simple and straightforward methods. I met someone, examined them, made a diagnosis, decided what was needed, and provided it. The medical model I was taught focused on what I as a physician thought, perceived, and decided, what I as a physician knew. Since then I've discovered that basically I do not know what is needed much of the time, and, even more surprising, I do not need to know. But I know that if I listen attentively to someone, to their essential self, their soul, as it were, I often find that at the deepest, most unconscious level, they can sense the direction of their own healing and wholeness. If I can remain open to that, without expectations of what the someone is supposed to "do," how they are supposed to change in order to be "better," or even what their wholeness looks like, what can happen is magical. By that I mean that it has a certain coherency or integrity about it, far beyond any way of fixing their situation or easing their pain I might devise on my own.

So I no longer have many theories about people. I don't diagnose them or decide what their problem is. I simply meet with them and listen. As we sit together, I don't even have an agenda, but I know that something will emerge from our conversation over time that is a part of a larger coherent pattern that neither of us can fully see at this moment. So I sit with them and wait.

The Celestine Prophecy offers a simple and helpful description of the possibility within all human relationships. It says that there is a way of relating to others such that one deliberately listens for the hidden beauty in them. The place of their beauty is often the place of their greatest integrity. When you listen, the integrity and wholeness in others moves closer. Your attention strengthens it and makes it easier for them to hear it in themselves. In your presence, they can more easily inhabit that in them which is beyond their limitations, a place of greater freedom and sanctuary. Eventually they may be able to live there.

As a counselor to people with cancer, I used to be ashamed of not being able to provide a more cognitive framework for what I do or offer a theoretical rationale for why I say what I say. I no longer feel this way. I also used to believe that things that could be expressed in numbers were truer than things that could only be said in words. I no longer believe that either. It has been my experience that presence is a more powerful catalyst for change than analysis and that we can know beyond doubt things we can never understand.

In some mysterious way, the life in someone may even use us to strengthen itself. Many years ago when I prepared for the final session with every patient, I used to review in my mind the milestones and turning points in our work together that had led to their healing. I would come up with a list of these in which I played a rather central role. Carefully I would go through my notes and document the thoughtful intervention I had made back in March or the powerful interpretation I had offered last September. But when I asked the people themselves to talk about their own experience of healing, they would rarely come up with more than half of my list. The rest of the time, they would share things that surprised me, chance remarks and facial expressions that they had interpreted in ways that evoked in them some profound and liberating insight. Then they would give me example after example of how they were able to use this insight to change their lives. Nodding sagely, I would have no recollection of the event at all.

Clearly, I had been used to delivering a message of healing to them that did not originate in me. This has happened so often that I have become accustomed to it. It can be a little hard on the ego, but only at first.

We may even believe we are serving others in one way and be actually serving impeccably in quite another. An internist told me about his experience as a Fellow on a large inner-city AIDS ward. It was a while ago, before protease inhibitors and other drug therapies had become available, and all the patients who were admitted to his service died. Many of them were young men quite close to his own age, people whose lives mattered deeply to him. After a few months of this, he became overwhelmed by a sense of futility. He had felt that way for the whole rest of the year.

Joe happens to be a Buddhist, and it has always been his practice to pray for his patients. When a patient dies even now, he lights a candle on his altar at home and keeps it burning for a month. For the whole time he was at San Francisco General, he prayed for each dying young man and lit a candle on his altar for them. Many years afterward he tells me of this with a smile. It has made him wonder. Perhaps the reason he was there was not what he had thought. He had expected to serve by curing and rescuing his patients. When their problems proved resistant to his medical expertise, he had felt useless. But maybe he was not meant to be there to cure people. Perhaps he was there so that no one would die without someone to pray for them. Perhaps he had served every one of his patients flawlessly.

SEEING THE BUDDHA SEED

THE ACT OF seeing can transform the person who sees and cause us to see differently for the rest of our lives. Flying back from Florida a week before Christmas, I found myself seated in a section of the plane completely taken over by dozens of small boys and their parents who were returning from a national baseball competition for seven-year-olds. Their team had come in second, and emotions were high. So was the noise level. The kids were over the moon and even their parents shouted to one another, sharing the scores of whatever game was on their Walkman. All the children had bags of fast food: french fries and burgers. I sat among the shrieks and the high fives as french fries flew through the air and a desperate stewardess tried to get everyone in their seats so we could take off. I seemed to be the only stranger in this crowd. I was not happy.

Seated next to me was a very heavy black woman with a cranky two-year-old. She seemed to be planning to hold this child on her almost nonexistent lap all the way to San Francisco. This did not strike him as a great idea, and he let her know this at the top of his voice. It didn't strike me as a great idea either. Noticing that he had marked my slacks with his shoes, she shook him slightly and told him to hush and then took his shoes off. Standing, I found the stewardess and asked if I might change my seat. But there wasn't another seat on the plane.

Finally we were able to take off. Dinner was served and turned out to be an ordeal. I had a Coke poured on me by a freckled, redheaded kid who mumbled, "Sorry, Grannie," as he ran on down the aisle. Finally, my seatmate turned her toddler loose and he disappeared forward amid the welcoming shouts of the older children.

Reading or any sort of work was impossible. Resigned, I started a conversation with my neighbor, asking her about the baseball league. She began to tell me about the time she spends with the team, the hours of cheering them on, of going door to door to raise money for equipment and travel, and why she was here now with two of her sons. "You can't just keep having kids," she said. "You gotta keep them alive." In her neighborhood many boys were dead or locked away by twenty, victims of drugs or violence. The league was her life insurance for her kids. I looked at her with new respect. She had four, all under the age of ten. The little guy was her baby.

She asked me about my own life, and I told her about my work with people with cancer. A sadness filled her eyes and she began to tell me about her neighbor, a woman like herself, a single mother with four little kids. Six months ago she had been diagnosed with cancer. "The chemo she has to take is terrible," she told me. "It makes her so sick, sometimes she can hardly get out of the bed. I sure hope she can make it through."

She spoke of her neighbor's symptoms, her neighbor's fears, the nightmares that awakened her almost every night. As she unfolded the story, I began to wonder how she knew so many of the intimate details of her neighbor's life, and so I asked her this question. Her answer stunned me. When tragedy had struck next door, she had simply moved her neighbor and all her children into her own home. They had been there for the past five months. I looked at her closely. There was not the slightest air of martyrdom or self-congratulation about her, just this natural reaching out to a person in trouble whose life was next to her own.

Shortly afterward her youngest returned, and she once again held him on her lap, feeding him french fries from his bag with her fingers until he fell asleep. After a while the lights were turned down for the movie. Exhausted, many of the children had fallen asleep and many of their parents were sleeping too. I took out my book, found some Christmas music on my headset, and began to read. We flew on over the heart of this country. After a while I glanced over at my seatmate. She too had fallen asleep, her face beautiful and serene, her sleeping baby in her arms, clasped against her great belly. On his head was the gift the fries and burger company had given all the children, a paper hat in the shape of a small golden crown.

SIMPLY NATURAL

A WOMAN ONCE told me that she despaired of the selfishness of her children. She could not understand how they had turned out this way as she had always set them a good example. "And how did you do this?" I asked. "By serving them generously," she replied. But perhaps we don't help people to become generous by giving to them but by involving them as we give to others.

My mother was a public health nurse. She worked long hours, and often I did not see her a great deal during the week. When I was small, I remember accompanying her as she made home visits in the slums of New York City. When she invited me to come with her, she told me that she needed me to help her by carrying her black bag. But perhaps she had asked me to come with her for far deeper reasons than this.

Her mother, my grandmother, was a rebbitzen, a rabbi's wife. In this role she often called on the sick, bringing food or helping with the household tasks. As a child in Russia, my mother went with her and helped her to feed people, bathe them, and even clean their houses. Whatever was needed. These were special times for my mother. She was one of six children and rarely got her mother to herself. She remembered this time spent together helping people as a privilege, a time of love.

Service was a way of life in my mother's family. It was not a way of life in New York City in the forties or even later. Like many children, when I was little I used to give away my toys, my mittens, and sometimes even my shoes. If another child wanted my pail and shovel in the playground, I would not ask for it back; and if someone had no mittens, I would give them one of mine. This was seen by my teachers and many of the other adults around me as a problem that I would need to outgrow.

Often I would be sent home from school without half my crayons or, once, without my shoes and with a note from my teacher explaining how I needed to learn to stand up for myself and have the courage not to let others take advantage of me. My mother would never scold me about these things but would, when necessary, simply replace whatever was missing. It never occurred to anyone else that I was doing exactly what I wanted to do.

Perhaps service does not need to be taught. It may be a natural impulse in all people. As such, we may only need to strengthen it. In *Children, the Challenge,* his revolutionary book on parenting, Dreikurs tells a story about a mother returning from the store and putting her bags of groceries down on the kitchen table. She opens the refrigerator, takes out the empty plastic containers that hold the eggs, and sets them on the table next to the bags. Then she begins to put the groceries away.

Returning from the pantry, she sees that her two-year-old has climbed onto the table, opened the egg carton and, two handed, is transferring one egg at a time into the egg container. "No, no," she cries out in alarm, "that's not for little girls, you'll break them," and she lifts her daughter who has begun to cry down from the table and puts away the rest of the eggs herself. Fourteen years later she will probably still be putting the eggs away herself and perhaps cleaning up her daughter's room as well.

Chances are that any helpful two-year-old will break some eggs.

We are often not very good at things when we are new. But there may be an important choice to make at such moments. Do we support and protect the innate wish to be of help to others in our children, or do we protect the eggs? Hard as it seems, the greater mother wisdom may lie in a willingness to clean up broken eggs or replace a mitten and a box of crayons.

ALL IN THE FAMILY

WE CAN DO violence to life in many ways. Many years ago, I was invited to hear a well-known rabbi speak about forgiveness at a Yom Kippur service. Yom Kippur is the Day of Atonement, when Jews everywhere reflect on the year just past, repent their shortcomings and unkindness, and hope for the forgiveness of God. But the rabbi did not speak about God's forgiveness.

Instead, he walked out into the congregation, took his infant daughter from his wife, and, carrying her in his arms, stepped up to the bimah or podium. The little girl was perhaps a year old and she was adorable. From her father's arms she smiled at the congregation. Every heart melted. Turning toward her daddy, she patted him on the cheek with her tiny hands. He smiled fondly at her and with his customary dignity began a rather traditional Yom Kippur sermon, talking about the meaning of the holiday.

The baby girl, feeling his attention shift away from her, reached forward and grabbed his nose. Gently he freed himself and continued the sermon. After a few minutes, she took his tie and put it in her mouth. The entire congregation chuckled. The rabbi rescued his tie and smiled at his child. She put her tiny arms around his neck. Looking at us over the top of her head, he said, "Think about it. Is there anything she can do that you could not forgive her for?" Throughout the room people began to nod in recognition, thinking perhaps of their own children and grandchildren. Just then, she reached up and grabbed his eyeglasses. Everyone laughed out loud.

Retrieving his eyeglasses and settling them on his nose, the rabbi laughed as well. Still smiling, he waited for silence. When it came, he asked, "And when does that stop? When does it get hard to forgive? At three? At seven? At fourteen? At thirty-five? How old does someone have to be before you forget that everyone is a child of God?"

Back then, God's forgiveness was something easily understandable to me, but personally I found forgiveness difficult. I had thought of it as a lowering of standards rather than a family relationship.

TRANSMISSION

I SPENT A few weeks one April in the Four Corners area of Utah in a little town called Bluff, celebrating the birthday of a friend of mine. On Easter morning we attended an Episcopal church service celebrated by a Native American bishop. With the exception of my friends and myself, the congregation was mostly Navaho people. The bishop was a middle-aged man of great personal integrity, and the service was beautiful. Dressed in a white robe with a woven scarf of Native American symbolism around his neck, he seemed deeply moved by the occasion and the story of the resurrection.

Most of the sermon was in Navaho, the bishop reading from the Bible in a voice filled with emotion. Then he glanced over toward us. We had not understood a word. With a deep courtesy he began to repeat the sermon and the reading for us in English. His English was perfect, but the passion of the first reading was simply not there. He struggled on, trying to make the English words transparent to the profound meaning of the story. Finally he looked up and, abandoning his Bible, spoke to us from the depths of his heart. "This man Jesus," he said and paused. "This man Jesus, He *is* good medicine."

This moment changed me profoundly. For years I had tried to be a good doctor and practice good medicine. I had taught many others to practice good medicine, first pediatrics and then mind/

body medicine. But the bishop's words pointed to something more, and in the depths of my being I recognized what this was. Perhaps what is needed is not only to learn good medicine but to become good medicine. As a parent. A friend or a doctor. Sometimes just being in someone's presence is strong medicine.

BEARING WITNESS

AFTER A DOZEN years, Alzheimer's disease had virtually destroyed Muriel's brain, erasing her memories and with them all of her sense of who she was. Confined to a nursing home, she was adrift and frightened, given to pacing back and forth in a seemingly endless fashion filled with a nameless anxiety. Such repetitive pacing is common in people at the last stages of this disease, almost as if they are being driven to search for something hopelessly lost.

All of the staff's efforts to ease her fear had failed. For a long time she was at rest only when she slept, and her unending movement had caused her to become painfully thin. Then one day, quite by accident, as she passed the full-length mirror that hung to the left of the door to the courtyard, she caught sight of her own reflection in the glass. Becoming still for the first time in many months, she stood before it, fascinated, an odd expression on her face. She looked as if she had just met a friend from long ago, someone whose face was vaguely familiar but whose connection to oneself cannot be immediately recalled.

As a result of her disease, Muriel had not spoken in many months. But drawn to the image in the mirror for reasons long forgotten, she began to speak to it in a language all her own. Day after day she would stand and talk to the woman in the mirror for hours on end. It made her calm.

The nurses welcomed this new behavior with relief. Her endless pacing and anxiety had made her very difficult to care for. Accustomed to much random senseless behavior on the part of their patients, they paid little further attention to how she now spent her time. But her doctor saw this differently. Every day on his rounds, he would stop at the mirror and spend some time with this patient. Standing next to her, he too would talk to the woman in the mirror with his usual kindness and respect. Once at the end of one of his longer chats with Muriel's reflection, he was deeply moved to notice that Muriel had tears in her eyes.

I was deeply moved as well. Unable to cure his patient's brutal disease, this true physician instinctively strengthened her last connection to herself with his simple presence and validated her worth as a human being.

Another colleague, a psychologist, told me this story. In the eighties, when she lived and practiced in New York City, she had decided to attend a two-day professional workshop based on twenty or so short films of one of Carl Jung's last pupils, the great Jungian dream analyst, Marie-Louise von Franz. Between the showing of these films, a distinguished panel consisting of the heads of two major Jungian training centers and Carl Jung's own grandson responded to written questions from the audience sent up to the stage on cards.

One of these cards told the story of a horrific recurring dream, in which the dreamer was stripped of all human dignity and worth through Nazi atrocities. A member of the panel read the dream out loud. As she listened, my colleague began to formulate a dream interpretation in her head, in anticipation of the panel's response. It was really a "no-brainer," she thought, as her mind busily offered her symbolic explanations for the torture and atrocities described in the dream. But this was not how the panel responded at all. When the reading of the dream was complete, Jung's grandson looked out over the large audience. "Would you all please rise?" he asked. "We will stand together in a moment of silence in response to this dream." The audience stood for a minute, my colleague impatiently waiting for the discussion she was certain would follow. But when they sat again, the panel went on to the next question.

My colleague simply did not understand this at all, and a few days later she asked one of her teachers, himself a Jungian analyst, about it. "Ah, Lois," he had said, "there is in life a suffering so unspeakable, a vulnerability so extreme that it goes far beyond words, beyond explanations and even beyond healing. In the face of such suffering all we can do is bear witness so no one need suffer alone."

Perhaps a willingness to face such shared vulnerability gives us the capacity to repair the world. Those who find the courage to share a common humanity may find they can bless anyone, anywhere.

THE TRAJECTORY

BLESSING LIFE OFFERS us a certain immortality. Our love outlives us and strengthens others, even after we ourselves are gone.

On special occasions, I wear the necklace my father gave my mother at their engagement, seventy-eight years ago. Recently, coming home from one of these events on the East Coast, I found that it was no longer around my neck. I had traveled two thousand miles and I had no idea where I might have lost it. I was never able to find it again.

I was talking about this loss to a sympathetic friend at dinner when she told me about a loss of her own. Her grandmother, her mother's mother, had left her a bracelet, a delicate Victorian thing of filigree and seed pearls. As the middle child in an alcoholic family, she had been very close to this grandmother. Her mother had been distant, caught up in the emotional roller coaster generated by her father's drinking, often with no time for the troubles of a little girl. It was her grandmother who had been there for her, who had soothed her fears and bandaged her knees. She had hugged and fed and listened and believed. She had been there in the night. "Grannie was my strength," she told me. "I don't think I would have survived my crazy family without her. I was an adult when she died, but I was devastated."

It had meant a great deal to her to have this bracelet, something that belonged to her grandmother. For years, she had kept it in a leather box in her bureau drawer and worn it only when she had felt the need for her grandmother's sort of unconditional support. She had last worn it at her wedding.

Shortly afterward, her new apartment had been robbed. Many valuable things including her wedding gifts had been taken. Over time she had replaced them all, except for the bracelet. She had mourned its loss for a long time.

A few years after the robbery, when she was in early labor with her first baby and packing to go to the hospital, by habit she opened the drawer where she had kept the bracelet, thinking to take it with her. Finding it gone, she had felt a pain as sharp as the day it had been taken. The stress and anxiety of the upcoming birth had overwhelmed her then, and she had sat down on her bed and begun to cry.

As she wept, she had experienced a light touch on the top of her head, so gentle that she was not completely sure that she had felt it. But the faint smell of Chantilly, her grandmother's perfume, was unmistakable. Suddenly she remembered something she'd forgotten: her grandmother had given birth to ten children, all of whom lived, and her mother had safely delivered four. She felt a great calm settle on her, and, holding tightly to her lineage, she had left for the hospital with her husband.

Nothing like this had ever happened again, she told me. But in difficult times she now asks herself what her grandmother would say about the situation that she is in. "We were so close, Rachel," she told me, "that it is not hard for me to know how she would see things. Her responses are often far less judgmental and more loving than my own." She also finds that she feels closer to her grandmother now than when she had her bracelet. "She's in my heart, not on my wrist," she told me.

My beloved grandfather died when I was seven, and my parents were concerned about how I would take the blow of his loss. When

I did not speak of it for several weeks, my worried mother had asked me what it was like for me now that Grandpa was gone. I do not remember saying this, but apparently I had told her that things were different now. Now I could take him to school with me. I do remember having a sense of his closeness that faded only after many years. Certainly I talked with him for a long time in much the same way as we both used to talk with God. As Mitch Albom writes in *Tuesdays with Morrie,* "Death is the end of a lifetime, not the end of a relationship."

HOLDING ON TO THE HEART

SOME TIME AFTER one of my patients died of breast cancer at thirty-seven, I arranged to spend an hour with her husband and her four-year-old daughter. The little girl had been devastated and was only now slowly learning to live in a world without her mother. Her father, overwhelmed by his own grief, had tried his best to be there for her, but it wasn't always possible. But they both were doing a little better now, he told me. Kimmie was able to sleep through the night, and he had started back to work. We sat in silence watching Kimmie as she gently patted my cat. Feeling herself watched, she looked up. With a smile, she abandoned the cat and climbed into my lap. Reaching into her tiny pocket, she took something out and put it into my hand. It was a small stuffed velvet heart, obviously handmade.

I looked at her father. "It's a feelie heart," he said. "She never goes anywhere without it."

A friend had sent it from Bridges, a bereavement center in Tacoma, Washington, that serves children who have been touched by death. Small enough to put into a little pocket and take to school to hold and rub, these soft little hearts give children permission to hold their own hearts tenderly and to grieve. To remember that they were loved and know that they can love. Children carry them for as long as they need to, finding comfort in the softness when thoughts of their loss might otherwise overwhelm them.

Deeply moved, I held the little heart out to Kimmie. She took it and held it against her cheek for a long moment. Her mother had loved her fiercely. Perhaps that love could be a place of refuge for Kimmie now.

More than 30,000 little hearts have been made for Bridges over the past ten years by a group of volunteers who sew them by hand out of old bathrobes, shirts, and running suits—anything that is velour or velvet. Bridges gives these hearts to grieving children at many of their own public events, in their support groups, and sometimes even at funerals.

No two hearts are exactly alike, and each has a life of its own. Stories about that life abound. It is common for children who have grieved to give their feelie heart to other children who are going through hard times. One little girl gave her heart to her father when her parents divorced. A small boy sent his to his teacher when her own little boy died. When we have the freedom to grieve, loss often turns naturally into compassion.

For the past nine years I have run a Continuing Medical Education program for physicians who work intimately with death. The physicians who come are seeking the deeper meaning of their difficult work and the inspiration to go on. A large part of this program involves healing loss. Physicians are trained to feel shame about their personal responses to the loss of a patient and to view these responses as unprofessional. We do not hold our own hearts tenderly. Many of us repress our losses and carry our own pain ungrieved, often for years. We have become numb, not because we don't care but because we don't grieve. Grief is the way that loss heals. The program has been in part about creating a community of professional peers who grieve together and give each other the permission and the courage to feel again.

Some time ago, I wrote to the women who make the feelie hearts for Bridges to tell them about this work, about the oncologists, emergency-room physicians, surgeons, and internists who have spent time with us and about the fifty first- and second-year UCSF medical students who take our course on the art of healing every year. They sent us hundreds of little velvet hearts. They fit into the pocket of a white coat perfectly.

Several of the students have told me that they find that if they hold their feelie heart while they study, it relaxes them. But perhaps it does more than this. The first- and second-year medical students at our school and at every medical school are remarkable young people, on fire with the spirit of service. They are people who care deeply and passionately. Research at medical schools throughout the country shows that often this passion does not survive the rigors of the training. Sometimes I think of one of these young people, late at night, struggling to memorize the countless facts on which the scientific practice of medicine is based and holding on to a little velvet heart. The image fills me with an irrational sense of hope.

LOST AND FOUND

IMMY WAS A frail little girl, the only child of older parents. At three, she was only as big as the average eighteen-month-old toddler. She was unable to walk more than a few blocks without tiring and did not have the strength to play games you could not play sitting down. A desperately wanted and long-awaited baby, she had been born with a hole in her heart and a badly formed heart valve. Only the most careful medical management had helped her to live until she was big enough to undergo extensive open-heart surgery. She had been followed since birth in our Pediatric Cardiology Clinic at the New York Hospital, and many of the pediatricians knew her and her family. Despite her physical difficulties she took full possession of all the hearts around her, including mine.

When the time for her surgery finally came, her parents were deeply anxious. These were early days for many cardiac surgery techniques, and the risks were considerable, but without surgery, she would not survive childhood. As the senior pediatric resident, I met with Immy's parents before the surgery to do an intake interview and summarize Immy's long story. They were committed and ready and very pale. As we spoke, they sat close together holding hands. Afterward I took them with me to the children's ward to examine Immy. She greeted us with her wonderful take-no-prisoners smile. She was holding a new teddy bear. Someone had put a white bandage across its chest.

I examined Immy carefully. Her heart sounds bore no resemblance whatever to the organized sounds of a normal heart. Once again, I marveled at her endurance. As I helped her to dress, I noticed a Saint Christopher medal pinned to her tiny pink undershirt. "What is this?" I asked her parents. Hesitantly her mother told me that a family member had made a special trip to Rome to have the medal blessed and then dipped into the healing waters at Lourdes. "We feel that it will protect her," she said simply. Her husband nodded. I was touched.

Immy spent the next day or two undergoing tests, and I saw her several more times. The medal had been moved from her shirt to her hospital gown. It had seemed so important to her parents that I mentioned it in passing to the cardiac surgery resident as we sat writing chart notes in the nursing station on the evening before the surgery. He gave me a cynical smile. "Well, to each his own," he said. "I put my faith in Dr. X," he said, mentioning the name of the highly respected cardiac surgeon who would be heading Immy's surgical team in the morning. "I doubt he needs much help from Lourdes."

I made a note to myself to be sure to take the medal off Immy's gown before she went to surgery in the morning so it wouldn't get lost in the OR or the recovery room. But I spent that morning in the emergency room, as part of a team working on two children who had been thrown from the back of their father's pickup truck onto the roadway. By the time I reached the floor, Immy had been taken upstairs to surgery.

The surgery had lasted almost twelve hours, and things had not gone well. The bypass pump, a relatively new technology, had malfunctioned for several minutes and Immy had lost a great deal of blood. She was on a respirator, unconscious and unresponsive, in the Intensive Care Unit.

On the day after surgery, Immy's mother told me in a shaking voice that Immy's gown had been removed in the operating room and thrown into the hospital laundry. The medal was gone. Concerned, I called the surgery resident and told him what had happened. "Why are you telling me this?" he asked me.

"Perhaps you should tell Dr. X," I told him. He began to laugh. "Don't be absurd," he said.

That night I could not sleep. At two in the morning I dressed and returned to the hospital to look in on Immy. She was no better. Her parents had not left the ICU waiting room, and several other family members had joined them there. We sat together talking for awhile, but I had no news and could offer little comfort. My heart ached for them and for Immy.

Back in the house staff residence, once again I undressed for bed, but I still could not sleep. I kept thinking of the lost medal and what Immy's parents had told me. At last, I took some paper and wrote to Dr. X, telling him what had happened and how important the medal was to Immy's family. Folding the note in half, I dressed once more and went back to the hospital to tape it to the closed door of Dr. X's office. I had signed it and on the way back to my bed I began to worry. What if I had done something really foolish? If the surgical resident didn't care about such things, why should Dr. X?

I was off call the next day and, exhausted, I spent most of the time asleep. When I returned to the hospital for the evening shift, the pediatric day resident told me that Immy was no better. For the next few hours I took care of whatever was most urgently needed on the service, but later in the evening I stopped by the Intensive Care Unit to examine Immy and speak with her family. I found her parents in the waiting room. Together we went to see Immy. She was still unconscious. Leaning over to listen to her chest, I suddenly noticed a medal pinned to her hospital gown. Turning to her parents in relief, I asked if it was another one. "No," her mother said, "it was the same one that was lost." Dr. X had come that afternoon and brought it to them. I told them how glad I was that it had been found. "Yes," her father said. "We are too." Then he smiled. "She is safe now, no matter what happens," he told me.

The following morning, the surgery resident told me how the medal had been found. On the previous day, Dr. X had made his patient care rounds much as usual, followed by a dozen of the young surgeons he was training. But instead of ending the rounds in the ICU, he had taken them all to the laundry department in the subbasement of the hospital. There, he explained what had happened, and then he and all his residents and fellows had gone through the pediatric laundry from the day before looking for Immy's gown. It had taken half an hour but they had found it, neatly folded, with the medal still attached.

I was astonished. "The people who work in the laundry room must have been very surprised to see you all there, and especially with Dr. X himself. Did he say why he asked you to do this?"

"Oh, yes," the resident replied. Surrounded by mountains of clean sheets and towels, Dr. X had told the elite young surgeons he was training that it was as important to care for people's souls as it was to care for their hearts.

FINDING NEW EYES

One of my former patients, Josh, is a gifted cancer surgeon who had sought help because of depression. A highly disillusioned and cynical man, he was thinking about early retirement. "I can barely make myself get out of bed most mornings," he told me. "I hear the same complaints day after day, I see the same diseases over and over again. I just don't care anymore. I need a new life." Yet, through his extraordinary skill, he had given just that to many hundreds of others.

Proust said that the voyage of discovery lies not in seeking new vistas but in having new eyes. New eyes can often be found in very simple ways. Drawing on the work of Angeles Arrien, the author of *The Four Fold Way,* I sometimes suggest to people like Josh that they review the events of their day for fifteen minutes every evening, asking themselves three questions and writing down the answers to these questions in a journal. The three questions are: What surprised me today? What moved me or touched me today? What inspired me today? Often these are busy people, and I tell them that they do not need to write a great deal: the key thing is in reliving their day from a new perspective and not the amount that they write about it. I asked Josh if he would like to try this as an experiment.

He was dubious. "Less expensive than Prozac," I told him. He laughed and agreed to try. I was not surprised to hear from him in a few days. He sounded irritated on the phone. "Rachel," he said,

"I have done this for three days now and the answer is always the same: 'Nothing. Nothing and nothing.' I don't like to fail at things. Is there a trick to this?"

I laughed. "Perhaps you are still looking at your life in old ways," I told him. "Try looking at the people around you as if you were a novelist, a journalist, or maybe a poet. Look for the stories." There was a brief silence. "Right," he said. I sighed. But he did not call me back.

Josh did not mention the journal again for several weeks. Our sessions focused on relieving some of his stress and reducing his workload a bit. He seemed to be getting better, and I was optimistic. And then, six weeks after his phone call, he came in with a little bound book and began to tell me about what he thought was really helping him.

He had trouble with the journal at the beginning and had wondered how he could be so busy and living such an empty life. But slowly he had begun to find some answers to the three questions. He opened the journal and began to read some of them to me.

At first, the most surprising thing in a day was that a cancer had grown or shrunk two or three millimeters, and the most inspiring thing was that a new or experimental drug had begun to work. But gradually he had begun to see more deeply. Eventually he saw people who had found their way through great pain and darkness by following a thread of love, people who had sacrificed parts of their bodies to affirm the value of being alive, people who had found ways to triumph over pain, suffering, and even death. I was deeply moved.

In the beginning, he told me, he would only notice the things that surprised him, moved him, or inspired him several hours after they happened, in the evening in the privacy of his home. "It was like one of those fairy tales," he said. "Like being under a spell. I could only see life by looking backwards over my shoulder." But gradually this lag time became shorter and shorter. "I was building up a capacity I had never used. But I got better at it," he told me. "Once I began to see things at the time they actually happened, a lot changed for me."

I was puzzled. "What do you mean?" I asked him.

"Well," he replied. "At the beginning I couldn't talk about it and I just wrote everything down. But I think when I began to see things differently, my attitude started to change. Maybe that showed in my tone of voice or in some other way. People seemed to pick up on it because their attitude seemed changed, too. And after a while, I just began talking to people about more than their cancer and its treatment. I began talking about what I could see."

The first patient he spoke to in this way was a thirty-eight-year-old woman with ovarian cancer who had undergone major abdominal surgery followed by a very debilitating chemotherapy. In the midst of a routine follow-up visit one morning he suddenly saw her for the first time, her four-year-old on her lap and her six-year-old leaning against her chair. Both little girls were shiny clean, well fed, happy, and obviously well loved. Aware of the profound suffering caused by her sort of chemotherapy, he was deeply moved by the depth of her commitment to mother her children, and for the first time he connected it to the strength of her will to live. After they spoke of her symptoms, he had commented on this. "You are such a great mother to your kids," he told her. "Even after all you have been through, there is something very strong in you. I think that power could maybe heal you someday." She smiled at him, and he realized with a shock that he had never seen her smile before. "Thank you," she told him warmly. "That means a lot to me."

He was very surprised at this, but he had believed her. Encouraged, he began to ask other people one or two questions that he had not been taught to ask in medical school. "What has sustained you in dealing with this illness?" or "Where do you find your strength?" and found that people with the same disease had very different things to say. Things that he really wanted to hear about. In some way what they said was true for him, too, as he struggled to deal with the difficulties of his own life. "I knew cancer very well, but I did not know people before," he told me.

He has always been a superb surgeon whose outcome data are remarkable, but in the past few months for the first time people have begun to thank him for their surgery, and some have even given him gifts. He sat in silence for a few minutes, and then he reached into his pocket and brought out a beautiful stethoscope engraved with his name. "A patient gave me this," he said, obviously moved. I smiled at him. "And what do you do with that, Josh?" I asked him. He looked at me, puzzled, for a moment and then he laughed out loud. "I listen to hearts, Rachel," he said. "I listen to hearts."

Most of us lead far more meaningful lives than we know. Often finding meaning is not about doing things differently; it is about seeing familiar things in new ways. When we find new eyes, the unsuspected blessing in work we have done for many years may take us completely by surprise. We can see life in many ways: with the eye, with the mind, with the intuition. But perhaps it is only by those who speak the language of meaning, who have remembered how to see with the heart, that life is ever deeply known or served.

STRENGTHENING LIFE

So many books have been written on becoming a healer and so many techniques of healing have been developed that people who love someone with cancer may become concerned that they are not helping in just the "right" way. But we all strengthen the life around us in ways that are uniquely our own. Sometimes we draw on our own life experience and sometimes on the deepest instincts of our hearts. And, in the end, it may be simply our commitment alone that has the power to reach across and spark the will to live. When someone's life matters deeply to us, the life in us may speak to the life in them directly and have a far greater healing effect than saying the right words or using just the right imagery or the right ritual.

Years ago, I cared for a desperately sick two-year-old boy with bacterial meningitis. Deeply unconscious, Ricardo lay in a nest of IV lines and monitor cords, his tiny body almost hidden by the technology that supported and documented his struggle to live. His mother, a slight Filipina woman, sat at the foot of his bed day after day. She even slept there, sitting in her chair and leaning forward across the mattress. Whenever any of us came to examine Ricardo or draw blood from him, we would find her there, often with her eyes closed, one hand under her baby's blanket. She was holding on to his foot.

After he began to recover and the life-support equipment was withdrawn, I asked her about this. She smiled and looked away, a little embarrassed. But she told me that for all those days she had felt that his life depended on her holding on to his foot. Moved, I asked her what had been going on in her mind all that time. Had she been praying for his recovery? No, she told me, while she was holding his foot, she would just close her eyes and dream her dreams for him.

Day after day she would watch him grow up. She would imagine taking him to his first day of school, see him learning to read and to write and play ball, sit in church at his first communion, watch him graduate from high school, dance at his wedding. She would imagine him as the father of her grandchild. Over and over and over again. She flushed slightly. "Perhaps," she told me, "it made a difference."

Sometimes we may strengthen the life in others when we have an image of the future and hold on to it fiercely, much as Ricardo's mother did. My colleague Hal also strengthens the life in others but does it quite differently. Soon after his wife was diagnosed with cancer, Hal began folding white paper cranes. Being Japanese, he had been taught how to do this by his grandfather when he was a small boy. Origami, the art of folding paper, is part of a tradition reaching back centuries. One can make many different animals and objects of great beauty.

In addition to their beauty, the paper cranes have a deeper symbolic meaning. It is believed that the crane is the symbol of long life, the bringer of harmony and balance, and so people who are ill will sometimes fold a thousand paper cranes in the hope of finding the strength to heal. This tradition meant something to Hal, but origami was not a part of his wife's way. Sick at heart over her illness and feeling helpless to affect her suffering, one day Hal began to make a thousand cranes in her behalf.

Early each morning at the start of his workday, he would sit at his desk and, with his long-fingered surgeon's hands, intricately fold a pure white sheet of paper in support of his wife's healing. It took about four or five minutes. During this time he would meditate on his wife's recovery and experience the importance of her life. As he completed each new crane he would put it with the others in a large box. He planned to give them to her someday, when there were a thousand of them.

Some months later, as he put away that day's paper crane and began to review the charts of the people on whom he would operate the next day, he suddenly realized that his intense wish for his wife's healing was not altogether different from the way he felt about his patients. These lives mattered to him, too. Reaching for the stack of white paper he kept in his desk drawer, he made two more cranes, one for each patient. It felt quite natural to him to meditate on their healing in this way. Taking the cranes with him to his pre-op meetings, he gave one to each patient, explaining what it symbolized and why he had made it for them. He has done this for many of his patients ever since.

I also meet with my patients on the day before they are to have surgery. I first saw one of Hal's cranes when one of my patients came to see me directly from his office. I had been very concerned about this woman. Deeply frightened by her diagnosis, she had felt that she would not be able to recover from surgery and had delayed making this necessary and important decision for several months. We had worked hard together to help her find a trust in her own ability to heal. She was ready, but just barely. I had hoped that her resolve would hold. But that day she was radiant. She set a shopping bag down beside her chair and very carefully took from it a large white paper crane, maybe eight inches across. It was a marvel, intricately folded and absolutely exquisite. We both admired it in silence for a few moments. I was awed that such a thing could be made from a piece of paper.

"What an amazing thing," I exclaimed. "Where did you get it?"

"My surgeon made it for me," she said and told me the story of the thousand cranes. "Can you believe how beautifully it is made?" she said in wonder. "The man who is going to operate on me tomorrow can make such a thing with his hands. And he made it for me. How could I possibly not heal?"

I have wondered for years why some surgeons have far better outcome data than others who are equally well trained. Maybe this is simply a question of subtle differences in operative technique and maybe not. Perhaps some have found their own way to strengthen the will to live in their patients long before they meet them in the operating room.

THE FRIEND

I LEARNED ABOUT yoga from a friend who has taught this practice for a good part of his life. The word *yoga* actually means union or joining, the path of return to God. In the yogic tradition there are many types of practice, all of which enable us to find our way back to God, among them Jnana yoga, the way of self-knowledge; Bakti yoga, the way of devotion; Buddhi yoga, the way of wisdom; Dhyana yoga, the way of meditation; Hatha yoga, the way of the physical mastery; Tantric yoga, the way of sexuality; Rajah yoga, the way of mental mastery; and Sannyasa yoga, the way of renunciation. As a person who does not have a formal practice, I have always been drawn by the idea of Karma yoga, the way of action: living in such a way that one's life becomes one's practice. Living in this way has been something my friend has long aspired to.

At the age of forty-five, this friend unexpectedly suffered a stroke so severe that many of his physicians did not expect him to live. In the Intensive Care Unit when he awoke and first realized what had happened to him, his greatest fear was that he would no longer be able to teach yoga or do the many other things he had done all his life to help others live from the heart. Early on, long before he was able to speak or move his legs, he began to pray. He knew he might never ride his beloved mountain bike again or drive a car or even walk. Although these things were very important to him, he did not pray for any of these things. He prayed to be able to somehow find a way to continue his life's work.

Despite all predictions to the contrary, he has survived. Although he continues day by day to recover his ability to function and his strength, many things have changed for him. At first he was deeply troubled that he could not recall anything about the stroke itself or the weeks that he was in the Intensive Care Unit. Unable to remember, he had felt damaged and broken. But when he spoke to a friend about this, one of those who shared a twenty-four-hour watch over him for many days, she had told him that the time in the hospital had been very hard and frightening for them all. She felt that it must have been even more difficult for him. Perhaps not remembering was his way of taking care of himself. He had thought it a strange thing to say at the time. But several days later, as he was walking down a street in Berkeley, it seemed to him that he felt his own arms go around himself, holding him close. "It was a very new experience," he told me. "I have done everything else to myself, I have doubted myself and blamed myself and judged myself. But I don't think I have taken care of myself ever before."

Since his stroke, his ideas of service have changed. When he was stricken, many people responded. He received hundreds of letters and cards and phone calls. People offered help of all sorts from across the country and even from around the world. Friends traveled great distances to be with him and offer support. Some loaned money, others offered their medical or legal skills without charge, still others organized themselves into teams to deliver twenty-four-hour-a-day care. He was never alone. People around the country prayed for his healing. Even total strangers, hearing of his plight from their friends, formed prayer groups on his behalf. This has gone on now for many months. My friend is a modest and simple man, and he was deeply surprised by this profound response. He feels it has been one of the great teachings of his life.

Sitting in his home in the late afternoon sun, he speaks of his gratitude for what he has received from others. It seems to him that he has been enabled to touch and open the hearts of those around him far more profoundly through his illness than he ever did as a yoga teacher. It has made him wonder if Karma yoga is different than he had thought, less a question of choice than a matter of surrender. "Rachel," he tells me, "before this happened, I had chosen to devote my life to the teaching. Now I seem to have become the occasion of the teaching, and I am willing to be that, whatever it takes."

He allows more silences now. At the close of one of these, he shakes his head in wonder. "They say that people may choose such illness in order to learn something," he says in disbelief. "Who would choose such a thing? And what could be learned that might be worth such a price?" He falls into another of his silences. "I think I have learned one thing," he tells me. "I am not afraid to be with people, no matter where their lives have taken them. There is no place I cannot belong."

WISDOM

When I was six and in the first grade, our school became ecumenical. Besides decorating a little Christmas tree in every classroom, each class participated in the lighting of the Hannukah candles, which our teacher told us is what Jewish people did instead of celebrating Christmas.

On the first day of Hannukah, she showed us a Hannukah menorah, a special candlestick with a place for eight candles, and explained how each day at sunset another candle would be lit until there was a candle burning in each of the eight places. Then she told us the Hannukah story about the Maccabees, fierce Jewish warriors who had long ago fought a great battle to defend the Jewish people, fighting on until all provisions had run out, even the oil for the eternal lamp over the altar in the synagogue. This lamp, lit when the synagogue was first consecrated as a house of God, was never allowed to go out. Its burning presence meant that God's spirit lived among the Jewish people.

Everyone had believed that the end was near; once the lamp went out, God would abandon them and they would be lost. But the lamp had continued to burn for eight days without oil to feed it, and the Maccabees had triumphed over their enemies. "Hannukah is about the Miracle of the Light," our teacher told us.

While I liked lighting the candles a lot, I found the story rather boring. I especially did not like the part about the war. Despite what my teacher said, my grandfather, who was a rabbi, had told me that the spirit of God is with all people, and I did not really believe this story about God playing favorites.

Every afternoon I stayed with my grandfather for an hour or so after school drinking tea and eating cookies until my mother could come from her work to take me home. That afternoon, I told my grandfather what our teacher had said about Hannukah and asked him if he knew the story about the war, too. He smiled and said that he did. "War is a time of darkness, Neshume-le. The Hannukah story is one of many stories about darkness and light that people have told each other at this time of the year." I looked out his kitchen window. It had begun to snow.

"But why, Grandpa?" I asked him.

"Winter is a time of darkness also, Neshume-le," he told me. "The nights start earlier and last longer. So in the dark, people tell each other stories about the light to strengthen their hope. The story of the Maccabees is very old, but it is not the oldest story about darkness and light.

"Come," he said, and, taking me into his study, he opened a drawer in his desk and lifted out a menorah. My teacher's menorah was made of clay but my grandfather's was much larger and made of silver. He had brought it with him from Russia, he told me. It had once belonged to his father, my great-grandfather. He drew out a box of wooden kitchen matches and a box of candles also and lay them out on his library table. The candles my teacher had used were small and brilliantly colored, but my grandfather's candles were large and white. "They will burn through the night until the sun rises," he told me.

Handing me one of the candles to hold, he put a single candle into the menorah. "Tonight is the first night of Hannukah," he said, "and so we will light one candle."

He took up his Bible and opened it to the first page. "The oldest story about darkness and light is the story of the beginning of the world," he told me, and he began to read. "In the Beginning, darkness was over the waters and the Spirit of God moved in the darkness like a great wind over the face of the waters. And God said, *'LET THERE BE LIGHT!'* " I looked at my grandfather, his face shining with the power of these words. I was enthralled. "This is how the world begins, Neshume-le," he said to me. "Life and all of its blessings begin with God's gift of light.

"Now," he said, "I will turn out the lamps and there will be darkness like there was in the Beginning. We will see what it is like to receive this gift." At the time I was afraid of the dark, and the thought of turning out the lights was not easy for me. "Will you stay right here with me in the dark, Grandpa?" I said a little shakily. "Of course, Neshume-le," he replied. "I will be here and God will be too. Tell me when you are ready to start." When I nodded, my grandfather reached behind him and turned out both the lamps.

The old study was a room without windows, lined floor to ceiling with books. It was very dark indeed. After a minute or so, my grandfather struck a match and lit the candle I was holding. It did not give much light, and I could barely make out the menorah on the table. The rest of the room was filled with shadow. I held on to my candle tightly. Pointing to the single candle in the menorah, he told me to light it with my candle. Then he took my candle from me and placed it in the menorah, too. I looked at the two candles burning together and felt a little better. "Tomorrow," said my grandfather, "we will light another one."

The next afternoon at sunset we sat together in the darkness again. This time my grandfather had placed two candles in the great candlestick. When he lit my candle, I carefully lit the two candles from its flame, first one and then the other. We sat and watched the three of them burning for a long time.

We did this every day for a week. As the days went by I lit three and then four candles until, on the final day, I lit all seven candles with my candle and the room was filled with light. I sat back and looked at the menorah with all its candles burning. It was so beautiful that my heart ached and tears filled my eyes. "It's beautiful, Grandpa," I told him.

"Ah yes," said my grandfather. "But God's menorah is even more beautiful, Neshume-le. God's menorah is made of people, not of candles."

Puzzled, I turned to look at him. "The story of Hannukah says that God's light burns in the darkness even without oil, and it is so," said my grandfather. "That is one of the miracles of the light. But there is more. There is a place in everyone that can carry the light. God has made us this way. When God says *'LET THERE BE LIGHT,'* he is speaking to us personally, Neshume-le. He is telling us what is possible, how we might choose to live. But one candle does not do much in the darkness. God has not only given us the chance to carry the light, he has made it possible for us to kindle and strengthen the light in one another, passing the light along. This is the way that God's light will shine forever in this world."

After many years I have found that often we discover the place in us that carries the light only after it has become dark. Sometimes it is only in the dark that we know the value of this place. But there is a place in everyone that can carry the light. This is true. My grandfather said so.

III.

FINDING STRENGTH, TAKING REFUGE

MANY YEARS AGO I had an odd dream. It was only a single image, but I awoke deeply disturbed. I had no idea what the dream meant, but it felt like some sort of a message to me. It aroused strong feelings of sadness and a sense of being trapped. The image was very vivid. I saw a daffodil bulb planted in the earth. Lying on top of it was a large and very heavy rock. Because of this rock, the daffodil was unable to bloom.

For several weeks, I could not get this simple, powerful dream out of my mind, and eventually I described it to a friend who had a deep interest in dreams and their meanings. She had looked thoughtful. "Perhaps there is a conversation going on between the rock and the daffodil," she had said. "Why not listen in?" With surprise, I realized that I knew this conversation well. The rock was saying, "It's a dangerous world. DON'T BLOOM! I will keep you safe."

I began to laugh. "That rock sounds just like my father," I told her. She laughed. "And mine," she said. Still laughing, she asked me if I could hear the other side of the conversation. What was the bulb saying to the rock? "I need to bloom," I told her. "Blooming is my whole purpose for being alive." We sat together thinking about this for a while. Then she frowned. "It should feel good to have that heavy rock between you and danger, shouldn't it?" she asked. "But it doesn't, really." Suddenly my eyes filled with tears. I had no idea why. We let the matter drop there. From time to time I would think of this strange dream, and once I even dreamt it again. It was just as disturbing.

Some years later I was agonizing over a major career change.

The stress of this decision became intense, and one morning I awoke with a severe pain in my back, just to the right of my spine. Annoyed, I thought that I had slept wrong and took two aspirin. But the pain did not go away. After the third or fourth day I went to see my doctor, who told me that the pain did not correspond to anything anatomical that he knew about. It did not correspond to anything I knew about either. "Stress," he said, looking at me. "Yes," I replied, but privately I did not think so. He had nothing more to offer.

The pain went on for weeks. Finally someone suggested that I consult an acupuncturist to see if I might find some relief. This was not the usual thing to do at that time, but I had become desperate and so I had gone. Dr. Rossman had taken my pulses for a long time and examined me carefully. Then he ran his finger lightly down my back. When he touched the place that was hurting, the pain was so intense I cried out. "Ah," he said, "this is an acupuncture point. The life energy, the chi, is stuck here." With my permission, he would try to release the block by putting an acupuncture needle in that spot. I had never had an acupuncture treatment and I was skeptical, but the pain had gone on for so many weeks that I was willing to try. So I lay down on my stomach on his examining table and closed my eyes.

As soon as I felt the needle, the old, half-forgotten image of the daffodil bulb and the rock reappeared to me with extraordinary clarity. Suddenly I understood how the rock felt. The rock was afraid to let the bulb bloom. It knew the daffodil's value and was determined that it must not come to harm. If it bloomed and became visible, it could be hurt. I also understood for the first time that if it did not bloom, the daffodil might die.

Survival was a high priority in our family. My father, and indeed many other members of my family, had been made fearful of life by the Depression and the war. They had become experts at surviving. Surviving was a question of tenacity, of putting safety above all other considerations. Living, on the other hand, was a matter of passion and risk. Of finding something important and serving it. Of doing whatever was needed in order to live out loud.

As a child of my family, I had not understood the difference in this way before. Perhaps survival was not the goal of life at all. As I anxiously began to wonder if it was possible to protect something without stopping the life in it, in my mind's eye the rock spontaneously began to change its shape. As I watched in surprise, slowly it became taller and thinner and more transparent until I realized it was becoming a greenhouse. Inside it, the daffodil bulb put out a spike and bloomed. The yellow of the flower was extraordinary—as if it were made, not of petals, but of light. Lying there on Dr. Rossman's table, I began to weep.

In the blink of an eye, things had turned inside out. The reason the rock had given the bulb for not blooming was the very reason it was important to bloom. It was a dangerous world, a world of suffering, loneliness, and loss. Daffodils were needed.

My family had actually cultivated fear. After I was bitten by a stray dog as a child and underwent a painful series of rabies shots, I became terrified of all dogs. My father encouraged this, believing that it would keep me safe. It had never occurred to me before that fear might be the wrong sort of protection.

After the first treatment, my pain never came back. When I revisited Dr. Rossman to discuss this with him, he told me that every acupuncture point has a name. The one where my life energy had been blocked was called the "Heart Protector."

Shortly afterward, I left my secure and respectable faculty position at Stanford and moved down the peninsula to join with others who also dreamt of finding a new way to practice medicine. I had been fortunate to find an old Victorian house to rent in Marin. It had survived the great earthquake and had been owned by my landlord's family for generations. I adored it. A few months after I settled in, I began to work in its lovely overgrown garden. When I finally cleared away the ivy that covered over the front gateposts, I found the name the house had been given in 1890 carved into one of them. It was called LA CASA VERDE.

I knew that *casa* meant "house," but I had to look up *verde* in my Spanish/English medical dictionary. It means "green."

Perhaps finding the right protection is the first responsibility of anyone hoping to make a difference in this world. Caring deeply makes us vulnerable. You cannot move things forward without exposure and involvement, without risk and process and criticism. Those who wish to change things may face disappointment, loss, or even ridicule. If you are ahead of your time, people laugh as often as they applaud, and being there first is usually lonely. But our protection cannot come between us and our purpose. Right protection is something within us rather than something between us and the world, more about finding a place of refuge and strength than finding a hiding place.

THE MEETING PLACE

Of all the ways that people commonly deal with suffering—denial, rationalization, spiritualization, substitution—few are places of refuge. Most will disconnect us from the very life we hope to bless and serve and may defeat us in fulfilling the purpose of our lives. The sad part of this is that we can never hide from suffering. Suffering is a part of being alive. Hiding ourselves means only that we will have to suffer alone.

In the presence of suffering, everyone needs to find refuge. The difficulty we have in knowing where to find our strength came home to me when I taught a group of beginning medical students a class on genetic disease. The woman who had generously agreed to be interviewed for the class was a young mother who had recently discovered that she carried a gene that would arrest the brain growth of both her young children. Her loss was beyond words, its dimensions instantly understandable by mothers since the beginning of time. I wondered how she would find a way to go on, and sitting there, listening to her tell her story, I began to silently pray for her.

The students were young, and I was not sure how they would respond to her. Immediately after she left the room there was, in fact, a moment of silence when something genuine, intimate, and profoundly human was in our midst. Sadly, it disappeared as the students rushed to a discussion of the disease entity that had caused this tragedy. For the next half hour they analyzed, labeled, and shared research data and vast amounts of information about mental retardation. Slowly, I began to understand that the suffering we had witnessed had far exceeded the life experience in the room. No one had yet accumulated the wisdom to respond to it or the strength to be present for it. Confronted by something so vast and so impervious to all medical expertise, the students were struggling to contain it by understanding its pathology. They had sought refuge from suffering in their science. But life does not work that way. Science is not a place of refuge. It cannot protect us from suffering. Hiding from suffering only makes us more afraid.

Suffering is all around us. We may have friends and family who have lost a breast to cancer, or who have AIDS or Alzheimer's; and no matter how young we are, we may have friends and family who die. It was a very short time ago that only those with a professional degree became intimately involved with such things, and almost everyone who died, died in a hospital. No longer. Suffering has escaped from hospitals and institutions and met us in our own living rooms.

We avoid suffering only at the great cost of distancing ourselves from life. In order to live fully we may need to look deeply and respectfully at our own suffering and at the suffering of others. In the depths of every wound we have survived is the strength we need to live. The wisdom our wounds can offer us is a place of refuge. Finding this is not for the faint of heart. But then, neither is life.

PEARLS OF WISDOM

SOME OF THE oldest and most delightful written words in the English language are the collective nouns dating from medieval times used to describe groups of birds and beasts. Many of these go back five hundred years or more, and lists of them appeared as early as 1440 in some of the first books printed in English. These words frequently offer an insight into the nature of the animals or birds they describe. Sometimes this is factual and sometimes poetic. Occasionally it is profound: a pride of lions, a party of jays, an ostentation of peacocks, an exultation of larks, a gaggle of geese, a charm of finches, a bed of clams, a school of fish, a cloud of gnats, and a parliament of owls are some examples. Over time, these sorts of words have been extended to other things as well. One of my favorites is pearls of wisdom.

An oyster is soft, tender, and vulnerable. Without the sanctuary of its shell it could not survive. But oysters must open their shells in order to "breathe" water. Sometimes while an oyster is breathing, a grain of sand will enter its shell and become a part of its life from then on.

Such grains of sand cause pain, but an oyster does not alter its soft nature because of this. It does not become hard and leathery in order not to feel. It continues to entrust itself to the ocean, to open and breathe in order to live. But it does respond. Slowly and patiently, the oyster wraps the grain of sand in thin translucent layers until, over time, it has created something of great value in the place where it was most vulnerable to its pain. A pearl might be thought of as an oyster's response to its suffering. Not every oyster can do this. Oysters that do are far more valuable to people than oysters that do not.

Sand is a way of life for an oyster. If you are soft and tender and must live on the sandy floor of the ocean, making pearls becomes a necessity if you are to live well.

Disappointment and loss are a part of every life. Many times we can put such things behind us and get on with the rest of our lives. But not everything is amenable to this approach. Some things are too big or too deep to do this, and we will have to leave important parts of ourselves behind if we treat them in this way. These are the places where wisdom begins to grow in us. It begins with suffering that we do not avoid or rationalize or put behind us. It starts with the realization that our loss, whatever it is, has become a part of us and has altered our lives so profoundly that we cannot go back to the way it was before.

Something in us can transform such suffering into wisdom. The process of turning pain into wisdom often looks like a sorting process. First we experience everything. Then one by one we let things go, the anger, the blame, the sense of injustice, and finally even the pain itself, until all we have left is a deeper sense of the value of life and a greater capacity to live it.

THE WAY THROUGH

SOMETIMES THE VERY things that threaten our life may strengthen the life in us. Loss and crisis often activate the will to live. When this happens, we may grow larger than the obstacles that face us and free ourselves from problems that never go away by living beyond them. One of my patients, a young man with juvenile diabetes, was shown this way to freedom in the form of a dream.

David was diagnosed with juvenile diabetes two weeks after his seventeenth birthday. He responded to it with the rage of a trapped animal. Like an animal in a cage he flung himself against the limitations of his disease, refusing to hold to a diet, forgetting to take his insulin, using his diabetes to hurt himself over and over. Fearing for his life, his parents insisted he come into therapy. He was reluctant, but he obeyed them.

He had been in therapy for almost six months without making much progress when he had a dream, so intense that he had not realized he had been asleep until he awoke. Something deep and unsuspected in him had pointed its finger and shown him the wisdom in his situation.

In his dream, he found himself sitting in an empty room without a ceiling, facing a small stone statue of the Buddha. David was not a spiritual young man, and he might not have recognized this statue except that the image is a part of our culture in California. Although he had seen many pictures of the Buddha, this statue was different. He was surprised to feel a kinship toward it, perhaps because this Buddha was a young man, not much older than himself.

He struggled to describe how the statue had looked. "Its face was very still and peaceful, Rachel," he told me. But there was something more he could not easily put into words. He fell silent, and then he told me that the Buddha seemed to be listening to something deep within himself. The statue had an odd effect on David. Alone in the room with it, he had felt more and more at peace himself.

He had experienced this unfamiliar sense of peace for a while when, without warning, a dagger was thrown from somewhere behind him. It buried itself deep in the Buddha's heart. David was profoundly shocked. He felt betrayed, overwhelmed with feelings of despair and anguish. From the depth of these feelings had emerged a single question: "Why is life like this?"

And then the statue had begun to grow, so slowly that at first he was not sure it was really happening. But so it was, and suddenly he knew beyond doubt that this was the Buddha's response to the knife.

The statue continued to grow, its face as peaceful as before. The knife did not change either. Gradually, it became a tiny black speck on the breast of the enormous smiling Buddha. Watching this, David felt something release him and found he could breathe deeply for the first time in a long time. He awoke with tears in his eyes.

Often when someone tells a dream, they find a deeper understanding of its meaning. As David told me his dream, he recognized the feelings he had when he first saw the dagger. The despair and anguish, and even the question "Why is life like this?" were the same feelings and questions that had come up for him in his doctor's office when he heard for the first time that he had diabetes. As he put it, "when this disease plunged into the heart of my life." But his response had been very different from the Buddha's.

David had seen this dream much as the opening of a door. When his doctors had told him that his disease was incurable, his response had been rage and despair. He had felt that the life in him had been stopped and there was no way to move forward. But in the most exquisite way possible, life had shown him something different. His dream offered him the hope of wholeness and suggested that, over time, he might grow in such a way that the wound of his illness might become a smaller and smaller part of the sum total of his life. That he might yet have a good life, even though it would not be an easy life. Nothing his doctors had told him had suggested this possibility.

Often people with chronic illness may become trapped and invalidated, not by the force of their disease but by the power of their beliefs about it. Disease is at various times brutal, lonely, constricting, and terrifying. But the life in us may be stronger than all that and free us even from that which we must endure. Sometimes someone dreams a dream for us all. I think of this as one of those dreams.

RIGHT PROTECTION

OVER THE YEARS, many people in the midst of major life transitions have told me that they have not really lost anything because loss is an illusion. "There is no loss, there's only learning," they have said, obviously sincere in their belief. But I wonder. Perhaps at the highest level of personal enlightenment this may indeed be true. But it is questionable if anyone has ever reached this nirvana without experiencing their losses first.

At the level of daily life, there certainly is loss. If we spiritualize it away, we cannot use it to grow. If, as Ram Dass suggests, life is the ultimate spiritual teacher, we cannot learn unless we attend school. This usually means allowing ourselves to be touched by life, to participate in it. We learn by experience. The unexperienced life does not teach anybody anything. There are no spiritual shortcuts.

We cannot protect ourselves from loss. The best we can do is to avoid feeling our losses. Some of the ways we do this are truly breathtaking. Two weeks after she completed an extremely difficult chemotherapy, one of my patients lost all her possessions when her house burned to the ground in a fire in Oakland, California. Not a shred of clothing, not a letter, not a piece of jewelry, not a picture of her children or her parents or her wedding remained. I was horrified to hear this, and when she came to the office the following week I put my arms around her, telling her how sorry I was to hear of her loss. She hugged me close for a moment. Then, stepping back, she looked me in the eye. "I never really liked the kitchen," she said.

The important thing about the many strategies we use to shelter ourselves from feeling loss is that none of them leads to healing. Although denial, rationalization, substitution, avoidance, and the like may numb the pain of loss, every one of them hurts us in some far more fundamental ways. None is respectful toward life or toward process. None acknowledges our capacity for finding meaning or wisdom. Pain often marks the place where self-knowledge and growth can happen, much in the same way that fear does.

Grieving is the way that loss can heal. Yet many people do not know how to grieve and heal their losses. This makes it hard to find the courage to participate fully in life. At some deep level, it may make us unwilling to be openhearted or present, to become attached or intimate. We trust our bodies to heal because of the gift of a billion years of biological evolution. But how might you live if you did not know that your body could heal? Would you ride your bike, drive a car, use a knife to cut up your dinner? Or would you never get off the couch? Many people have become emotional couch potatoes because they do not know that they can heal their hearts.

Unless we learn to grieve, we may need to live life at a distance in order to protect ourselves from pain. We may not be able to risk having anything that really matters to us or allow ourselves to be touched, to be intimate, to care or be cared about. Untouched, we will suffer anyway. We just will not be transformed by our suffering. Grieving may be one of the most fundamental of life skills. It is the way that the heart can heal from loss and go on to love again and grow wise. If it were up to me, it would be taught in kindergarten, right up there with taking turns and sharing.

FROM THE HEART

ALMOST FIFTY-EIGHT YEARS ago, I attended preschool in the little park around the corner from our apartment in upper Manhattan. As the shy and timid only child of older parents it had taken me a long time to feel safe in the company of other children, and my mother or my nana often sat on a bench within eyesight to give me the courage to remain in the group.

Eventually I was able to stay there alone. One day close to Halloween, my nana left me at the park, and I spent the morning with the other four-year-olds making masks. Close to noon the teachers threaded string through our creations and helped us to put them on. I had never worn a mask and I was entranced. About this time, mothers began arriving to pick up their children, and as soon as I saw my own mother walking toward the class I stood and waved to her. She did not respond in any way. She stopped just inside the door, her eyes searching the room. Suddenly I realized that she did not know who I was and I began to cry, terrified. All her efforts to soothe me and explain why she had not recognized me failed to comfort me. I simply could not understand why she had not known me. I knew who I was with my mask on. Why didn't she? I never went back to the nursery school again. I felt too invisible, too alone, too vulnerable.

Most of us wear masks. We may have worn them so long, we may have forgotten we have put them on. Sometimes our culture may even demand we wear them.

A young woman named LaVera told me of something that happened when she was a first-year medical student. Those were anxious times, and it was not uncommon for people to work and study eighteen hours a day for weeks on end. In the evening, members of her class were in the habit of releasing the day's tension by playing basketball on the court in the basement of the medical students' residence. No one kept score, and people would drop in and out of the game for fifteen minutes or a half hour—however long it was before their anxiety about needing to study took them back upstairs to their desks. Often the game went on for hours, and the two teams that called it quits had no players in common with the teams that had started the game.

About four months into the year, in the midst of one of these games, one of her classmates had suddenly collapsed and died surrounded by other freshman students who had no idea of how to help him. He was twenty-one years old.

Although many of the students were deeply shaken by the event, nothing further was said about the matter. The school made no opportunity to acknowledge either the tragedy of the death or the feelings of the class. The young man's belongings had been packed up and sent to his parents who lived in another state. No one from his class or from the school had attended his funeral, which was held near his home.

The pace of the first year was intense and the competition fierce. Despite their shock and distress, the members of the class simply went on. Few talked about their classmate even at first, and by the spring of the year, the incident seemed almost forgotten.

At the beginning of their second year, the class began the study of pathology. In one of the laboratory sessions on congenital anomalies the instructor began passing around trays, each holding a preserved human specimen that demonstrated a specific birth defect. Wearing gloves, the students examined each specimen and then passed it on.

One of these specimens was a heart with a congenitally malformed anterior coronary artery. As it was being passed hand to hand through the class, the instructor commented in a casual way that it was the heart of the young man who had died the year before.

Without lifting her head, LaVera looked out of the corner of her eye. No one around her seemed to react. All her classmates wore expressions of detached scientific interest. A wave of panic rose up in her until she realized that she, too, was wearing a mask of professional detachment. No one could possibly know the terrible distress she was feeling. She was flooded with relief. She remembers thinking that she was going to be able to DO this. She was going to be able to become a real physician.

LaVera closed her eyes as she finished her story and sat in silence for a moment. She rocked back and forth slightly and began to cry.

After more than thirty-five years as a physician, I have found at last that it is possible to be a professional and live from the heart. This was not something that I learned in medical school.

Medical training instills a certain scientific objectivity or distance. Other perspectives may become suspect. In particular, the perspective of the heart is seen as unprofessional or even dangerous. The heart with its capacity to connect us to others may somehow mar our judgment and make us incompetent. Such training changes us. We may need to heal from it. It has taken me years to realize that being a human being is not unprofessional.

My training encouraged me to give away vital parts of myself in the belief that this would make me of greater service to others. In the end I found that abandoning my humanity in order to become of service made me vulnerable to burnout, cynicism, numbness, loneliness, and depression. Abandoning the heart weakens us.

The heart has the power to transform experience. No matter what we do, finding fulfillment may require learning to cultivate the heart and its capacity for meaning in the same way that we are now taught to pursue knowledge or expertise. We will need to connect intimately to the life around us. Knowledge alone will not help us to live well or serve well. We will need to take off our masks in order to do that.

WHOLENESS

WHEN I FIRST met Jeanne, her psychology practice was barely above water. She shared offices with a group of physicians, and, desperate to be accepted and work under what she perceived as the umbrella of their credibility, she took whatever crumbs fell from their professional table. Hers was the smallest office in the complex and hers the only name not listed on the office door. It was obvious from the first how dedicated and gifted a therapist she was, and this compromising attitude troubled me. But Jeanne felt validated by the association and certain that she needed referrals from these physicians in order to have patients. She would stay there almost two more years.

Jeanne was a shy person, a little apologetic and sometimes hesitant in finding the right words. She was also just the slightest bit clumsy. All this made her very endearing. You felt somehow at home with her and safe. Her patients adored her.

One day at lunch, she told me that she was moving from her present office. Pleased, I asked her why she had decided to leave. "They do not have wheelchair access," she said. I looked at her in surprise. She looked away. "Rachel," she said, "I have not told you everything about myself. Years ago when I was young, I had a very serious stroke. I was not expected to recover." I was astonished. "I had no idea," I said. She nodded. "I know," she replied. "Nobody does."

I had noticed her occasional troubles with words and her awkwardness. But even with my training, I had not guessed. Jeanne was a miracle. I could barely imagine the focus and determination she had drawn upon all these years, that she drew upon still, to live her life every day. "But why have you kept this a secret, Jeanne?" I asked, astounded.

Almost in tears, she said that for years she had felt damaged and ashamed. "I wanted to put it behind me," she said. "I thought if I could be seen as normal I would be more than I was." And so she had guarded her secret closely. Neither her colleagues nor her patients knew. She had felt certain that others would not refer to her or want to come to her for care if they knew. She was no longer sure this was true.

"And what do you plan to do now?" I asked her. She looked down at her hands clasped in her lap. "I think I will just be myself," she told me. "I will see people like myself. People who are not like others. People who have had strokes and other brain injuries. People who can never be normal again. I think I can help them be whole."

Over the past five years, Jeanne has become widely known for her work. She has been honored by several community groups and interviewed in the newspapers. She speaks often and consults for businesses and hospitals. The many people she has helped refer others to her. For the first time, her practice is full. Her own name is on her door. All that she needed in order to serve was the courage of her vulnerability.

THE LINK

IN *THE ONCE and Future King,* that luminous book about the youth of King Arthur, T. H. White suggests that when we strengthen the life in others we transcend time, and those whose lives we have once blessed are strengthened by us still.

At the beginning of this story, Arthur is a child, a foundling who has been taken in by a good knight and raised with the knight's own son. Only Merlin, who has hidden the infant king away in this fashion, knows his true identity. He contrives to meet the little boy and undertakes his education so that someday he will be able to fulfill his royal destiny.

This teaching does not take place in a classroom. As a magician, Merlin knows that life itself is the wisest teacher, and he uses his magic over the years to transform the little boy into various animals, birds, and insects so that he can befriend them and learn, firsthand, their life wisdom. As an ant, he learns that great things are accomplished little by little; as a hawk, he learns that once you take hold, never let go; as a fish, that your strength lies in your backbone. His education becomes an adventure as heartfelt as it is profound.

Gradually the years go by, and as the two boys grow older, Arthur is pressed into service as a squire for Kay, the knight's son, who is being groomed to be a knight himself. In this new role he accompanies Kay to his first tournament. Shortly before the tournament is to begin, it is discovered that young Sir Kay, in his nervousness, has forgotten his sword. Imperiously he commands his squire to fetch him another.

Arthur leaves the tournament on this quest and wanders through the shuttered and abandoned town hoping to find an available sword. There is no one to ask for help as everyone is at the tournament. He eventually comes to the deserted church square and there, standing before the church doors, is a magnificent new sword stuck through an anvil and embedded in the stone below. He takes this to be some sort of war memorial. He is so excited that he does not notice the words written on the sword which say, "Whosoever Pulleth Out This Sword of This Stone and Anvil, Is Rightwise King Born of All England." In the simplicity of his wish to be of service, he is delighted to find what his young master needs.

After a few worries about taking a sword that belongs to someone else, he tells himself it is after all for a good cause and, besides, he will return it at the end of the tournament. And so he steps up to the sword, puts his hand on its hilt, and pulls. Nothing moves. "Stuck fast," he says to himself.

And so, here is Arthur's moment, the opportunity of knowing at last his life's purpose and who he really is. Such moments often have the power to create a tuck in time, or perhaps they transcend linear time itself. Suddenly with a rustling of wings and a scampering of feet, with a slithering, squeaking, growling, cheeping, and baaing, the empty square fills with the spirits of all the creatures who have generously shared the wisdom of their own lives with Arthur, who have loved him over all the years and made him their friend. The badgers and nightingales, the hares and falcons and fishes, the hedgehogs and griffins are there, the hawk and owl and corkindrill, and even the wasps and the ants. Long gone from his life, they are nonetheless with him, supporting and encouraging him, reminding him of the experiences they have shared together that have made him ready. And strengthened by their love and all that he has learned from them, he reaches forward again and pulls the sword from the stone as if it were butter.

The Arthurian myth is a powerful archetype. Everyone will have moments when their true identity is offered to them, their integrity and with it their life direction. Quite often it is when they are looking for something else. Anyone who has ever believed in them, strengthened their wholeness, and offered them their love will be there with them then, no matter how long ago it was or how far away.

GETTING CLEAR

After listening to Patricia's fears for more than six months, one day I told her that for the next four weeks she was simply not allowed to be afraid. She had looked at me in confusion, unable to imagine what I had meant. Carefully I explained that I had observed that her first reaction to just about everything was fear and that when people had one reaction to everything, that reaction became suspect. In short, I did not believe that all her fear was true.

Abruptly she had become angry, telling me that I was not compassionate and indeed did not see her or understand her. "No," I said, "I believe that after all these months I do see you. This fear that has so little to do with who you are got in the way."

Calmer, she asked again what it was I was suggesting that she do. She reminded me that she experienced fear many times every day. "I know," I told her, "and I am proposing an experiment." I suggested that whenever she felt fear that she think of it as only her first response to whatever was happening. The most familiar response, as it were. I encouraged her to look for and find her second response and follow that. "Ask yourself, 'If I was not afraid, if I were not allowed to be afraid, how would I respond to what is happening?' " She was reluctant, but she agreed to try.

At first, Patricia had been discouraged to notice how many times she experienced fear every day. But she was surprised to find that often she could step past her initial stab of fear with some ease and that then she had a wide variety of different reactions to the events in her life. It had never occurred to her to challenge her fear in this way before.

After a few weeks, she even began to wonder whether she, herself, was afraid. For the first time she questioned if the fear that had been her life's companion was just a sort of habit, a knee-jerk response to life that she had learned years ago. Over the next few months whenever she felt fear, she would stop and ask herself if it were true, looking closely to see if she really was afraid. Surprisingly often, she discovered she was not.

Over time, she found that she was not afraid to submit her work to others, not afraid to try when she was not sure she could succeed, not afraid to speak out in defense of her values, not afraid to introduce herself to someone and offer them her help, not afraid to confront an angry person. Her mother had been afraid of all these things.

Staying safe had been the most important thing in her mother's life. Slowly Patricia came to realize that it was not the most important thing in hers. Her mother had lived a narrow and unhappy life. It had been a close call. "Rachel," she told me, "if you carry someone else's fear and live by someone else's values, you may find that you have lived their lives."

As a child, I was surrounded by my father's fear. Many years ago as I was trying to sort myself out from the ways I had lived and inhabit the way that I am, my companion in this process, a therapist, had given me the gift of an exquisite antique silver bracelet. She had it engraved with the single word *clear.*

She had known that a silver bracelet was something that I would take seriously. For more than a year I never took it off. A few months after she gave it to me, I asked her why she had had it engraved with the word *clear* and not with my name. "Look it up," she said, "but only in a very large dictionary."

I looked it up in the *Random House Dictionary of the English Language* and found that it had more than sixty meanings, many of which have to do with freedom: free from obstruction; free from guilt; free from blame; free from confusion; free from entanglement; free from limitation; free from debt; free from impurities; free from suspicion; free from illusion; free from doubt; free from uncertainty; free from ambiguity; and so on. And, of course, its ultimate meaning, which is "able to serve perfectly in the passage of light."

Sometimes it takes a lifetime to become clear. No matter. It may be the most worthwhile way to spend the time.

BEING FED

"I'VE BEEN INVITED to a luncheon in San Francisco for His Holiness the Dalai Lama," my colleague said one morning. "Why don't you come with me?" I hesitated, wondering if I really had the time. But here was a chance to be in the presence of someone who many believe to be enlightened, and enlightenment was something that I wondered about. I had met a few "enlightened" people over the years and had felt little difference between them and others. I had expected to feel some sort of difference, and this had troubled me. But here was another such opportunity. I decided to go.

The luncheon was held in one of San Francisco's most exclusive hotels. Naively, I had imagined that thirty or forty people would be there. But this was not the case. We were shown into a very large reception room crowded with many of San Francisco's wealthiest and most politically powerful. Men whose suits cost thousands of dollars and women in fabulous designer dresses stood holding drinks and talking, waiting for the appearance of His Holiness.

It was not an easy gathering. The noise level was intense. One had the feeling that anyone speaking to you was looking over your shoulder to see if someone else more important was there with whom they could more profitably spend their time. It made me uncomfortable and shy. My colleague was equally ill at ease, and we had begun to move slowly toward the door when His Holiness arrived and began to greet people. A somewhat informal line organized itself, and by chance we found ourselves close to the head of it.

My colleague had brought with her three photographs of an inspired approach she has developed for working with people with cancer. She had hoped to show these to His Holiness and ask him a single question. These pictures were quite large and had been mounted on heavy poster board. She was carrying them in a string shopping bag, and, as the line advanced, she began to try to untangle them from the bag. In the press of the crowd, this was no simple matter. She was still struggling to free them when she found herself standing with His Holiness. With some difficulty she at last managed to extract them and let the string bag fall to the floor.

She spoke to His Holiness of this work and they looked at the pictures together. Standing behind her, I had a close view of the interaction. It was completely unhurried, as if they were alone in the room. As their conversation drew to a natural and gracious close, His Holiness smiled. And then he stooped and picked up the string bag at my colleague's feet. In the most seamless way imaginable, he opened it and held it out to her so that she could easily replace the pictures in it.

It is not easy to say why this small gesture had such power. Thinking back on it later, I realized that few of the other men in the room might have done such a thing. But I do not think that is why I remember it.

It was not so much what His Holiness had done but the way in which he had done it. In this tiny interaction I felt something purely joyful in him go forward to meet with her in the problem. In that moment getting three large, stiff pictures into a flexible string bag was not her problem or his. It was not even a problem. It was an opportunity to meet. Of all those in the world who could have picked up a string bag and held it out, I doubt anyone else could have done it in quite this way. For some inexplicable reason, a place in me that has felt alone and abandoned for all of my life felt deeply comforted, and I had a wildly irrational thought: "This is my friend." In that moment it seemed absolutely true. It still does.

WHEN SOMEBODY KNOWS

I HAVE HAD Crohn's disease for forty-seven years. In 1981, after feeling quite well for a long time, I began to have mysterious and frightening symptoms. Sometimes, in the midst of some ordinary activity, I would begin to shake uncontrollably, and within minutes my temperature would rise to 106. Other times I would grow flushed and experience the acute onset of such profound fatigue that, if I were out, I would barely be able to get home. My physicians ordered progressively more sophisticated tests without finding any answers. My numbers were normal, but I decidedly was not.

Over a period of several months, these symptoms grew more frequent and severe. I continued to visit my doctors regularly, more because I did not know what else to do than because I thought they could offer any explanation or help. Eventually, I stopped telling them some of the more unusual things that I was experiencing. I felt they no longer wanted to hear.

As things became worse, I began to feel that something very dangerous was happening to me that no one could even name. The fear this caused is impossible to describe. It seemed to me that I was looking at the world through a plate-glass window, caught up in a set of events that dominated my life, and that no one else experienced or understood. In desperation, I made an appointment to see yet another doctor, a surgeon who had sat with me on the advisory board of a research project.

Dr. Smith was the head of the department of surgery in a large

HMO, a prepaid health plan whose protocol legislated the length of time that a doctor could spend with a patient during any single visit. We would have fifteen minutes together. Sitting in his tiny examining room waiting, I regretted making this appointment. It would probably be a waste of time. What could this man possibly do to be of help in fifteen minutes when several other physicians had not been able to offer much despite hours of their time?

There was a soft knock on the door and Dr. Smith entered. He greeted me and then spent a few minutes sitting quietly and reading over the lab results and X-ray studies I had brought with me. Then he leaned toward me and said, "Tell me why you have come."

I looked into his face and saw a genuine concern. I began to tell him all the things I was experiencing, starting with the more commonplace and finally including such things as the strange taste that often awakened me from sleep, and the times when I suddenly lost all sense of direction and was unable to remember how to get home. My voice shook a little. He continued to listen.

Slowly I began to tell him other things, things I had not told anyone else. How the doctor who first diagnosed my illness had told me I would die before I was forty, that my father had unexpectedly died a few months previously because of a medication error and I had brought my mother, ill with severe heart disease, across the country to live with me. I shared my anxiety about being able to care adequately for her complex needs, the worry that my present health problems might cause me to let my own patients down, the loneliness I felt when friends went on without me because I could no longer keep up. Eventually I said it all and then I just cried.

It took no more than nine or ten minutes to tell my whole story. Dr. Smith said nothing to interrupt and just listened closely. When I had finished, he asked a few questions that showed me that he had heard and fully understood. Then he reached for my hand and told me that he realized how hard things were. He validated my concerns. Despite the strangeness of these happenings, this was not all in my head. "There is no question that there is something going on that we do not yet understand," he told me. He reminded me that my lab studies had ruled out the truly life-threatening possibilities. He assured me that eventually whatever this was would declare itself more clearly and when it did, if there was a surgical solution, he would be there. He looked at me and smiled. "We will wait together," he told me.

Like the others, he had no diagnosis. What he offered was his caring and companionship, his willingness to face the unknown with me. In fourteen minutes he had lifted the loneliness that had separated me from others and from my own strength. In some way that I didn't understand then, this made all the difference. Someone else knew, someone else cared, and because of this I found I had the courage to deal with whatever was going to happen. Several months later when the great abscess hidden deep in my abdomen finally appeared on an X ray, it was he who did my surgery.

A PLACE OF REFUGE

PERHAPS THE MOST important thing we bring to another person is the silence in us. Not the sort of silence that is filled with unspoken criticism or hard withdrawal. The sort of silence that is a place of refuge, of rest, of acceptance of someone as they are. We are all hungry for this other silence. It is hard to find. In its presence we can remember something beyond the moment, a strength on which to build a life. Silence is a place of great power and healing. Silence is God's lap.

Many things grow the silence in us, among them simply growing older. We may then become more a refuge than a rescuer, a witness to the process of life and the wisdom of acceptance.

A highly skilled AIDS doctor once told me that she keeps a picture of her grandmother in her home and sits before it for a few minutes every day before she leaves for work. Her grandmother was an Italian-born woman who held her family close. Her wisdom was of the earth. Once when Louisa was very small, her kitten was killed in an accident. It was her first experience of death and she had been devastated. Her parents had encouraged her not to be sad, telling her that the kitten was in heaven now with God. Despite these assurances, she had not been comforted. She had prayed to God, asking Him to give her kitten back. But God did not respond.

In her anguish she had turned to her grandmother and asked, "Why?" Her grandmother had not told her that her kitten was in heaven as so many of the other adults had. Instead, she had simply held her and reminded her of the time when her grandfather had died. She, too, had prayed to God, but God had not brought Grandpa back. She did not know why. Louisa had turned into the soft warmth of her grandmother's shoulder then and sobbed. When finally she was able to look up, she saw that her grandmother was crying as well.

Although her grandmother could not answer her question, a great loneliness had gone and she felt able to go on. All the assurances that Peaches was in heaven had not given her this strength or peace. "My grandmother was a lap, Rachel," she told me, "a place of refuge. I know a great deal about AIDS, but what I really want to be for my patients is a lap. A place from which they can face what they have to face and not be alone."

Taking refuge does not mean hiding from life. It means finding a place of strength, the capacity to live the life we have been given with greater courage and sometimes even with gratitude.

COMING HOME

A HOSPICE WORKER once told me that it is rare for people to change at the edge of life. People die in character, she said, in much the same way that they have lived. Sometimes this is so. But just as often this has not been my experience at all.

The only daughter of one of my patients, a physician herself, wrote the following to me after her father's death:

> In the weeks before his death, my father, a blustery man's man of a guy who had difficulty communicating anything that was not a strongly held opinion, became someone else who I had vaguely sensed was there in him but had never before met. I could talk to this other father in ways that would not have been possible in all the years before. As you know, my father was outstanding in his profession and in one of these last conversations I had asked him what he felt was the contribution he had made to the world that made his life feel worth it to him. I had thought he would point to one of his many award-winning projects but he had smiled and said, "You, of course." I do not recall ever having another word of praise from him in my whole lifetime, but it was enough.

Surprisingly, we may find sanctuary in the presence of death, a place of refuge from everything that is not genuine in our culture and in ourselves. Many of us have learned to cover over what is most authentic in ourselves in order to protect ourselves or gain the approval of others. We may have lived this way so long that we no longer know that it is not our way. But many people who are dying have taken their masks off and let go of lifelong roles and self-expectations, ways of being that are not genuinely their own. At first they may let go of these things because they do not have the strength to hang on to them, but later they let go because it has become clear at last that these things do not really matter. They have come home to themselves. In their presence, we can come home to ourselves as well.

Places of death are often places of a greater wholeness, times when we, too, can discover what matters and the value of our love. Relationships, once cast in stone, can soften and assume a more authentic shape. Despite the pain of loss, such changes often endure. Over the years, I have seen such profound healings happen that I have even come to wonder if dying is not some sort of an act of service. Whenever someone has found the courage to live more deeply, more courageously than before, no matter how short a time it may be, they hold open that door for anyone who tries to follow.

IN THE GRAY ZONE

A WOMAN WITH metastatic cancer once told me that through the experience of her illness she had discovered a basic truth. There are only two kinds of people in this world—those who are alive and those who are afraid. She had smiled at me and said that many of the people she had met who were afraid were doctors.

Perhaps such fear is a natural outcome of the wish to be in control. A patient whose physician told him several years ago that he had three months to live told me in bewilderment that the doctor had seemed "satisfied" as he made this heart-stopping statement. "He seemed sorry to be telling me this but he seemed pleased that he had the information to give me, almost as pleased as if he had told me that he had the right drug to eradicate my cancer. He told me of my death with an air of authority as if it were he who had decided when it would be and in doing so had somehow gained mastery over it. As if when he could not control my cancer, he could at least control the time of my death. I was angry for a long time, but I now think he was as out of control and vulnerable as I was. Too bad we could not have talked man to man on that level instead of reaching for a false certainty."

Perhaps the most basic skill of the physician is the ability to have comfort with uncertainty, to recognize with humility the uncertainty inherent in all situations, to be open to the ever-present possibility of the surprising, the mysterious, and even the holy, and to meet people there.

The need for certainty is not just a problem for medical professionals. We wish for certainty as ardently as our doctors do, are seduced by it as profoundly and are as disappointed with the uncertain nature of the world. We all yearn for mastery. But mastery is always limited. Sooner or later we will come to the edge of all that we can control and find life, waiting there for us.

The wish to control floats like a buoy above the hidden reef of fear. More than any single thing, fear is the stumbling block to life's agenda. Perhaps it is only the things we fear that we wish to control. No one can serve life if they are unconsciously afraid of life. Life is process. When he was very old, Roberto Assagioli, the founder of psychosynthesis, reminded one of his young students of this: "There is no certainty; there is only adventure," he told this young man. "Even stars explode."

FINDING THE CENTER

MEANING IS A form of strength. It has the power to transform experience, to open the most difficult of work to the dimension of joy and even gratitude. Meaning is the language of the soul. Few works of service can endure unless they are sustained by a lived sense of their meaning and purpose.

About ten years ago a hospice director invited me to facilitate a day-long retreat on stress reduction and renewal for the staff. "Is this workshop for the professional staff?" I asked her. "No," the director said, "for everyone that works here."

The hospice occupied a whole building, and more than forty-five people staffed it. At that time, some hardly knew one another and there was an unspoken but tangible dividing line between those who offered direct patient service and the support staff. It had been like this for many years. This was of deep concern to the director. As she described the way the hospice functioned, I could not help thinking of the caste system in India. "In addition to stress reduction, I would like every person who works at hospice to feel that they are a valued part of a single service organization," she told me. "Perhaps you might do that in the morning session."

As she went on to talk about her goals for the afternoon, my heart sank. I couldn't think of any way to make her agenda happen, and certainly not in a single morning. But I have my resources. As soon as I could I called Marion Weber, the Coordinator of Experiential Learning in the physicians' postgraduate program at Commonweal. Marion is an artist who has a fine understanding of the unconscious mind and a profound and intuitive approach to healing and the building of community. "What do you think?" I asked her. "No problem," she said with a laugh. "It really is one organization and everyone there is an important part of it. You don't need to make that happen, Rachel. You just need to make it visible."

Over the next fifteen minutes, she worked out a group exercise for the morning session. Following her suggestion, I sent a letter to everyone who would be at the retreat welcoming them and asking them to bring with them a small object from home that symbolized to them the meaning of their own work at hospice. The letter said nothing about the purpose of these objects, and a great deal of curiosity was generated. "Should I tell them more?" I asked Marion. "Certainly not," she said.

By the morning of the retreat I had many reservations. I had never done this sort of thing in such a large group before. Neither had Marion. I felt it quite possible that things would not go as she had predicted. But there is a deep river of truth that runs beneath our daily experience. Sometimes tapping into it in the simplest of ways will have profound and moving outcomes.

The exercise Marion suggested was very simple. I began by asking everyone to sit in a single large circle on the rug. There were almost fifty people in the room. I do not believe that they had ever sat in the same room before, and people were not completely comfortable. When everyone was settled, I invited whoever would care to go first to say their name aloud, show us the object that they had brought, and tell us about it and how it represented the meaning of their work at hospice to them.

There was a silence at first. Then a young man stood. Saying that his name was John, he showed us what he had brought. It was a small ceramic bridge, which he had taken from his aquarium that morning. Holding the bridge in his hands, he told us that he had brought it because he felt that his work was a bridge between the fears and needs of dying people and their families, and the healing power of the hospice. This work was important to him because his mother had died frightened and alone when he was a teenager. "Where do you work in the hospice?" I asked him. "I am one of the telephone operators," he told me. The room was absolutely still. Moved, I asked him to put the bridge on the rug in the middle of the circle. He set it down carefully and went back to his place in the circle. Fifty pairs of eyes looked at it in silence. Something frozen in the room eased slightly.

The next person to speak was a middle-aged woman who had brought a crystal paperweight in the shape of a heart. She told us that her work was about listening to what was spoken and what was unspoken. She said that she had been trained to listen with her mind but through this work she had learned to listen with her heart. This had been important to her because for a long time she had not known that she had a heart. She was a social worker at the hospice. She set her object in the middle of the floor next to John's. Then person after person spoke about their objects and the meaning of their work. The things they brought were unique and varied. There was a tiny lighthouse, pictures of family members, a statue of Kwan Yin (the goddess of compassion), a nightlight, a cross made of two nails, a ragged teddy bear from someone's childhood, and even a pair of newborn baby shoes. Every object reflected one of the many facets of the hospice's profound work of service. People who had barely said hello to each other before listened to each other with absolute attention and respect. Slowly something ineffable began to become visible in the center of the room. Although they had never seen it before, people knew it had always been there in their midst and that they were a part of it.

The director had taken me aside before the morning session began and told me that she had forgotten to bring an object. She was certain that this would not matter. "I think it does," I told her and suggested that she find something that symbolized her work, either from her car or from the beautiful natural setting that surrounded the meeting room. She looked at me doubtfully but she went in search of something.

About three quarters of the way through the exercise she stood. She told the group that she had forgotten the object that she had meant to bring and had gone outside to find another one. The one she had found was far better than the one that she had meant to bring. It was the right one. Reaching into her pocket she took out a rock, about as big as a hand. It was very ordinary and there was still some dirt clinging to it where she had dug it out of the ground. She held it up and everyone looked at it, puzzled.

"This is what I bring to this hospice," she said quietly. "It is not soft and it does not change easily. It is steadfast. You can count on it and you can build on it." And walking forward she gently laid the rock down among the candles and hearts and statues of the Buddha. The group contemplated it in absolute silence. Among the other symbols of the hospice's work this was truly one of a kind. Yet perhaps only one of this kind was needed. In the silence I could feel a sort of shift happen in the room, the sort of experience I sometimes have in a therapy session just before someone sees the familiar in a new and deeper way. The strength and determination of this visionary woman that others had sometimes found daunting had become their Rock of Gibraltar.

At the close of this exercise we stood and slowly walked around the fifty objects lying in the middle of the room so that everyone could see them from all sides. In the elegant language of symbolism, something that mattered deeply to everyone present had become fully visible. The objects had been brought by nurses, doctors, telephone operators, cleaning women, social workers, and file clerks, among others. But it was not possible to tell by looking what had been placed there by a nurse or a telephone operator and what had been added by a file clerk or a doctor. In two hours people had gone beyond the divisiveness of their expertise to experience the deep unity of their purpose. Many were in tears.

There is in all work of service a deep soul. Something that has called those who participate to this work and sustains it. The experience of this can become lost in the daily, the mundane, the routine nature of the work. But it is important to evoke it now and then, to make it tangible and even visible. That which sustains the work will sustain us too and bless us with its strength.

IN THE BEGINNING

I DID NOT speak at all until I was almost three years old. The pediatrician caring for me had told my parents that they must not expect too much as my birth had been difficult and I had been so terribly premature. I might be late in speaking. Or I might never speak at all. My parents became frantic with worry. They did everything possible to help me to speak, pointing to objects and saying their names, repeating words slowly and carefully and reading to me for hours. There was talk of mental retardation, but my grandfather would hear none of it. "Look into her eyes," he would say firmly. "She is there." He always spoke to me as if I understood everything he said. As it happens, I did.

To everyone's great relief, I said my first words at a Thanksgiving dinner a few months before my third birthday. I was usually fed in the kitchen, but because of the holiday I was allowed to eat in the dining room with the grown-ups. Seated at the table on two telephone books, I turned to my mother halfway through dinner and said, "MAY I HAVE THE SALT."

I have heard this story about my first words many times. When I was a child, it would make me smile because these were not my first words at all. My first words were in Hebrew, patiently taught to me by my grandfather when I was about two years old. For countless generations, Orthodox Jews have taught these same six Hebrew words, the *Sh'ma,* to tiny children as soon as they are able to speak. Translated into English, they are "Hear, O Israel, the Lord

God, the Lord is One." Traditionally the *Sh'ma* is also said in times of great danger and at the moment of death. It is a statement of the fundamental nature of the world.

These words were the first of the many secrets that I shared with my grandfather. When I was older, I asked him to explain to me what the *Sh'ma* really meant. "Neshume-le," he answered, "to me these words have always meant that despite suffering, loss, and disappointment, life can be trusted."

Puzzled, I asked him why he had taught me this when I was so small. He smiled and said that perhaps the most difficult thing we are asked to do is to choose to live as a person. Being a person is hard on the soul. It takes great courage to live as a person, and sometimes souls who know this may delay their decision to be here or may be simply overwhelmed to find themselves here in a body.

"Your birth was very difficult, Neshume-le," he said. "And so your soul discovered how hard things could be from the very beginning." He had thought that because I had been born so far ahead of time, perhaps my soul had even been taken by surprise and had not been ready to choose life. In the time I had been in the incubator, it wavered back and forth between staying and leaving. Even afterward, it had been fearful and cautious, like a little bird. He had felt its uncertainty, its indecision. He told me that he had taught me the *Sh'ma* because in those long months before I spoke, it had seemed to him that my soul had been listening for something to hold on to. He had hoped that once I found this, I might be willing to begin.

CALL HOME

AFTER TWENTY YEARS of working with people with cancer, I have come to realize how much stress is caused by the sad fact that many of us believe in one way and live in quite another. Stress may be more a matter of personal integrity than time pressure, determined by the distance between our authentic values and how we live our lives.

This may explain why many people in the face of what one might imagine is the most overwhelming stress, life-threatening illness, notice their stress level has actually diminished and they feel more joy. Certainly their disease causes them concern, worry, and often fear; yet they report that their lives are less stressful now than when they were well. Such people seem to have found through their suffering a deep sense of what is most important to them, and the courage to bring their lives into alignment with it for the first time. Rather than using their strength to endure situations and relationships that betray their deepest values, they have used their strength to make needed change.

In the midst of her treatment, a woman with breast cancer told me how surprised she was to notice this change in her stress level:

> For the first time I am sailing my boat by my own star. My God, have I sailed it by everything else! And allowed everyone else to take a turn at the tiller. All of my life I've headed against myself, against my own direction. But now I have a

deep sense of my way, and I am loyal to it. This is my boat and it was made to sail in this direction, by this star. You ask why I seem so much more peaceful now? Well, I am living all in one piece.

Each one of us has such a star. It is called the soul. Unfortunately it is often easier to see it and follow it after it has grown dark.

Perhaps the root cause of stress is not overbearing bosses, ill-behaved children, the breakdown of relationships. It is the loss of a sense of our soul. If so, all the ways in which we have attempted to ease stress cannot heal it at the deepest level. Stress may heal only through the recognition that we cannot betray our spiritual nature without paying a great price. It is not that we have a soul but that we are a soul.

There are many practices that can awaken us and deepen our sense of the soul, among them prayer, meditation, chanting, fasting, and ritual. One of the most surprising of these is the experience of great loss. I have learned much about the power of the soul from people who have lost almost everything they once thought was important.

Some years ago, one of my patients, a woman with breast cancer, told me a dream. A self-made woman of considerable means, one night in the middle of her rigorous chemotherapy she dreamed that she was watching a woman build a mountain. Sweating and straining, the woman put rock on top of rock, climbing as she went, working night and day, until she had constructed a magnificent snow-capped peak and stood on its very top.

"A remarkable image," I commented.

"Yes," she replied, "and familiar. It was my life, my old life. Working, always working, building my beautiful homes, my corporation, my increasingly powerful role in the international business community. Watching her standing there at the top, I felt such a familiar thrill of pride. How competent she was! How disciplined and determined! How powerful!

"Then, to my horror, I saw a great crack begin to open in the mountain close to the base. From where I was standing, I could see it begin to collapse in on itself. Terrified, I tried to call out a warning, but I had no voice and could only watch. Finally the top of the mountain itself begin to give way. The woman stood frozen, paralyzed. And then, at the very last second, just as the whole thing crumbled beneath her, she found that she knew how to fly."

Awed, I asked her what this dream had meant to her. Smiling, she said that what we imagine is our strength may be very different from what our strength really is.

The soul is not an idea or a belief; it is an experience. It may awaken in us through dreams, music, art, or work or parenthood or sometimes for no reason at all. It overtakes us at times in the midst of daily life. Spiritual experience is not taught; it is found, uncovered, discovered, recovered. These sorts of experiences are common. They happen to all of us, sophisticated and unsophisticated, educated or uneducated, often when least expected. Many people discount them or devalue them or simply barely notice them. Yet they can change our lives.

A neighbor, a down-to-earth and practical person, shared such an experience with me and asked me what I thought it might mean. She had been cleaning her house, mopping and waxing a floor and thinking of nothing in particular, when suddenly it was as if her life were passing rapidly in front of her and she became aware of something she had not recognized before, that there was a coherence and direction that ran through it like a thread. The choices and events of her past, which at the time had seemed quite random, fit together seamlessly in an entirely new and purposeful way. Though she had never experienced this direction before, it was familiar to her. It was as if she had been following something unseen for many years and she had not known.

"What do you think?" she asked me. "I think it's a very important experience," I replied. "Well," she said, "that's not all."

As she stood in her kitchen, holding her mop and filled with this new awareness, she became deeply certain that what was true of her personally was also true of life in general. Everything was unfolding according to a direction. It underlay all existence, binding it all together. For a heartbeat, it seemed to her that she could experience this directly. "A steady unseen force, like a wind," she told me. It was the foundation on which all else rested, the very nature of life itself. Suddenly she knew that, despite external appearances, life could be trusted, and she began to weep with joy.

"You know," she said, "I tried to share this with several people, but it was very hard to talk about. Funny, when it's so real for me."

"Is it still real for you?" I asked. "Oh yes," she replied instantly. "It's not as strong, but it's still there. Especially the part about my own direction. It seems to me that I have my own star to follow—you know, like the old sailors. Perhaps we all do." She smiled at me. "Makes no sense, does it? But I feel less stressed and alone."

Experiences like this make me wonder. There are many ways of knowing, and sometimes we can know in a flash things that we can never understand. It is possible to be standing in your kitchen and feel the breath of God. Perhaps each of us has an inner compass that points to our true self. Whether we follow it or not, it will not diminish in power; it always points in the direction of integrity, the way home.

BROKEN

I HAD NOT expected to like Jon. Our relationship began with a phone call from the director of the pediatric training program at an East Bay hospital. "One of our residents has an attitude problem," he told me. "He's smart and a good doctor, but he has insulted or offended almost everyone here. Either this changes or we can't keep him. Are you willing to see him? He's not going to be easy to handle." I thought briefly about the three other young people who were currently my patients, all of whom had cancer. It would be good to see someone who was well.

"Sure, send him on over," I said, and we arranged an appointment for early the next week.

I had thought perhaps he might not come, but Jon was prompt. He was a slender young man, dark-haired and intense, wearing rumpled whites, the traditional uniform of doctors in training. His stethoscope was draped around his neck like a pilot's scarf. He sat down opposite me, folded his arms, and looked at me bitterly. I smiled at him. His expression did not change.

"Good morning, Jon," I said to him. "Why are you here?"

"They told me that I had to come or they will not let me finish my training," he said flatly. I had not realized that Jon would be made to come here in this way. *Not a good start,* I thought.

"Are they giving you this time?" I asked.

"They're paying for it," he told me grimly. I nodded.

"So how do you want to use it?" I asked him.

We looked at each other in silence, taking each other's measure. I was impressed by the passion I could sense in this young man and wondered what it was that was important to him. "I guess I'll just talk," he said finally. I leaned toward him and began to listen.

Within minutes, it became clear that the attitude that I was expected to fix was Jon's resentment toward the medical system. Jon was intensely angry about how the system was treating him. He told me that he was expected to work an eighty-hour week for less than the hospital paid people to collect the garbage. He had to endure the condescension of older physicians who underestimated his knowledge and then treated him as a servant. He was not allowed enough time to sleep or to eat properly. No one cared. He felt that the residency director was a hypocrite who was more interested in pleasing the hospital administrator than standing up for the needs of the residents.

Jon was also angry at his colleagues for what he felt was their careless ways of treating patients. He had witnessed some of his fellow residents discussing the diagnosis of a retarded little girl in front of her as if she could not hear or understand; another resident had forgotten to order pain medication for a toddler with a broken leg, too young to talk and say how much it hurt. Over and over he had seen anxious parents belittled and made to feel as if they were in the way, asked to leave when they wanted to stay to comfort their children. He told story after story, a furious indictment of his colleagues, his hospital, and his profession. I listened until the end of the hour and then made another appointment with him.

The next few sessions went in much this same way. I said very little and just listened. It was clear that Jon felt that most of those around him were callous, stupid, or uncaring, and his rage about this went very deep. Sometimes his feelings were so intense that he could not stay in his chair and would pace around the room as he talked. It was like being in a firestorm.

But then things changed. Close to the end of the fourth session, he was expressing his feelings toward another resident who had not returned a parent's phone call for two days. "This is their child. Doesn't she understand that these people are frightened? Doesn't she care that they feel helpless?" His face was red with anger. "Jon," I said to him. "Perhaps these are not the real questions. Is there a larger question that you have not let yourself ask?" He stared at me, silent for a few heartbeats. Then in a choked voice that sounded very young, he said, "Why are things *like* this? Why are children *suffering?"* I caught a glimpse of the depth of his pain and was shocked into silence. He looked at me pale and stricken, and before he could stop himself he started to cry. A single tear rolled down his face and he quickly brushed it away. Instantly he stood and left the office.

For Jon this represented a great loss of control, and so I was not at all sure that he would come back. But he was there the following week at the appointed time. "I've come to tell you that I won't be coming here anymore," he said. "That's fine," I told him, "but since you are here already we might as well have a final session." He hesitated and I smiled at him. "It's paid for," I said.

Surprisingly, he agreed. As this was our last meeting, I suggested that he might want to try using some imagery. At first he refused, saying that he was not interested in such things as he was a scientist. I said nothing. He sat opposite me, thinking it over. "Ah, why not?" he told me.

So I invited him to make himself comfortable in his chair and close his eyes. We sat together quietly for a few minutes, and gradually his breathing slowed. I was startled by how gentle and tender his face looked with his eyes closed. After a few minutes I suggested that he allow an image to come that was related to the suffering and the meaning of his work as a pediatrician. Jon found an image immediately. When I asked him to describe it to me, he said that it was a man about his own age.

"What does he look like, Jon?"

"He has long hair and a beard."

"And what is he wearing?"

"He's wearing white."

Thinking he might be wearing a white jacket and pants like Jon himself, I asked him about this. "No," Jon told me, "he is wearing a long white robe." He hesitated for a moment. "And sandals." I was surprised.

"How do you feel about him?" I asked.

"He's sort of embarrassing," he told me.

"What's embarrassing about him?"

"He's, you know, *SOFT.*"

"How do you know that he is soft?"

Jon's voice filled with disgust. "Just look at his face, look at his eyes," he told me. "This guy is *SOFT.*"

He paused briefly. Then he told me, "This is too embarrassing. I'm going to open my eyes." I encouraged him to stay with his imagery for a few more minutes. "Keep watching him, Jon. What is he doing?"

"He's not *doing* anything. He's just standing there."

"Keep watching."

"He's just standing there looking at me."

"How is he standing?" I asked him.

"He has his arms out."

"Show me," I said.

Silently, he held his arms out wide in front of him, palms up.

"Yes," I told him, "keep watching him."

"He is so *stupid*. He's just standing there with his arms out."

"Keep watching."

"He's just *standing* there and looking at me with those soft eyes." I said nothing and simply watched Jon sitting with his arms outstretched and his eyes closed. The room had become very still. Finally Jon spoke again. In a voice filled with impatience he told me, "This guy could stand there with his arms out like this forever . . . and ever and ever."

There were another few seconds of silence. Then suddenly and unexpectedly Jon's arms dropped to his sides and he began to cry, not one or two tears, but great choking sobs as if his heart were broken. He cried uncontrollably for a long time with his eyes still closed. When he became calmer, I asked him what had happened. "A little bird has come. It is sitting in his hand." There was a long pause. Still with his eyes closed, Jon smiled. "It is safe with him," he told me. And then of course we both recognized that the image was St. Francis of Assisi. As a former pediatrician myself, I was deeply moved. Perhaps, buried under his anger and his pain, this was Jon's hope for himself and his work.

Jon opened his eyes almost immediately. "I don't know," he told me quickly. "Isn't this just because we are here in San Francisco?"

"Perhaps and perhaps not," I told him. "There may be some personal truth in it. Let's talk about it a little." So we began to explore his past, looking for St. Francis's footprints, as it were. They were everywhere. He had several books about St. Francis, and the only video he owned was *Brother Sun, Sister Moon,* a story about St. Francis's life. He had watched it many times. We found other things, too. He had always loved animals and was good with them.

As a child he had brought many hurt animals home and cared for them. He had even thought about becoming a veterinarian, but his father had steered him toward medicine.

We sat together for awhile thinking things over. "It's just so hard," he said, looking away, his face still soft and vulnerable. Privately, I agreed. I leaned toward him. "Yes, I know," I told him, "but perhaps it could become a little easier." He looked at me. "How?" he asked. "Well," I told him, "what your imagery suggests about pediatrics seems true to me and so it may be just the right work for someone like you." We sat in silence for a few heartbeats. "Why did you choose it, Jon?" I asked him.

He drew in his breath. "I thought I could become a friend to innocent life," he said softly. I smiled at him. "You actually do this every day," I told him. There was a silence.

"I guess I focus a lot on how badly others are doing, don't I?"

"Yes," I said. "And they may be doing badly."

"But I let myself forget why I'm here in the first place."

"Yes," I said. We sat together for some time, both thinking things over. I began to smile at him again. "Talk to St. Francis, Jon," I suggested. "No one needs to know." He nodded and then he began to smile, too. "Maybe I will," he said, and with the briefest of thanks, he left.

I never saw him or heard from him again. But about two years later I had a phone call from the same residency director, referring another problem doctor, this time a woman. Cautiously I asked him about Jon. He laughed and said, "That's why I'm sending her over. He really straightened up; an extraordinary doctor. Very dedicated. An inspiration to us all. Maybe you can fix her, too."

Maybe, I thought. *Maybe she isn't broken, either.*

Sometimes when people don't fit into an existing mold, it is because they belong to something larger than the present. Something they will never find because they will someday build it for themselves and others. Over the years, I have met many young people of vision who suffer from a deep sense of difference. They may first need to abandon their resentment of the way things are in order to begin repairing the world.

PROMISES, PROMISES

IT IS POSSIBLE to befriend uncertainty, to remind yourself and others of the fluid, ever-changing nature of things. To remain awake to all possibility.

Like many Orthodox Jews, my grandfather never made an appointment or spoke of any event in the future without adding the words "God willing." It is actually a teaching of Orthodox Judaism that one does not make any promise without this tip of the hat to the authority of God. So whether someone said "I'll see you next Tuesday," or "We will have dinner in an hour," Grandpa would invariably respond, "God willing." God might, after all, end the world sometime between now and the chicken soup. There was never any fear in his voice when he said this, just a simple reminding of himself and those around him of the nature of things.

Life required us to hold things loosely, not to be attached to a particular outcome. The lunch appointment, the pot roast, the graduation, or the marriage—all were in God's hands. To be alive was to wait for the will of God to reveal itself. And one waited with curiosity. A sense of adventure. Much in the way you read a detective story at bedtime, struggling to stay awake in order to discover what is true, to see how things will turn out.

If the fulfillment of every promise or plan rests on God's approval, then God's hand is hidden in everything that happens. According to my grandfather, all tragedy or blessing was a part of some unknowable and dynamic purpose. One might not always get one's own way, but one trusted the Way absolutely. At any given time, the will of God might be unknown, but the presence of God was certain and was the only certainty anyone needed in order to live.

These days, my appointment calendar has places for entries three years ahead. There is a certain hubris in this, and, even as I write my commitments down, I remember this other way of living. I exchange letters of confirmation, I make plans, I even buy plane tickets, but deep inside I hold these things loosely. Lightly. I make my promises, and then I wait to find out. In my heart, I still hear my grandfather say, "God willing."

IV.

THE WEB OF BLESSINGS

IT HAS TAKEN me a long time to realize that I have an effect on the people around me. Like many people who were different when they were young, I suffered for years from shyness and a lack of self-worth. All but invisible to myself, I believed I was invisible to others as well and that my presence or absence had little or no influence on anyone. In early days, I would often not respond to a written invitation or return a phone message. Sometimes I would leave a party without a word to anyone, including the host or hostess. It simply never occurred to me that anyone might notice that I had not responded or that I was no longer there. That it might matter. Years later, I was stunned to discover that all those years I had been seen as aloof and rude. And that my behavior often hurt people.

Many people do not know that they can strengthen or diminish the life around them. The way we live day to day simply may not reflect back to us our power to influence life or the web of relationships that connects us. Life responds to us anyway. We all have the power to affect others. We may affect those we hardly know and those we do not even know at all. Many of the people with cancer whom I have met over the years have been taken completely by surprise by this power. Until they had cancer, they had simply not known how many lives touched their own.

Without our knowing, we may influence the lives of others in very simple ways. When Sara became ill many years ago, bulimia was not yet a household word. Filled with guilt at her uncontrollable behavior, she was taken to specialist after specialist until someone able to identify the problem as something more than a teenage rebellion hospitalized her for a year. This had saved her life. Slowly she fought her way back from the edge, surrounded by concerned adults who could not understand why she was bringing this on herself. She did not understand it either.

As she described it to me: "Rachel, I was just so *alone,* I could not stop myself, and at the worst of it I was not sure that it was possible to survive this. I was very afraid. I remember thinking that somewhere there must be someone else who has this problem, someone who has been able to heal from it. If they could live, maybe I could live too." Sara did not meet another person with bulimia, but after many years of difficulty she had somehow found her own way through and was able to recover. She cannot really say why.

A few years ago, she was reading her evening newspaper and came across an announcement for a meeting of a bulimia support group. Sara is a middle-aged woman and has not suffered from this problem for many years, but the idea of a support group intrigued her, and she decided to attend a meeting to see what it was like. It had been a powerful experience. The desperately ill young people there had touched her heart, and, while she felt unable to help them, she cared about them and so she continued going back. Other than saying that she had bulimia as a girl she had not revealed a great deal more about herself but had simply sat and listened to the stories of others.

As she was about to leave one of these meetings, she was stopped by a painfully thin young girl who thanked her for coming and told her how much it had meant to know her. Her eyes had been filled with unshed tears. Sara had responded with her usual graciousness, but she had been puzzled. She could not recall ever speaking to this girl and did not even know her name. As she drove home, she wondered how she could have forgotten something so important to someone else. She was almost home before she understood. Her husband, who met her at their front door, was surprised to see that she had been crying. "Sara, what is wrong?" he asked in concern. "I have become the person I needed to meet, Harry," she told him and walked into his arms.

Sometimes life's power shines through us, even when we do not notice. We become a blessing to others then, simply by being as we are.

It is sometimes possible to affect people's lives in major ways through very minor actions. An educator who is now happily married once shared with me a single incident that freed her to change her life. She had been living for several years with a charming, highly educated man who was physically and psychologically abusive to her. He was deeply respected in the community, and to the outer world theirs was a perfect marriage. But their private life was something far different. Over and over he told her that she had provoked him and had brought the abuse on herself by her stupidity and her other shortcomings. She would try even harder, but no matter how hard she tried she was never good enough. Over the years she had become so diminished and uncertain of what was real that she had come to believe him.

All this changed one day on a street corner in New York City. As Elaine and her husband were standing at a crosswalk waiting for the light to change, she had looked across the street and noticed a building with exceptionally beautiful prewar architecture. She had called his attention to it. "Look, Melvin," she had said. "Isn't that building beautiful?" Thinking they were alone, he had responded to her in the tone of absolute contempt that he reserved for their private conversations. "You mean the one over there that looks exactly like every other building on the street?" he sneered.

She had flushed with shame and fallen silent. And then a woman standing next to them, a complete stranger who was also waiting for the light to change, turned and fixed him with a glare. "She's absolutely right, you know," she said with a strong New York accent. "That building *is* beautiful. And you, sir, are a horse's ass." When the light turned green, this woman crossed the street and walked away.

It was the defining moment in the relationship, my colleague told me. Suddenly all was crystal clear. She knew then that she would find the strength to leave him. It would take some time but she knew she could do it.

To recognize your capacity to affect life is to know yourself most intimately and deeply, to recognize your real value and power, independent of any role that you have been given to play or expertise you may have acquired. It is possible to strengthen or diminish the life around you in almost any role. One of the ways in which we may become dangerous to others is to assume that our role or our expertise has in it such an inherent capacity for good that we, occupying that role, can do no harm. There is no role that absolves us of the responsibility to listen, to be mindful that life is all around us, touching us.

BELONGING

BASICALLY SERVICE IS about taking life personally, letting the lives that touch yours touch you. These days, many people seem to think that being touched is a form of weakness, even if the life that touches you is your own. If you are under thirty, the thing to be is "cool." Been there, done that. But why would anyone want to be "cool"? Should I live to be very old, I expect that I will not remember the times when I was "cool" but will be warmed only by the times when I cared passionately, risked everything to make a difference, and knew who I was.

Not only have we disconnected from life, but many of us have disconnected from each other as well. Such qualities as self-reliance, self-determination, and self-sufficiency are so deeply admired among us that needing someone is often seen as a personal failing. A hundred years after the end of the frontier we still inhabit its culture. Self-sufficiency was critically important when you lived a hundred hostile miles away from your nearest neighbor. But we live in this way still, three thousand to a city block. Needing others has come to require an act of courage. Is it surprising that so many people are secretly lonely and afraid to grow old?

Perhaps it is this striving for excessive independence that is a weakness, that makes many of us so vulnerable to isolation, cynicism, and depression.

It is doubtful that independence and individualism will enable us to live in the deepest and most fulfilling way. In order to live well, we may need to know and trust one another again. To touch and be touched by those around us. Service is the way that this world can heal.

True service is not a relationship between an expert and a problem; it is far more genuine than that. It is a relationship between people who bring the full resources of their combined humanity to the table and share them generously. Service goes beyond expertise. Service is another way of life.

Many times when we help we do not really serve. Those who help see life differently from those who serve and may affect life differently as well. It is hard not to see the person you are helping as someone weaker than yourself, someone more needy. When we help we become aware of our strength because we are using it. Others become aware of our strength as well and may feel diminished by it. But we do not serve with our strength; we serve with ourselves. We draw from all our experiences. Over the years I have discovered that everything I know serves and everything I am serves. I have served people impeccably with parts of myself that embarrass me, parts of which I am ashamed. The wholeness in me serves the wholeness in others and the wholeness in life. The wholeness in you is as worthy as the wholeness in me. Service is a relationship between equals.

As I serve, I become aware of my wholeness and more accepting of it. In using it to serve, I may come to see and understand its power. Many times my limitations have become the source of my compassion, my wounds have made me gentle with the wounds of other people, and able to trust the mysterious process by which we can heal. My loneliness has made me able to recognize the loneliness in others, to respect that place where everyone is alone and meet others in the dark. Most humbling of all, I have found that sometimes the thing that serves best is not all my hard-earned medical knowledge but something about life I may have learned from my Russian grandmother or from a child.

A helping relationship may incur a sense of debt, but service, like healing, is mutual. Service is free from debt. The wholeness in me is as strengthened as the wholeness in you. Everyone involved is fortunate to have had the chance to participate. In helping, we may find a sense of satisfaction; in serving, we have an experience of gratitude.

Serving is also different from fixing. One of the pioneers of the Human Potential Movement, Abraham Maslow, said, "If all you have is a hammer, everything looks like a nail." Seeing yourself as a fixer may cause you to see brokenness everywhere, to sit in judgment on life itself. When we fix others, we may not see their hidden wholeness or trust the integrity of the life in them. Fixers trust their own expertise. When we serve, we see the unborn wholeness in others; we collaborate with it and strengthen it. Others may then be able to see their wholeness for themselves for the first time.

Perhaps fixing is only a way to relate to things. Relating to another human being in this way is to deny and diminish in some profound and subtle way the power of the life in them and its mystery.

Over forty-seven years of illness I have been helped and fixed by a great number of people. I am grateful to them all. But all that helping and fixing left me wounded in some important and fundamental ways. Only service heals.

All who serve, serve life. What we serve is something worthy of our attention, of the commitment of our time and our lives. Service is not about fixing life, outwitting life, manipulating life, controlling life, or struggling to gain mastery over life. When we serve, we discover that life is holy.

Service is closer to generosity than it is to duty. It connects us to one another and to life itself. When we experience our connectedness, serving others becomes the natural and joyful thing to do. Over the long run, fixing and helping are draining but service is renewing. When you serve, your work itself will sustain you, renew you, and bless you, often over many years.

The best definition of service I have come across is a single word, *BELONGING*. Service is the final healing of isolation and loneliness. It is the lived experience of belonging.

LIFELINE

My father was in the hospital for ten days after his heart surgery. The long incision that ran from the front of his chest all the way around to his back was healing well, and he was able to eat and walk in the hall. "He's doing just fine," his nurses said. "But he's not talking," I replied, concerned. "Maybe he's just tired," they told me.

My father was born talking. He had an opinion on everything. As the days went on, his silence frightened me. He seemed to understand everything that was said to him, but he had no response. He had been in surgery for almost ten hours. He had never even been sick before.

Since the surgery he had not said a single word. He seemed numbed, frozen in some way. Thinking about it, I had a sense of my father, hanging out in the vicinity of his body, shocked out of it by the pain and the unimaginable invasiveness of the procedure, uncertain of whether to put himself in harm's way again and get back in. It seemed like a vulnerable time, as if some decision about continuing on had yet to be made.

The days passed and things did not get better. One afternoon as I sat with him, I could barely hold back my tears and I realized how afraid I was for him. His body was there in the room with me, walking, eating, healing, but he had gone somewhere else, and it seemed that no one but me had noticed. He lay in his bed, with his eyes closed, looking small and somehow deflated, as if the life had leaked out of him and he had collapsed like an empty balloon. I did not know what to do.

Deeply distressed, I took the hand lotion from his bed table and uncovered his feet. Standing at the foot of his bed, I began to slowly rub his feet with lotion. His eyes remained closed. Unable to bear seeing him this way, I kept my eyes focused on his feet. After a while, I began to talk to him.

I started at the beginning of our relationship, telling him what I could remember of him as a little girl, the things we did together when I was very small. And then I just continued on. I reminded him of how he had pushed my swing for hours in the swing park, how he had taken me to school the first day and stood at the bottom of the steps taking my picture over and over again until I was late, about the time that I had broken my arm and he had carried me at a dead run all the way to the neighborhood doctor's office, singing nursery rhymes to me at the top of his lungs. I reminded him of the many hours he had helped me do my homework, of the times he had played gin rummy with me and let me win, of the night he drove me and my date to our high-school prom, wearing a rented tux himself. I reminded him of the long drive to college, and how we had both cried when he left, of the many late-night phone calls of encouragement. And how, when I hugged him minutes after graduating from medical school, he had told me, *"Now* you can join the circus," and then burst into tears. And all the while I rubbed his feet. Finally I reminded him of the conversation we had just last week when he had given me pages and pages of instructions about what to do if he did not come back from the operating room. "But you didn't die, Papa," I told him. "You made it through."

One of my father's feet moved slightly. I looked up. My father was looking at me. The numb and distant look of the past weeks was gone. Suddenly he threw back his head and began to laugh. Indescribably relieved, I began to laugh, too. "I am a tough old bastard," he told me. "And a good thing, too. What would you do without me?"

Connection strengthens the life in us. Sometimes the life in us is strengthened by discovering that others need us. Other times we are strengthened by discovering beyond a doubt that our love matters to someone more than we realized possible or that someone loves us just as we are.

Recently a woman, long recovered from breast cancer, told a group of other women about her husband. "Richard is my blessing," she told us. This was a second marriage for both of them, and they loved each other and each other's children dearly. Richard was a widower when they first met; his first wife had suffered a long and painful death from cancer.

Less than a year into their courtship, when Celia found a lump in her breast, she had not thought much about it. She had found lumps in her breasts before. She had gone to the doctor alone and was alone when she received the devastating news: This lump was not like the others. This lump was malignant.

Almost her first thought was of Richard and his children. They had been profoundly wounded by cancer only a few years before. They were still healing from it. How could she bring this terrible thing into their lives again? She had called Richard immediately and, without telling him why, had simply broken off their relationship. For several weeks she had refused his phone calls and returned his letters. But Richard had not given up and had continued to pursue her, begging her to see him.

Finally she had relented and arranged to meet with him and tell him good-bye, thinking perhaps this would convince him to stop pursuing her and go on with his life. Richard appeared to be under great strain. Gently he had asked her why she had broken with him. Almost in tears, she told him that she had found a lump in her breast and that it was malignant. She had undergone surgery a few weeks ago and would begin chemotherapy the following week. "You and the children have lived through this once already," she told him. "I won't put you through it again."

He had looked at her, openmouthed. "You have cancer?" he asked. Dumbly, she nodded, the tears beginning to run down her cheeks. "Oh, Celia," he said, beginning to laugh with relief. "We can do cancer . . . we know how to do cancer. I thought that you didn't love me."

Perhaps we can only truly serve those we are willing to touch, not only with our hands but with our hearts and even our souls. Professionalism has embedded in service a sense of difference, a certain distance. But on the deepest level, service is an experience of belonging, an experience of connection to others and to the world around us. It is this connection that gives us the power to bless the life in others. Without it, the life in them would not respond to us.

LEARNING TO SERVE

COMPASSION BEGINS WITH the acceptance of what is most human in ourselves, what is most capable of suffering. In attending to our own capacity to suffer, we can uncover a simple and profound connection between our own vulnerability and the vulnerability in all others. Experiencing this allows us to find an instinctive kindness toward life which is the foundation of all compassion and genuine service.

Ours is not a culture that respects the sick or the old or the vulnerable. We strive for independence, competence, and mastery. In embracing such frontier values we may become intolerant of human wholeness, contemptuous of anything in ourselves and in others that has needs or is capable of suffering. The denial of a common vulnerability is the ultimate barrier to compassion.

My medical training was not an opportunity to learn compassion. The way I was trained, in order to serve you had to be strong. John Wayne is not the Father of Medicine, but you could not have guessed this from the way we all lived and worked. Denial of vulnerability was the very basis of the program. My own chronic illness made this especially clear to me.

By the time I was an intern, I had been taking large doses of steroids every day for several years. Often my appearance changed radically, depending on how much medication was required to keep the symptoms of my Crohn's disease in check. Sometimes my face would become round and swollen and I would grow a five-o'clock shadow. Other times I had severe acne. My weight cycled so wildly that I owned clothing in every size from 8 to 16. I would wear almost all these things in the course of any given year. I was frequently in significant pain. During this time, I worked closely with dozens of other doctors every day. In all my training, no one ever said a word to me about any of this nor did I mention anything about it to them.

After years of daily treatment with high-dose steroids, severe osteoporosis—a thinning and weakening of the bones—is common. Once, as senior resident, I was leading the morning ward rounds, pushing a rack of patient charts as five of us went from room to room discussing the needs of each patient and planning for their day's treatment. About halfway through the hour, I heard a crack and felt my right leg give way. No one seemed to notice. We were in the corridor at the time and we finished the rounds there, a matter of another twenty minutes or so of discussion during which I put my weight on one leg, leaned on the chart rack, and breathed into the pain. By the time the rounds were over, I was drenched in sweat. After the younger residents went off to begin the day's work I asked the ward nurse, the only other woman on the rounds, for her help. In the emergency room, it was found that I had a spontaneous fracture in my right leg.

My leg was casted, and the following day I returned to the ward on crutches. The only person who said anything to me about this was the resident who had taken my call the night before, and even he did not mention my cast or ask me how I was feeling. He just wanted to know which of his on-call nights I was going to cover to repay the time I owed him.

I must say that there was a certain professional pride in all this. The few women on the medical staff were living as equals in a macho culture. The men asked no quarter of each other or of us, and none was given. As physicians we all expected to function far beyond our personal needs, whatever they might be, and we respected one another for the style in which we did this.

But of course wisdom is something quite different. Soon after this, I was to catch a glimpse of it. One of the few women doctors on the faculty at that time was a middle-aged internist, a full professor of medicine. Although I had never actually spoken with her, I had followed her career and her achievements closely. She was the model of the sort of physician I hoped to be, and I admired her greatly.

She too was a single woman, and her passion and dedication to her work were legendary. A superb researcher, clinician, and teacher, she was deeply respected by the younger doctors and by her colleagues. She was strong and vigorous, and when I heard that she had found a lump in her breast I was stunned.

The chief of the department did her surgery, and the mass turned out to be malignant. She had asked him to come and tell her what he had found as soon as she awakened from the anesthesia. He had gone to the recovery room with this hard news. Leaning over her gurney, he had awakened her and gently told her the results of the frozen section. She was still so drugged from the anesthesia that he was not at all certain that she had understood that she had cancer, and so he had told her this twice. Afterward she had closed her eyes for a brief time. Thinking she had fallen asleep, he had turned and taken two steps toward the door when he heard her voice. So softly as to be barely audible she had said, "Now someone will have to take care of me."

The news of her diagnosis was accepted by the rest of the medical staff without much comment, but her words had a very powerful effect on me. They had cut me to the heart. As soon as I could, I fled to the privacy of an on-call room and sat on the bed deeply shaken. My own cast had been removed just days before. For the six weeks that I had worn it, I had never asked for help nor had help been offered. For the first time, I questioned this way of living.

It had taken cancer for Dr. Jones to give herself permission to be cared for. Was this because she was so strong she had not needed care? But everyone needs care, even John Wayne. Surely she had been worthy of compassion even though she was strong. An emotion I could not easily name overwhelmed me. It crowded my heart almost beyond enduring. What had happened to Dr. Jones mattered to me, and I began to weep for her. I wept for a long time, for her and for everyone else who suffers unseen and alone.

WE ARE ENOUGH

MANY PEOPLE HAVE found healing in the cancer retreats at Commonweal. Yet, a lot of what we do is to grieve our losses together. This is not something I was taught to do in my training. Medical school taught me to fix pain, not share it. But a degree is only the beginning of an education. Over time, I have seen that when people can show their pain and suffering to others who genuinely understand, much of what has stood between them and their wholeness disappears.

We start sharing on the first evening of the retreat. Eight people with cancer who barely know each other's names talk intimately about their losses, surprised to be able to say things they have not been able to say before. When someone speaks, everyone present simply listens generously and no one asks for explanations. No one needs to. So, in the end, people find they are able to belong just as they are. A place that can accept your suffering without dismissing you is a safe place. A place where you can become whole again.

I remember talking about these early sessions to someone who commented that it sounded like we were encouraging victimization and self-pity. But it simply doesn't happen that way. In being able to talk this openly, people often are able to see for the first time that which their suffering has covered over: the courage, the strength, the faith. The will to live and its power. During these first retreat evenings, I have watched wounded people strengthen the life in each other over and over again. At the beginning it may seem like a group of victims; but, as it turns out, it is usually a room full of warriors.

The healing that people find in such situations is profoundly natural. It is not the work of experts. Healing does not require our intent; often we heal others simply because of who we are. Then, by some Grace, our very wounds can serve to strengthen the life in others. Although I have witnessed this many times, I still find something mysterious in such occasions, as if something unknown, finding us worthy, has used us just as we are to be an instrument of healing.

Some years ago, a patient gave me a small square of glass with a quote from St. Francis written on it. It has hung in my office window for many years. It says, "Lord, make me an instrument of thy peace." This does happen, and without your changing a hair on your head.

This is not to say that healing is always pleasant or easy. Sometimes when a cancer retreat group is going to be unusually difficult, I can sense it from the moment I first sit down. Within minutes after I joined this group of eight women with cancer, even I began to feel unsafe. Yet eventually much healing would happen among us.

From the first, it was not a group that could listen well. One of the participants had a brain tumor that made it hard for her to track a conversation, and she often responded inappropriately; another, older woman was almost totally deaf and constantly asked the others to speak up; another was a Harvard psychiatrist who offered a Freudian interpretation of every feeling anyone expressed. In addition there was an aggressive and contentious lawyer who challenged everyone's opinions and offered hers as pronouncements, and a gifted artist whose mother had died of cancer when she was three. Deeply wounded, she seemed to have stopped growing emotionally at about that age. No matter what was being said, she redirected everyone's attention toward herself and her issues. And there was a young woman who sat in a corner, her arms wrapped around her knees, seemingly unable to make eye contact or speak. Her name was Beth.

It was so hard to feel safe in this first morning meeting that it was no surprise when another staff member told me that Beth had come to him at lunch and said that she wanted to go home. I had been concerned about her even before she arrived. On her application she had stated that she had stopped her treatment—a chemotherapy known to be 95 percent effective in curing her type of cancer—halfway through the recommended course. She had offered no explanation of this choice, and I had wondered about it.

The staff member had listened to Beth's distress. The room had felt "abusive" to her. She did not feel certain I would be able to protect her from the aggressiveness and indifference of some of the other women. She had cried then and told him that she had experienced physical abuse for most of her childhood. Her mother had beaten her unmercifully, sometimes with a belt, sometimes with a riding crop. She had stopped chemotherapy because it had brought many of these memories of purposefully inflicted pain flooding back and she could not go on.

When she had finished, he gently reminded her that she had come a long way to be here and might want to give it more of a chance. He suggested that she speak to me about her fears. She said that was out of the question as she had great difficulty in trusting older women like her mother. She would, however, try one more time.

The second morning went a little better. The artist, Faith, began the session by confronting Beth and demanding, "Are you going to say anything today?" Beth shrank back, and I took this heaven-sent opening to clarify that there was no need to say anything in these meetings. I suggested that we might still benefit even if we sat here silently every morning, each one of us simply caring about the others. I watched Beth out of the corner of my eye. By the end of the session, she seemed slightly more at ease.

As the week progressed, the group came together in a very interesting way. Often there is a single word or quality which sums up the relationships in these groups that is different for every group. In this case, it was *acceptance.* The women found ways to care for and support one another without taking offense at behaviors that were sometimes difficult. It was as if each woman extended to the others the sort of love they had given their children. Beth still did not speak or reach out to the others, but she listened intensely, obviously affected by what others were feeling and saying. She did not leave.

On the final morning of the retreat, the group had a frank and open discussion about sexuality. Women who had not shown their scars to their husbands and lovers showed them to each other. Including myself, most of us were women whose bodies had been profoundly changed by surgery, and we spoke candidly about our experiences and the way others had responded to us. Faith had just shared a touching and very funny story about a studly lover's reaction upon discovering that one of her breasts was false. Suddenly she turned to Beth, who was sitting next to her, and blurted out, much as a child would, "Well, I guess you don't have any stories, do you? Your kind of cancer doesn't show."

The gauntlet had been flung down again. I looked at Beth, hoping that she might be ready to meet the challenge this time. She was pale but she was more than ready. In a choked but dignified voice she replied, "That's not true. I have never allowed anyone to see or touch my back." The obvious emotion in her voice would have deterred someone more socially and emotionally mature, but Faith was oblivious to it. "Why not?" she demanded. Beth replied that her back was deeply scarred. "I was whipped many times when I was small," she told us.

There was a stunned silence. Almost anyone else would have backed down, but Faith continued on. With a small child's natural curiosity she asked, "Who hit you like that?" Beth turned toward her and looked her in the eye. "My mother," she said flatly.

There are the things that most of us would say at such a moment; one could be contrite or overcome with embarrassment. One could apologize. Faith did none of these things. Instead she responded as a very young person might. Her eyes became huge and slowly filled with tears that overflowed and ran down her cheeks. Beth, seeing for the first time another woman's genuine and heartfelt response to her suffering, reached out at last for Faith's hand and said softly, "Thank you. Oh, thank you."

A few months later we heard from Beth that she had resumed her treatment. After six years, it is apparent that it was successful.

Curing is the work of experts, but strengthening the life in one another is the work of human beings. Few experienced therapists would have interacted with Beth in the way that Faith had, and yet a professional might not have been nearly as effective. Perhaps Beth might not have trusted anything less genuine than what she was given. Sometimes the deepest healing comes from the natural fit between two wounded people's lives. It makes one wonder about the source of such healing.

FINDING THE CONNECTION

We strengthen life any time that we listen generously or encourage someone to find meaning, or wonder about possibility, or dream or hope or escape from self-judgment and inner criticism, or know that they matter. Anytime we share someone's joy, we bless the life in them.

Jesse does this as naturally as she breathes. Her own life has not been easy; nonetheless she is a celebrator, a deeply happy person. Although she has had two episodes of colon cancer and many professional disappointments, her joy in life is tangible. I smile whenever I am in the same room with her. So does everyone else. She is always one of the first to celebrate someone's birthday, to remember anniversaries, to congratulate people on their successes, whether she knows them well or not. So Jesse is one of the first people to call when something good happens to you or to someone you love. She is there to listen to the whole story with delight. Often when you finish talking to her you feel even better about what has happened, luckier than before.

Once as we were sitting together in a doctor's office, awaiting the lab results of her six-month chemotherapy checkup, I had asked her about her joy in life. Her own life had been so hard. Didn't she feel envious of others who had things she did not? She had smiled at the thought and shaken her head. "Then what is your secret?" I had asked her, laughing. Suddenly serious, she had replied that it seemed to her that joy was not something personal. When I looked at her, baffled, she explained she has found that if you are genuinely happy for them, people are very generous with their joy and share it with you openheartedly. "When something good happens to the person next to me, I am there to celebrate it with them. Their good luck makes me feel lucky. I rejoice with them about it as fully as if it was happening to me," she told me. "It makes me really happy." She paused and looked thoughtful. "Of course, then it *is* happening to me," she said with a grin.

When Jesse was first diagnosed, her cancer had spread beyond her bowel. Despite this, her surgeon had operated and removed as much of it as he possibly could, but he could not remove it all. "We need to keep her comfortable for as long as we can," he told me. But that was fifteen years ago. It makes you wonder. When you strengthen the life around you, perhaps you strengthen the life within you.

BREATHING IN AND BREATHING OUT

I BEGIN AND end every day with a very old ritual that was taught to me by a gentle elderly woman who is a Tibetan nun. Each morning, the first thing after awakening, you take a small empty bowl that you keep for this purpose and fill it slowly to the brim from a source of running water. Doubtless, the originators of this ritual had in mind some high mountain stream. I use my kitchen faucet, turning it on and letting it run for a while before passing my little bowl through the water to fill it completely.

As the bowl fills, you reflect on the particulars of your life, whatever they are. The people with whom you share your time, your state of health, whatever problems you face, what skills and strengths you have, your disappointments and successes, your worries, your personal gifts, your personal limitations, your home, all your possessions, your losses, your history as a human being. As the bowl fills, you receive your life openheartedly and unconditionally as your portion. Walking very slowly so as not to spill a drop out of the brimming bowl, you take it to a private place in your home, perhaps a personal altar, and place it there, dedicating all that it contains to the service of life. Leaving the full bowl in this place, you begin your day.

I find that this practice has been profoundly healing to me. The thought that all things can be used equally to befriend life seems to soften the edges of things, to break down the boundaries between one's sorrows and one's joys, one's wounds and one's strengths. They may be of equal value in serving life. Perhaps it is through such consecration that all things will ultimately reveal their true value and meaning.

Each evening, the last thing before going to sleep, you take the bowl outside and empty the water out onto the earth. Then you place the empty bowl upside down in its special place in your home, turn out your light, and rest. Perhaps this cycle of openheartedly taking on whatever one has been given, using it all to serve the life around you, then letting it go completely refers as much to the wisdom of living a lifetime as it does to the wisdom of living each day.

THE GIFT OF SERVICE

SERVICE HAS A life of its own. A single act of kindness may have a long trajectory and touch those we will never meet or see. Something that we casually offer may move through a web of connection far beyond ourselves to have effects that we may have never imagined. And so each of us may have left far more behind us than we may ever know.

When I was twenty-two and a third-year medical student, I was assigned to the wards of Bellevue, the great city hospital of the city of New York, for my first clinical experience. Bellevue Hospital has been rebuilt since then, but the old Bellevue was a colorful place to work, like Dickens in modern dress. I learned a lot of medicine there, and many other things as well.

In 1960, Bellevue was a place of refuge. Managed care was many years in the future, and so it was not uncommon for people to be admitted to the hospital with a chief complaint of "cold and hungry" or "homeless in winter." Often such "patients" helped out by making beds, carrying food trays, or even washing the floors. Bellevue was a place with its own culture, its regulars and its newcomers, and its politics. At that time it was probably simpler to place a bet, find a card game, or score drugs inside Bellevue than it was out on the streets of New York.

I started working on one of the men's general medicine wards. Each ward was a single huge room with three rows of beds, one along each of the side walls and one running down the middle of the room. Good news and bad news, examinations and treatments, family relationships, even deaths, happened in full view of everyone. It was one of my first experiences of community.

As a third-year student I was expected to come an hour or more before ward rounds every morning, pick up the resident's orders from the night before, and draw all the requested blood work. From the first, I dreaded this morning task. As a female student, I was a bit of an oddity and I attracted a certain curiosity. Under the watchful eyes of fifty men I would go from bed to bed, placing tourniquets on arms, hoping that my meager skills would be up to finding a vein and taking blood from it. As this was my first clinical rotation, my skills were new. Even though many of the men had done hard physical work most of their lives and had sinewy arms with veins as thick as ropes, I would often have to try several times before I was successful in drawing their blood. It was painful for them and agonizing for me.

During my second week on this service, I was working my way down the middle row of beds and had just stuck a man for the third time without success when I sensed someone close behind me. Turning, I found one of the "regulars" standing there, a big rough-looking man in the blue Bellevue patient pajamas with tattoos covering both of his arms. Without a word, he reached out and picked up one of the unused syringes I had put on the bedside table. With one hand he tightened the tourniquet around the arm of the man in the bed and with the other he drew blood from him. It had been done in seconds. I stood there openmouthed. "Do you have a gauze pad?" he asked me. Silently I produced one and he pressed it on the man's arm, withdrew the needle, and handed me the full syringe. Hands shaking, I emptied it into the specimen tube. My eyes stung with tears.

Trying to hide my humiliation, I turned and went to the next bed, but he followed me. "Doesn't anybody teach you kids how to do this?" he asked me. Unable to speak, I shook my head. "Here, look," he said, and, more slowly this time, he wrapped the tourniquet around the patient's arm and found a vein. "See?" he said. "Keep the hole in the needle up and the vein won't roll away from you." Silently I put the new specimen into another tube, and we went on together to the next bed.

The man in this bed was smiling and extending his arm. "Here," he said, "you just try. Larry will show ya how to do better." I tried and missed. Larry showed me a better way to hold the syringe and it was much easier. We went on from bed to bed, Larry offering suggestions and showing me many tricks I had never seen before. By the end of the hour I was drawing every blood on the first try. "Not bad, kid, not bad," Larry told me, and he walked away.

The next morning he was there again, and we went to the bed of the first patient together. I placed the tourniquet around the man's arm and was about to draw from the large elbow vein that popped into view, but Larry shook his head. "This one," he said, pointing to a much smaller vein. I looked dubiously at the patient. He winked at me. "Do it," he told me. There were almost thirty bloods to draw that morning. By the last of them, I was able to take blood easily from veins I could barely see.

Larry came with me every morning. At the end of a week, I was able to find hidden veins by touch alone and draw bloods I would not have thought possible. Several of the men told me they could barely feel the needle. "A quick learn, kid," Larry said. "Lookin' good." It had meant a great deal to me. Praise was hard to come by in medical training.

The following year I returned to Bellevue for three more months and was assigned to work in the emergency room, one of the most famous in the world. Medically, it was an extraordinary experience, and I was giddy with the drama of it. All of New York City's suffering came through those doors: accidents, shootings, heart attacks, suicides, beatings, rapes. At the time, it was my idea of being a real doctor. So I was there the evening that Larry was brought in by police ambulance, shot to death over a drug deal gone bad. It had stunned me. Being very young, I had simply assumed that he had been an army medic. It had never occurred to me to wonder where he had learned to be so skilled with a needle.

It is almost forty years since I was a student at Bellevue and touched by Larry's kindness. There have been many times when my deftness with a needle has made a difference to someone and a few times in a tight situation when that difference was between life and death. Over the years I have taught Larry's secrets to hundreds of others and perhaps they have passed them on as well. Once this skill is learned, it is something no one ever forgets, like riding a bicycle.

FELLOW TRAVELERS

ONE NIGHT IN the emergency room, a young woman was brought in comatose, having taken a massive overdose of Elavil. Shortly after she arrived, her heart had stopped. The ER staff worked to resuscitate her for some time, not because they had much hope of success but because they knew it was important to those who survive to feel that everything possible had been done. They had not been successful. It fell to the physician who had led the Code Team to tell her husband that his wife had died. Despite the pressures of the busy emergency room, he had sat with this man for quite a while and listened to his story.

He and his wife had not lived here long. They were both children of violent and alcoholic families, and they had come to California with the hope of making something better for themselves. He was a mechanic; she waited tables in a bar. All they owned was a truck and his tools. A week ago, the tools had been stolen and there was no money to replace them.

Neither one of them was very strong emotionally. He had been depressed often and told the doctor that when his moods came on him, they would drive to the beach and he would sit next to the ocean for hours. She would wait in the truck, watching, to be sure that he did not go too far. She had suffered from depression also. Sometimes she would wake in the night and wander through their little place, and he would always hear her and awaken to sit with her in the dark. They were all each other had. But this night, he had not heard her awaken. She had gone to the medicine cabinet and taken down the bottle of Elavil she had been given at the mental-health clinic the week before. In it was a four-month supply of pills. She had swallowed them all. He thanked the doctor for his efforts. It had been too many pills, too much pain, many years too late to bring her back. Once again the doctor assured him that everything possible had been done. The man had sat quietly thinking it over. "Everything possible has been done," he said, nodding. "Everything."

The doctor was deeply moved by the simplicity of this man's life and the depth of his love for his wife. His heart went out to him in his loss. He had been a devoted husband. But she had been mortally wounded long before she had been loved so completely.

On several occasions over the next few days, he found himself thinking of this man and his wife. There in the waiting room, he had sensed in him a sort of acceptance that was bewildering. He was young, and it had never before occurred to him that some pain might be beyond the power of love to heal. He had found the thought humbling. Is that what this husband had known? Is that what he had accepted? If so, how had he found the courage to love her so completely? And having loved her in this way, how could he go on?

About a month later, on a busy night in the ER, one of the nurses came to tell him that a man whose wife had been seen the month before was waiting to speak with him. She did not know the man's name, and, certain that he would not remember the details of the case, he had asked the nurse to get the wife's chart before he went to see what was needed. But by the time the chart was found, the man had gone. He had left a message. "Tell the doctor she is healed and in Heaven now," he had said.

The doctor had been touched and puzzled by this message. But four years later in the anguished aftermath of his own wife's suicide, surrounded by many well-intentioned and impotent words of comfort, it was this man whose words he had remembered. "He understood the power of acceptance, Rachel," he told me. "It is the only way for those who survive to find peace and heal. I think in time I will be able to go on because I know that I could not have loved her more. No one could have. But she had been wounded long ago, long before I even knew her name. The man in the emergency room, he would have understood."

THE LAYING ON OF HANDS

WHILE WE CAN contribute to the lives of others at a distance, the sort of service that is mutual is usually handmade, something that happens in a deeply personal way between two people. At such times, we may come to know the true value and worth of our lives. The kind of service that transforms us the most has our fingerprints on it. It is rarely accomplished by simply signing a check.

At the age of forty-five, George had patented a part of a medical invention. For more than two decades since then, he was the CEO of a small but successful company that manufactures and distributes these parts worldwide. George was a fine businessman and a shrewd investor, a highly sophisticated man who traveled widely and collected many beautiful things. By most standards, he had led an enviable life.

Six months before he first came to my office, George had discovered that he had lung cancer. His cancer was widely metastatic at the time that it was found, and his physicians had told him that he did not have long. He told me this during his first visit to my office.

My office is not traditional. Elegantly and tastefully dressed, George seemed unfazed to find himself on a houseboat. The cat loved him immediately, and he held her on his lap as we spoke, unmindful of the potential for damage to his Armani suit. I loved him immediately, too.

His diagnosis had shaken George badly. I had expected that he would be depressed about the hopelessness of his situation, but this was not the case. There was a lot else on his mind. "I have wasted my life, Rachel," he told me flatly. "I have two ex-wives and five children. I support all of them but I don't know any of them. I never took the time to know them or anyone else. I have spent my life doing business, building my company from an idea in my basement to what it is today. I do not think they will miss me. I've nothing behind me but a lot of money." He looked away and shook his head. "What an old fool," he said. "A stupid old fool."

The thing that George invented and that his company manufactures is a part of a medical device that has enabled people whose chronic disease was previously unmanageable to live almost normally. Another of my patients uses this device. It has changed her life. Before it was available, she had been severely limited by her disease and almost housebound. Controlling her physical symptoms had occupied most of her time. She had been unable to work, unable to have any sort of normal life among people.

Soon after she was fitted with this device, she had gotten a job for the first time. There she had met people and begun to have friends. In time she had met and married a fine man and had a child. "The day they gave me this device, I was reborn," she had told me. And so she was.

It is a breach of privacy to give one patient's name to another, but I thought that perhaps Stephanie might be willing to write an anonymous note about her experience and I could give it to George. I resolved to ask her if she might be willing to do this.

When she discovered I knew the man whose invention had

made her device possible, Stephanie was speechless. She sat thinking over my request that she write to him to tell him about the difference his work had made in her life. Shyly she asked me if I thought he might be willing to come to her home for dinner so that she could show him the life he had made possible for her. I said that I would ask.

George was surprised that I knew a patient who used his invention. He was very touched that she might want to meet him and readily agreed. He offered to take her and her husband to dinner at one of our most elegant and expensive restaurants. "I don't think so," I told him. And so, an evening was found, and George went to dinner at Stephanie's home.

The week after this dinner, he sat in my office shaking his head in wonder. He had expected to have dinner with this young couple, but when he had arrived, George was welcomed by Stephanie's whole family. Her mother was there, her three brothers and sisters, several of her aunts and uncles, and a crowd of nieces, nephews, and cousins. Her husband's parents were there, too, and many of her friends and neighbors—the whole community of people who had sustained her in the years she was an invalid. They had decorated the little house with crepe paper, and everyone had cooked. It was an extraordinary meal and a wonderful celebration.

"But that was not the important part, Rachel," George told me. "They had really come to tell me a story; they had each played a part in it and had a different side of it to share. It took them over three hours to tell it. It was the story of Stephanie's life. I cried most of the time. And at the very end, Stephanie came to me and said, 'This is really a story about you, George. We thought you needed to know.' And I did. I did."

I had tears in my eyes. "How many of these things do you make every year, George?" I asked him. "Close to ten thousand," he said softly. "I just knew the numbers, Rachel. I had no idea what they meant."

CHOOSING YOUR BATTLES

AFTER YEARS OF running a discussion group for physicians, so many surprising things have happened that when an orthopedic surgeon reached into his designer attaché case and brought out a hand puppet, I did not blink an eye. The topic of the evening's discussion was the joy of practicing medicine, and he had brought the puppet because it was a part of the story that he wanted to tell the group. As he spoke, he slipped his hand into it and cradled it in his powerful forearms. It was a fuzzy gray bunny rabbit. From where I was sitting, it looked quite real.

His story concerned a three-year-old girl whose mother had brought her to his office because of a problem with her thumb. The moment he had opened the door of the examining room, she had begun to cry in terror. Closing the door again, he had gone to get this puppet, which he uses when he works with frightened children. Cradling it in his arms, he had gone back into the room and introduced the puppet to the child. She had been delighted, and they played together for a while. Then he examined her, using the puppet's paws to hold her hand and determine the limitation in the movement of her thumb. He had decided to follow her for awhile to see if surgery could be avoided, and he had asked her mother to bring her back again.

Several weeks later, when he noticed this little girl's name on his day sheet, he had remembered her fear and had gone to get the bunny puppet before he went in to see her. Cradling the puppet in his arms again, he had opened the door and found her sitting there on his examining table, smiling and waiting for him. She was holding a carrot.

This story was told in a drop-in discussion group open to any of the doctors who have attended one of the Continuing Medical Education retreats at Commonweal. This evening, a family doctor from Kentucky who was passing through San Francisco for a medical meeting happened to come by. By chance, he had been one of eight physicians present at a retreat years before when the surgeon had told another story that had completely slipped my mind. He reminded the surgeon of this older story and asked him if he would tell it again now.

In a quiet voice, the surgeon began to speak about an event in his life that had changed him. As a fourteen-year-old, he had been given the gift of a real bow and arrows. This had become the center of many hours of adolescent daydreaming in which he had imagined himself standing among the great company of fierce warriors who had carried such weapons into battle since the beginnings of time. His head filled with such fantasies, he would go out into the backyard after dinner and shoot at anything that moved. He had never actually hit anything, but this had not diminished the intensity of his warrior daydreams. One evening, when he was about sixteen, he had gone out with his bow shortly after sunset, and in the dusk of the backyard he had seen a little rabbit. Drawing back his arrow, he had aimed and, to his shock, had hit it. It had screamed once.

His dreams of fierceness had evaporated instantly. He had run forward, horrified, fallen to his knees and lifted up the small, furry body pierced by the arrow. In that moment he knew beyond doubt that there was nothing in him that had wanted such an outcome or was even capable of wanting it. Cradling the little rabbit in his arms, he had known for the first time the nature of his own heart. "I guess I'm not a warrior," he said.

There was a silence in the room. Hippocrates, the great teacher of Harmlessness, had reached across generations and touched many of us again. I looked at the surgeon, still holding the puppet cradled in his arms. Clearly, he had not realized its symbolism or made a connection between these two stories before. But the doctor from Kentucky, having traveled two thousand miles, had been there to make this connection for him. In his soft backwoods drawl, he said, "Perhaps you are among a great company of fierce warriors, Dick. It's just a different sort of battle."

We do things for many reasons, some of which we are largely unaware of. These things often have their own wisdom and a kind of language that may be poetic. The surgeon had chosen consciously to bring the rabbit with him in order to ease the fears of a little girl. Surely he had looked fierce to her, a stranger in white who might overwhelm her and hurt her. And, indeed, the tools he uses every day could easily become weapons.

So on one level the puppet is nothing more than a comfort for a frightened child, but, on another, the rabbit is his talisman, a symbol of the purity of his intent and the nature of his heart. In the elegant language of the unconscious, it is a reminder to him and a sign to his little patient that even with a very sharp knife in his hand he can be trusted to wish the life in her well.

HEAVEN AND HELL

THE WAYS AND means by which people serve may vary from time to time and from culture to culture, but the nature of service has not changed since our beginnings. No matter what means we use, service is always a work of the heart. There are times when the power of science is so seductive that we may come to feel that all that is required to serve others is to get our science right, our diagnosis, our treatment. But science can never serve unless it is first translated by people into a work of the heart.

Molly, one of my former patients, still laughs about something that happened while she was hospitalized with fractures of both her elbows. She had been in an automobile accident as she was driving to the airport in a city two thousand miles away from her home. When she awoke in the hospital, her arms were encased in rigid casts that went from her shoulders to her wrists.

Molly has multiple food allergies and other very special dietary needs and can become dangerously ill if she inadvertently eats the wrong things. Over the years she has learned from frightening experience what she can eat and what she cannot. It is a very tricky business. Soon after she was settled into her bed, a dietitian had come and carefully documented her unusual food needs. It had taken more than an hour. "The questions she asked were so thoughtful, Rachel," Molly told me. "She really knew her stuff. In all these years no one has ever asked me some of these questions or understood so quickly and completely how things were with me. I was really impressed."

Within a few hours, special food was ordered into the hospital and kept in the hospital kitchens to meet Molly's complex needs. Three times a day, this food was served to her by professionals who brought it to her bedside on a tray and put it before her on her bed table. Then they left.

"The first time this happened, I just sat there, looking at the food, unable to feed myself," she told me. "I was certain that someone would come to help me, but no one did. After a while, the woman in the next bed noticed that I could not eat. Trailing her own IV lines, she had gotten out of bed and fed me my dinner."

This had happened at every meal. In the four days that she was in the hospital without the use of her arms, no one on the staff had ever come to help her to eat. Day after day, the right food would be brought, and the patient in the next bed would feed it to her.

There is a parable about the difference between heaven and hell. In hell people are seated at a table overflowing with delicious food. But they have splints on their elbows and so they cannot reach their mouths with their spoons. They sit through eternity experiencing a terrible hunger in the midst of abundance. In heaven people are also seated at a table overflowing with delicious food. They, too, have splints on their elbows and cannot reach their mouths. But in heaven, people use their spoons to feed one another. Perhaps hell is always of our own making. In the end, the difference between heaven and hell may only be that in hell, people have forgotten how to bless one another.

THE WISE MAN

DURING MY TRAINING, it was generally assumed that those who had no families or whose families were not close by would volunteer to work Christmas Eve and Christmas Day so others could be with their wives and children or their parents. So for several years I spent every Christmas Eve in a hospital. In those years the peace and silence of the wards after dark became inseparably entwined with the holiness of the season. Something seemed close and clear and tangible then that was harder to see at other times. For a long time I could not imagine spending Christmas anywhere else, and it still seems to me to be one of the best places to be on Christmas Eve. But I did not feel this way at first.

The first Christmas Eve I spent in a hospital was at Bellevue, in New York City, in about 1960. As a single woman, I had been expected to sign on for this, and although I really had no other plans, I felt deeply resentful.

The week before Christmas, we tried to send as many patients as possible home, but some did not have anywhere to go. They would spend Christmas in Bellevue along with those few who were too sick to leave. By Christmas Eve, the wards were almost empty, and the drama I had come to associate with doctoring was gone. As a state-of-the-art young physician, I felt that being there was a waste of my skills and my time.

One of those who had nowhere else to go was Petey. He was a gentle elderly man, no longer exactly certain of his age, a derelict who had lived on the Bowery for more than twenty years. When he was admitted to the General Medicine Service, all he had with him was a change of clothes. He had chronic emphysema, which gave us an excuse for keeping him as it was winter and bitter cold out on the streets. We couldn't help him much medically, but he seemed to accept this without question. Shy, he was pleased just to be there with us and appreciative of anything we did for him.

All day on Christmas Eve, service groups like the Salvation Army had come through Bellevue's wards and distributed small gifts to the patients, usually fruit or cheese, occasionally recycled clothing, or even Bibles. But by nightfall even they had gone home. Outside, it was snowing, the ugliness of the city streets already softened and covered over. The great hospital was quiet, most beds unoccupied, the few bed lamps that were lit making little islands of light in the darkness. I moved from patient to patient checking IVs and inquiring about symptoms, offering pain medication to those who were hurting and sleeping medication to those who were still awake. Christmas is a time of memories, and many of those whose lives were now so hard wanted to talk of other times. As I moved from bed to bed, I often listened to the past.

As I approached his bed, Petey beckoned to me. "Missy Doc," he said, reaching over and opening the drawer of the battered bedside table. Inside was most of what he owned—a pocket knife, a toothbrush, a razor, a comb, some small change, and two beautiful navel oranges he must have been given earlier that afternoon. He held one of the oranges out to me. "Merry Christmas," he said shyly.

I saw in his face a deep pleasure at having something to give, and I was stunned into silence. I had felt that kind of joy once too. Other Christmas Eves came back to me, times from my own childhood. I had felt that joy then. But that was a long time ago. I had learned a great many things since, but I had also forgotten things. With a contraction of the heart, I remembered the resentment I had felt only a short time before. I had not even wanted to be here.

A long time ago, my grandfather had shown me by his example a way to live; it was the same way that Petey was showing me now. But Grandpa's voice had been covered over by the voices of my family, my colleagues, and my professors. Petey's old face folded into a smile. "Merry Christmas," he said once again. My eyes filled with tears, and I reached out and took his gift with both hands.

It takes many years to remember that everything of value we have to give was not learned from a book and that the wisdom to live well is not conferred with an advanced degree. But real teachers are everywhere. The life in us will be blessed by others over and over again until finally we have remembered how to bless it ourselves.

HOW THE WORLD IS MADE

IN *CAT'S CRADLE,* Kurt Vonnegut offers a wry view of how the world is made. The basic unit of God's organization of things is the Karass, a group of people who have been born in order to serve one of God's purposes and who serve it flawlessly, often without ever knowing they are doing this. A Karass may be as large as several thousand people or as small as two lovers. No matter. The lives of those in a Karass revolve around the holy purpose that has called them into being in much the same way that electrons revolve around the nucleus of an atom. Some orbit at a distance from the common purpose, others are very close to it, but all are held in relationship to it because it has magnetized their souls.

The people in any Karass differ widely in age, color, and creed; they may speak different languages, be educated or uneducated, rich or poor, foolish or wise. Some may actually know each other and even work together, and others may never meet in their lifetimes. No matter. Their lives fit together perfectly in the service of the purpose.

When I first read this, I imagined that the purpose of a Karass would be visible to the naked eye, and, indeed, this may sometimes be the case. There is surely a Karass behind the abolition of slavery, women's rights, most life-saving medical advances, and all ecological concerns. But just as often a Karass may have a purpose known only to God and understandable only from God's vast perspective, such as the saving of some single life who will become the great-grandmother of someone else whose work will cause a sweeping change for all of humanity.

In contrast to the Karass, Vonnegut describes another sort of group, the False Karass, or Granfalloon. This is a group of people who believe themselves to be related to one another but whose relationship is not "one of the ways that God gets things done." Some examples of a Granfalloon might be the Yale class of 1963, the American Academy of Cardiology, and the Republican Party.

I have begun to find this tongue-in-cheek description of the world more and more compelling over the years. It has explained a great deal of my own experience. And something else Vonnegut says rings true for me as well. Despite the apparent differences between them—the variations in social status, expertise, language, religion, age, gender, roles in life, and the like—should members of a Karass happen to meet, they will feel their kinship instantly even though it does not make sense to them. Life can be a lonely thing. In the presence of another member of your family of service, that loneliness may ease a little.

ONE LITTLE CANDLE

MANY HEALTH PROFESSIONALS have a deep regard for life and a wish to use their lives in service to others. This commitment goes deep and often enables them to go on despite significant difficulties, disappointments, and losses. Yet such things are rarely discussed in the doctors' dining room or at grand rounds. Most of those who have passed through the professional retreat programs at Commonweal say that while they have shared many difficult situations with their colleagues and have trusted one another's expertise and judgment absolutely, they have never discussed what their work means to them or what has brought them to it with another professional before. As professionals, meaning is a part of our secret lives.

It is hard to break these habits of silence, and during our retreats we often use symbolism as a way to open this sort of discussion among professionals. The group sandtray enables a level of dialogue that might not otherwise be possible. In a two-hour session, the eight professionals in the retreat have the opportunity to choose objects from our sandtray room that represent the meaning of their own work to them and use these objects to share this meaning with each other.

Marie, a young nursing administrator from a large urban hospital on the East Coast, took part in one of these sessions. As each person seated around the sandtray table placed the objects they had gathered into their section of the sand, I noticed that she had kept something back and put it beneath her chair. As the instruction is to use all the symbols you bring to the table, I had wondered about this. One by one the group members spoke about the objects they had chosen and how each symbolized a part of what their work meant to them. Marie listened closely and seemed deeply moved by what the others were saying. About halfway through, she began to speak about what she had put before her in the sand. When she finished, she fell silent for a few moments and then hesitantly told us that there was something she wanted to add that she did not want others to see. She asked us to close our eyes while she did this.

The group of nurses, physicians, psychologists, and social workers sat around the table with our eyes closed. In the silence, Marie reached under her chair for the object she had hidden. After a few moments she told us we could open our eyes, and we saw she had placed a slender white candle in a tall candlestick in the center of her part of the sandtray. It was unlit. Just showing it to us obviously had a deep emotional significance for her. I offered her a box of kitchen matches, and she sat holding them for a long time, unable to light the candle or even talk about it. Finally, she lit it, saying in a barely audible voice that it represented her real self. It was a touching and surprisingly intimate moment, especially powerful as the candle bore a striking resemblance to her own beauty, simplicity, and purity.

One at a time, others also shared their work, and then the woman seated next to Marie at the table began to speak. She, too, had an unlit candle in her tray. It was short and fat. She told us that it represented her dream of being a professional and working with an open heart. As she spoke, instead of lighting her candle with the matches, she picked it up, reached across the low wooden boundary between her section of the table and Marie's and lit it from the flame of Marie's candle. Marie burst into tears.

The woman, a sophisticated psychiatrist, began to apologize, saying that she had no idea why she had not used the matches and had not meant to invade Marie's sandtray. "Oh no," Marie told her, "it's that there is so much cynicism and judgment among us that I never show anyone at work what really matters to me. Only my patients know. I am afraid that people will laugh or that they will think less of me and so I hide myself.

"For me this work is holy. It is my calling. When you lit your candle from mine, I saw why it might be important to stop hiding. Perhaps I can find the courage to be who I really am. Perhaps there are others . . . like you . . . who are hiding, too." There was a moment of silence, and then these two women reached for each other's hands.

GREATER THAN THE SUM OF ITS PARTS

IN THE PARABLE about the three blind men and the elephant, he who takes hold of its trunk believes that the elephant is like a snake, he who touches its leg believes that the elephant is like a tree, and he who leans against its side believes that the elephant is like a wall. But this is not a story about elephants; it is a story about blindness.

It is often difficult to understand the nature of things. There may be an elephant in our midst and all our efforts to analyze our part of it, to describe in greater and greater detail our own experience, the nature of what we have taken hold of, will not help us one iota in knowing what is real. This is true no matter how compelling your experience of your part or how many others are convinced of that experience or even share it with you. The elephant is beyond us all.

But sometimes we may catch a glimpse of a pattern, the bones of a larger meaning. In such moments we may recognize that things of apparent diversity and randomness may be coherent and whole. Robert Samples in his book *The Metaphoric Mind* describes a radio talk show where an author, speaking about his intuitive sense of a larger wholeness, asked anyone in the listening audience who had such an experience to call in and share it.

A long silence ensued, during which the author and his interviewer covered their anxiety with small talk. Finally the phone rang, and a woman began to describe a powerful and spontaneous experience of the interconnectedness and unity of all life. When she had tried to share this understanding with her family, their response was disappointing. Her frequent references to it caused them to insist she see her family physician, who in turn referred her to a psychiatrist. She had simply stopped talking about her experience then, although she could remember it vividly and felt profoundly changed by it. Her phone call was the first time that she had generally shared it.

As Samples puts it, "All at once the entire board lit up. It became apparent that such glimpses are commonplace. Once they realized that this sort of experience might be normal, dozens of people were willing to call in and talk about it."

Perhaps there is a wholeness hidden in the world, and the experience of separation that causes so much of our suffering is an illusion. If the world is really one large elephant, the wisdom may lie in holding your part loosely and loving what you cannot understand. And in helping others, here in the dark.

V.

BEFRIENDING LIFE

I'VE SPENT MANY years learning how to fix life, only to discover at the end of the day that life is not broken. There is a hidden seed of greater wholeness in everyone and everything. We serve life best when we water it and befriend it. When we listen before we act.

In befriending life, we do not make things happen according to our own design. We uncover something that is already happening in us and around us and create conditions that enable it. Everything is moving toward its place of wholeness. Befriending life requires that we listen for that potential which is trying to actualize itself over time. It will be there whether we are listening to a tree, a person, an organization, or a society. It is always struggling against odds. Everything has a deep dream of itself and its fulfillment.

Befriending life is less a matter of knowledge than a question of wisdom. It is not about mastering life, controlling it or exerting our will over it, no matter how well intentioned our will may be. Befriending life is more about harmlessness than it is about control. Harmlessness requires connection. It means listening to life from the place in us that is connected to the wholeness around us. The place in us that is also whole.

Life has its own wisdom. In my family, where doctors are almost as common as people, it was assumed that knowledge was all that was needed in order to have what was worth having. The more information you accumulated, the more answers you had, the more that you understood, the more you could direct your life and achieve happiness. For many years I did not understand the difference between knowledge and wisdom. I was almost thirty-four years old when I remembered that there are other ways of knowing besides the intellect, ways that have great power. I was stunned to find that many of the things most worth knowing are not written in books or discovered through scientific effort. They are known by people who have been to school but just as often known by people who have never been to school, by people who can read and by people who have never read a word in their lives.

It came as a shock to discover that in order to live well you might need to learn to read life.

Life can speak to you through anyone, through a person who has never been educated or who does not speak your language, through someone who is ill or dying, through a child. It can speak without any words at all. I have learned a great deal about life from people who do not think of themselves as teachers.

There are few master teachers in life. The rest of us are learning still. Everyone presently human is unfinished. But there are many who can listen to life so well that they can hear the vastness in everything and in you. A teacher is someone who has learned how to listen to life. Someone who has found a way to listen well.

Any real teacher is only a pointing finger. In the end, we may find out more by not following our teachers but by following what our teachers follow for ourselves. From a good teacher you may learn the secret of listening. You will never learn the secrets of life. You will have to listen for yourself.

Some seek to find wisdom through focused intention or practice, a cultivation of the capacity to reach beyond the cage of the ego to feel and know the life around us. People meditate, or do yoga or tai chi. They invite silence, they chant or fast or pray. But none of these things will make you wise. All of them can enable you to hear something in yourself and beyond yourself a little better. Wisdom will still require that you experience life.

The wisdom to befriend life will find us anyway, whether or not we pursue it. We may live in a familiar circle of experience for many years among the attitudes, beliefs, places, and relationships that define our everyday world. But it is only a matter of time until something invites us or requires us to reach beyond the familiar, to experience something never before felt or seen, something perhaps not even imaginable. The experience can break open our sense of what the world is about and draw us closer to who we are. Such experiences usually involve either suffering or joy. Both will leave us wiser.

Learning from life takes time. I rarely recognize life's wisdom at the time it is given. Sometimes I am too distracted by something else that has caught my wandering eye, and not every gift of wisdom comes nicely gift-wrapped. I have often received such a gift only many years after it was offered. Sometimes I needed to receive other things first, to live through other experiences in order to be ready. Much wisdom is a hand-me-down. Like all hand-me-downs, it may be too big at the time it is given.

Befriending life may enable us to solve some of life's problems. It has become a common understanding that most problems cannot be solved by approaching them with the same consciousness that created them in the first place. It is doubtful that the solution to our present suffering will lie in greater technology and greater expertise. Our very survival may require that we do something new, something simpler and more human. That we become open beyond our expertise. That we learn to live closer to life, the life in us and the life around us and remember what we are serving with our technology and our expertise. That we pay enough attention to learn to trust life.

Bless anything that shows you wisdom. Anything that shows you wisdom has become a part of who you are and has drawn you closer to life. The Tibetans have reverence for those who have passed along to them the priceless gift of the wisdom to live well. Perhaps this means having reverence for all of life, the ant and the hawk, the enemy and the friend, the lover and the parent and the child. All have offered us the opportunity to know ourselves and to know life. The chance to befriend life. This is true of our wins and losses, our illnesses, our celebrations, our joys and sorrows. All offer us wisdom. Bless them all.

THE GAME

I WAS RAISED to read the tea leaves in life, to examine every life event to determine if it was fortunate or unfortunate. The fortunate ones were painless, easy, and happy; the unfortunate ones were not. Although I once was certain, I no longer believe that I can tell the difference. As my father, a dedicated and somewhat addicted gin rummy player, would say, "It's not in the hand; it's in the way that you play it."

Almost everyone in the family was drafted at one time or another to be my father's opponent at cards. My father was a scientific player, and he practiced constantly. Often after the first five or so cards had been played he would be able to tell you with a high percentage of accuracy what you held in your hand and what cards you probably needed to win. He based his conclusions on the cards that had been discarded and what was in his hand. He was rarely wrong. He would hold back the cards you needed in his own hand until he had picked the cards he needed to declare victory. He played with his buddies filling the kitchen with cigar smoke and winning almost every hand.

My mother played by pure intuition. She ignored every rule of the game, blithely breaking up lays and discarding matching cards, throwing back the very cards she had picked up only moments ago. He was never able to beat her.

I remember his outraged howls when she would discard one of the three jacks he knew she must be holding and pick another card. "Gladys, you can't do that," he would bellow. My mother would look at him with the most innocent and wicked of smiles. "But I have, Ray," she would tell him. "I have." Eventually he refused to play with her. "She does not play fair," he would tell me.

My parents' kitchen-table card games are among my favorite family memories. They were often hilariously funny. But they were important in other ways as well. These were some of my earliest lessons in the fact that the game may lie beyond the rules, that we can know many things that we can never explain, and that following your own deepest wisdom may be the best way of all to live.

KNOWING LIFE

ONE OF THE things that I have learned since my medical training is that it is possible to study life for many years without knowing life at all. Often things happen that science can't explain. Many very important things cannot be measured, but only observed, witnessed, and ultimately trusted. Life may not be limited by the facts. Science defines life in its own way, but perhaps life is larger than science.

A friend of mine, director of research at a nonprofit institute, had become interested in spontaneous remission of cancer. As his interest became more widely known, people would call or write him to tell him their stories of unexplained recovery from serious illness. One of these was a young man who claimed to have had a spontaneous healing from a dire form of bone cancer called osteogenic sarcoma.

He had been diagnosed many years ago as a college student. Noticing a hard lump in his right thigh, he had gone to see a doctor. A biopsy had confirmed the doctor's suspicion of cancer, and he and his parents had been called to a meeting. Sadly, the doctor told them of his findings and strongly recommended that he have his right leg amputated at the hip. He was nineteen years old. Despite the urging of several doctors and his parents, he had refused this surgery and had gone home to his parents' farm without any treatment to live out his life. Nothing further had been done for him except that the pastor of his church had asked those people who were so moved to pray for him at seven o'clock every night. People prayed for two years. Over time, the mass in his thigh had simply grown smaller and finally disappeared.

My friend was captivated by this story. Through his work he had developed a researcher's healthy skepticism, but the man seemed so genuine and matter-of-fact that he could not get the story out of his mind. Finally he called to ask a favor. Would I mind trying to track down the doctor who had made the original diagnosis and see if he would confirm this story or if he had kept medical records or a biopsy report? "How long has it been?" I asked. "Twenty years," said my friend ruefully. I started to express my doubts, but my friend interrupted. "Please try," he said. And so I did.

It turned out to be easy. The doctor, a relatively young man at the time he treated this patient, was listed in his state's medical association and still in practice. Encouraged, I called and got him on the phone. After the usual introductions, I told him that I was calling to see if he had kept the medical records on a former patient. It was so long ago that I doubted he would remember, and then I told him the man's name. His response was immediate. "Of course I remember him," he said with feeling. "I've thought of him many times over the years. What a senseless tragedy. Are you calling on behalf of the family?"

"No," I replied, and told him that the man was still alive. "Thank God," he said. "Where did he have his surgery?"

"He didn't have surgery," I replied. There was a pause. When he spoke again, I could detect a change in his voice. "Then what happened?" he asked. So I told him the story as it had been told to me. There was a long silence and then, without another word, he hung up the phone. I called him several times afterward, but he never returned my calls.

Most of us encounter a great deal more Mystery than we are

willing to experience. Sometimes knowing life requires us to suspend disbelief, to recognize that all our hard-won knowledge may only be provisional and the world may be quite different than we believe it to be. This can be very stressful, even frightening. But if we are not willing to wonder, we may have to hang up the phone on life.

LOVING LIFE

PROFESSIONAL WOMAN AND intellectual though she was, my Russian mother tied red ribbons to my crib and put them on my carriage. As I grew older she would often hide little pieces of narrow red ribbon in the pockets of my clothes or in my shoes. She would buy ribbon especially for this purpose and cut it into two-inch lengths. Although I never caught her inside my closet or going through my drawers, I would find these hidden bits of ribbon often. They became so commonplace that I hardly noticed them, and I always left them where I found them. They were there to protect me from the Evil Eye.

My mother left her ribbons in my pockets long after I was an adult. One day, I was cleaning out a favorite old purse and found one of them in the bottom of it. At that time, she had been dead for more than a dozen years.

These ribbons represented a worldview. As I remember it, a large percentage of my family's communication was about saving one another from danger. There were so many warnings: Button up! Watch your step! Watch your purse! Don't talk to strangers! Drive carefully! In my early years, I had actually thought that this was what a family was about: presenting a united front against risk, offering each of us the benefit of many other pairs of vigilant eyes. Later, I found the same sense of vigilance among my colleagues in medicine. Perhaps such watchfulness is an inside-out way of saying that life is valuable and important, too important to lose or misplace. If so, perhaps it would be wiser to celebrate it more and defend it less.

There is a great differencc between defending life and befriending it. Defending life is often about holding on to whatever you have at all cost. Befriending life may be about strengthening and supporting life's movement toward its own wholeness. It may require us to take great risks, to let go, over and over again, until we finally surrender to life's own dream of itself.

EGGS

IN MY GRANDMOTHER Rachel's kitchen, nothing was ever wasted. When she was a young wife in Russia, there was not always food enough, and sometimes the family went hungry. Her husband was the rabbi, and so whatever food they had was always shared with others who had less, and she had become skilled at making what they had go a long way. It had not been easy.

Perhaps this is why, in America, my grandmother's kitchen was overflowing with food. Here in this country she raised her daughters to keep an extra box and bottle unopened in the pantry for every bottle and box that was in use. Although she died before I was born, I was raised by her eldest daughter to do this same thing. Absentminded as I am, I often find I have accumulated two or even three extras of anything in my house.

But this abundance did not mean that things were to be wasted. Everything was always used to the full. Even the tea bags were used twice.

There is a family story told about my grandmother's icebox that may not be true, but then again, perhaps it is. I have heard it ever since I was quite small. Grandma's icebox was the deep source of a truly amazing outpouring of goodness. It was always full to the very edges, every shelf, every nook and cranny was put to use. Occasionally when someone, usually a child, opened it without sufficient caution, an egg would fall out and break on the kitchen floor. My grandmother's response was always the same. She would look at the broken egg with satisfaction. "Aha," she would say, "today we have a sponge cake!"

Befriending life is not always about having things your own way. Life is impermanent and full of broken eggs. But what is true of eggs is even more true of pain and loss and suffering. Certain things are too important to be wasted. When I was sixteen, just after the doctor came and informed me that I had a disease that no one knew how to cure, my mother had reminded me of this. I had turned toward her in shock, but she did not cuddle or soothe. Instead she reached out and took me by the hand. "We will make a sponge cake," she told me firmly. It has taken many years to find the recipe, the one that is my own, but I knew in that moment that this was what I needed to do.

Life wastes nothing. Over and over again every molecule that has ever been is gathered up by the hand of life to be reshaped into yet another form. The molecules in you and me and indeed in everyone are secondhand, borrowed for the occasion and returned when outgrown. How strange to think that great pain may be impermanent. Something in us all seems to want to carve it in granite, as if only this would do full honor to its terrible significance. But even pain is blessed with impermanence; slowly, drop by drop, it may be worn away until even the most devoted searchers cannot find it unless they look for compassion or some other form of wisdom.

FINDING THE WAY

IN THINKING ABOUT the special bond between grandparent and grandchild, I remember a birth that I attended long ago. The baby's father, a first-generation Mexican-American, was a graduate student at the university where I worked. He had married another student, a young woman from Boston whose family had been here for several generations. This was their first baby, and they wanted the very best of care.

The university clinics were prepared to offer that. The young couple had gone through childbirth training together and had attended parenting classes as well. They were ready and so were we with the full power of contemporary obstetrical and pediatric medicine to support us.

But things had not gone well. The labor was long and very difficult. After many hours, the obstetricians offered the couple a surgical intervention. But the young woman had been fearful of having a c-section and they had refused. Several more hours went by, during which the obstetricians called me in as a pediatric consultant. It was decided to offer the couple surgery again. Despite her exhaustion, her pain, and the pleading of her husband, the young mother was adamant. She would not have this surgery. She was too frightened. Another hour passed without much progress, and in desperation the young man called his mother-in-law on the East Coast and asked her to speak to Jennifer, his wife, about having the surgery. While they spoke, he went with me into the waiting room to tell his own father what was happening.

Although he had come to California from Mexico long ago, Michael's father spoke little English. He was a man close to the land, weathered and strong, at first a migrant farmworker and then, with the help of his sons, the owner of a small farm in the Santa Clara Valley. Michael was his eldest. He had been sitting in this room for many hours awaiting the birth of this first grandchild.

He listened carefully as Michael told him what was happening, his face growing serious and thoughtful. Then he nodded and said a few words in Spanish to his son and put an arm around his shoulders. I could see Michael relax a little. Afterward, we went back to the labor room to find that after speaking with her mother, Jennifer had at last decided to go ahead with surgery.

Jennifer, her eyes filled with tears, lay back in her bed, exhausted. Most of the obstetrical team went to prepare the operating room for the c-section, and I went up two floors to my office to let them know that I would be attending the surgery to care for the baby. I had barely reached my desk when I received a stat page from Jennifer's obstetrician. Before she could be taken to the operating room, Jennifer had rallied and with three great pushes had delivered her baby. "Everyone is fine," said the obstetrician, and over the phone, I could hear the baby crying. It was a boy.

Afterward, I asked Michael what he thought had happened. He replied that the obstetricians had offered him several explanations, but he actually thought it had something to do with his father. Seeing my look of surprise, he smiled. "My father is a great man," he told me. When he had gone to tell his father that the baby had been born without the surgery, the older man had smiled and nodded. "There had been much fear," his father had told him in Spanish. He had heard about his daughter-in-law's fear, and he had also felt the fear in his son Miguel. So he had known that the baby, too, was afraid. And so, sitting alone in the waiting room, he had spoken with his grandchild in his mind, encouraging him to come and be born.

He had shown the baby his many memories of the beauty of the land, its dawns and sunsets, the new crops and the rich harvests. He had told the baby that he looked forward to walking together on the earth. He had spoken of the goodness of life, of friendship and laughter and good work. And lastly, he had spoken of his love for the family. He had remembered his own father in Mexico and his wife, both now dead. One by one, he had spoken of the baby's uncles, his sons. Of their goodness and their strength. Of his pride in them and in the women they had married. He shared memories of Christmas and birthdays and weddings. Of the joy they took in each other's lives. He had offered the baby his heart. And the baby had come.

Over the years, I have attended many births, as a pediatrician or a birth coach, a family member or a friend. I sometimes suggest to parents in labor that they reach out to their unborn child in just this same way, showing their baby mental images of the world's goodness, sharing their love of life to strengthen and encourage their baby in this difficult passage.

WHEN IT WORKS

AT TEN O'CLOCK on a very quiet night in the emergency room, a distraught father rushed through the doors carrying his unconscious infant son in his arms and shouting for help. Within seconds the child was the center of an intensive team effort. At the time, I was an intern, and as three more senior and experienced resident physicians had been available to deal with this crisis, I was in the room mostly as a witness. Rapidly several bloods were drawn from the infant, IVs were placed in both his arms, and fluids were started. An EKG was connected, which showed a profound electrolyte imbalance and an irregular heartbeat. Based on the rapid downhill course and the history of severe diarrhea given by the parents to another member of the team, the infant was diagnosed as having life-threatening dehydration.

We had barely gotten all our monitors and IV lines in place when someone shouted that we were losing him, and all eyes swung to the EKG monitor. The baby was in ventricular tachycardia. In seconds, it became ventricular fibrillation, the most dangerous of the heart arrhythmias. Untreated, death occurs in minutes.

We had run out of time. The electrolytes and fluids pouring into the tiny veins would not be fast enough to reverse the chaotic electrical activity of the baby's heart. As one, the team turned to the pediatric defibrillator, two paddles attached to a machine capable of delivering an electric shock to the heart. It was our only hope of restoring a normal heartbeat.

The most senior resident stepped toward the table and placed the paddles, one behind the baby's back and the other almost completely covering the little chest. Holding the paddle handles he shouted "Back!" and everyone stepped away from the table to avoid being shocked. He pressed the button and delivered the first shock. We all looked toward the EKG monitor. It showed a total cardiac arrest. "Again," he said, and we all stepped back. Over the next few minutes, he shocked the baby four times without a response. The EKG was flat. The baby's heart had stopped.

He flung the paddles to the floor. "God DAMN it!" he said with intense feeling. Quickly he ordered epinephrine injected directly through the chest into the baby's heart. There was still no response. He turned and nodded to the other two residents, both men. "Time to talk to the parents," he told them, and without another word all three left the treatment room.

After the intensity of moments before, the room suddenly went very still. It was a room full of women, two nurses and myself. Silently we looked at the tiny body lying on the table. He was a beautiful little boy, perfect in every way. Something in me called out to him, much as you might call a child in from playing to dinner. He had been well just yesterday. Less than five minutes ago his heart had been beating. It seemed impossible that he could not come back. I was too young a doctor and too inexperienced to know that after four attempts at defibrillation, no one comes back.

Without thinking, I stooped and picked up the paddles from the floor. "Just one more time," I said to the nurses. Placing the paddles as I had seen the senior resident do, I waited for them to step back. And then I pressed the red button. As before, the tiny body lifted slightly from the table and fell back. In the silence that followed, I heard one of the nurses draw in her breath. "Look!" she whispered, and pointed to the EKG. The flat line was now the classic tracing of a normal heartbeat pulsing steadily across the screen. I let go of the paddles and picked up the baby in my arms, IV lines, EKG leads and all.

The relief in the room was indescribable. We crowded together, all of us talking at once, and we all had tears in our eyes. Then the door opened. In the doorway stood a distraught woman. Just behind her was a man, his face white and drawn, holding her by the shoulders. Behind them both stood the senior resident. Dismayed, I realized that he must have just given the baby's parents the bad news. Suddenly the baby began to cry. As the woman stumbled toward us, one of the nurses quickly took the IV bottles from their stand and carried them aloft. The other began to push the EKG machine. Halfway across the room we met her and put her son back into her arms.

Befriending a single life is usually the task of a community over time, many of whom will never meet each other or even be aware of each other's existence. Medicine is often like that. So is life. In the forty-seven years that I have been a patient, I have been served by hundreds and hundreds of people throughout the country, some of whom are professionals and many who are not. Often we do not get to see the outcome of our actions, and, in a sense, this may represent a sort of immortality. Trajectories of service to a single life may be decades long and come to fruition long after those who initiated them are dead. The dead act with great power in this world still. This is as true of service to an idea as it is to a person.

But there are other times when by grace you may be allowed to directly participate in events that make a profound difference. Times when, despite the odds, the limitations of science, or the pressure of time, things happen anyway. Such moments evoke a sense of gratitude in all who participate as if, even as we act, we are only witnesses to life fulfilling its dream of itself and realizing its own mysterious purposes.

HABIT

AMONG US THE habit of competition and individualism is so ingrained that we seem to have forgotten one of the basic laws of survival: Strength lies in community. But not every culture is as alienated as our own, and, in some, connection and service are simply a way of life.

A few weeks after I signed on as a leader to accompany a group on a tour of Fiji, the government was overthrown. Because of the extreme instability of the country, the State Department issued a caution to American tourists suggesting that travel plans be reconsidered. I had assumed that the trip would be canceled and was surprised to hear from the organization sponsoring it that they planned to go on.

Which is how we found ourselves in Micronesia in the midst of a civil war. The flight landed at a small airport, and, as we walked across the tarmac in the stifling heat, the other two staff leaders suggested that I go with the group to collect the luggage while they saw to our transportation. It was hot. The group was predominantly women in their late fifties and sixties. Some of the oldest among them had an unhealthy grayish look. For the dozenth time I regretted coming.

The baggage area was a large cinder-block room with an automatic carrier snaking through it. It was not air-conditioned. Even more disturbing, every ten to fifteen feet along the walls stood a uniformed soldier at full attention, his hand resting on the stock of a rifle, his eyes fixed on an invisible spot in the center of the room. The group of gray-haired women fell silent, awed. Huddled together we waited for our bags. It took a long time.

When the baggage finally came, my heart sank. Women of a certain age have a lot of baggage, and I doubted that I could lift most of it. But there was nothing for it but to begin. Pulling a dolly beside the carrier, I began to wrestle the heavy bags onto it. As I struggled to lift them, I became aware that the young Fijian men along the walls were growing uneasy. A certain tension began to build, and I became nervous. One or two of the other women felt it also and tried to help me with the bags.

Suddenly a soldier left his position and came toward us. I am a tall woman, but he was well over six feet, and the medals on his chest were right at eye level. I looked up, dreading to meet his hostility. But he was smiling. "May I?" he said, and he began effortlessly pulling luggage off the carrier and piling it onto the dolly. Then others came to help, filling dolly after dolly with our bags and helping us push them out of the baggage area into the parking lot. I was overcome with gratitude. As we left the building, I looked back. The men stood in groups talking. There were rifles leaning unattended against every wall.

I have thought about this many times since. As I came to learn, the Fijian culture is deeply altruistic. These young men, raised within it, had so profound a sense of their connection to others that even as soldiers they could never have watched us struggle with our bags without responding. Their lives were imbedded in a thousand-year-old lineage of kinship. The revolution had only started the week before.

THE GIFT OF NEW EYES

GIVING AWAY MONEY can be demanding and even lonely. A few years ago a friend of mine, obligated to yearly philanthropy by her inheritance, chose several of her friends and gave us each $20,000 a year to give away in any way that we saw best.

It was a steep learning curve. I was surprised at how quickly this task changed the way in which I saw things. I had developed a therapist's eye for growth in people, but I had never before noticed the places where things were trying to move forward in the culture, groups of people or individuals whose vision, if nurtured, could lead to a better world. I suppose that I never saw them because I did not think I personally had the means to be of help to them and so they had nothing to do with me. You might never notice plants struggling to grow around you, either, until someone hands you a full watering can. But I could see them now. They were everywhere.

One evening I was eating out in a local restaurant with a friend. The dining room was casually arranged. Along one wall there was a long padded bench in front of which stood a row of small tables three or four feet apart. My friend and I were shown to one of these tables. I sat on the bench and my friend sat opposite me on a chair. At the table next to us two men were dining.

My friend and I had been talking for some time when I gradually became aware of the conversation at this next table. One of the men was telling the other about a program he and some of his

Spanish-speaking colleagues had been running as volunteers. The program conducted a series of support groups for poverty-level Spanish-speaking families who had lost children to illness, accident, or violence. In the past, many of the hospitals in our city had contributed a small amount of support to this program, which barely covered hiring a small staff and renting places to hold these meetings.

The man speaking was obviously upset. So much good had come of this program, he told his friend. In the past few years over a hundred couples had been helped to preserve marriages torn open by grief and blame and parent their remaining children. But now many of the city's hospitals had merged or gone out of business or been taken over by organizations that had no interest in supporting such a program, and it had fallen through the cracks. Desperately he and his colleagues had tried to raise the money to continue this work, but they had not been successful. They had been able to raise only $500. This would not last much longer, and the program would close in a few months. As he spoke, he seemed close to tears.

His friend was sympathetic and concerned. "How much do you need to keep things going, Steve?" he asked. By now, I was eavesdropping shamelessly. "A great deal of money," said Steve sadly. "More than we could ever raise."

"How much is it?" asked his friend again.

"Four thousand dollars," Steve replied.

Reaching across the few feet between us, I touched Steve lightly on the arm. "You got it," I said, and, reaching into my purse, I pulled out my checkbook.

Without the generosity of my friend, I doubt that I would have responded to the conversation at the next table or even heard it. But because of her visionary program, I knew that I had something of value to give. I gave away her money for three years and an odd thing has happened. Now that I no longer have money to give away, I still notice the growing edge of things and I still respond to it. I give away my time, my skills, my network of friends, my life experience. You do not need money to be a philanthropist. We all have assets. You can befriend life with your bare hands.

MAKING A DIFFERENCE

HARRIET LEANED FORWARD in her chair, her twill-clad knees separated and her clasped hands dangling between them. In a flat and angry voice she told me she had studied and practiced medicine for more than twenty years, rising to the top of her specialty, first as a pediatrician, then as a neonatologist, and finally as an expert in the care of premature infants. Unmarried, she had dedicated her life to the survival of these smallest of people and had made herself one of the country's best in this demanding and highly technical specialty.

As she spoke, I had the chance to watch her. A big solid woman in a plaid shirt, without makeup or jewelry, she wore her hair short and simply combed, just as it came out of the shower. She looked genuine. Suddenly, I had a sense of being safe with her, that her capacity to be there for the vulnerability of others was total and absolute. I was deeply moved.

As she continued to speak of her work I began to sense something under the competence, below the anger. Something I could not name. I leaned forward to listen more carefully. In the past five years, she told me, more and more of her time was spent defending the needs of her tiny patients for care. She spoke of the hours she now spends every day on the phone, the blizzard of paperwork, the frustration of arguing with insurance company employees, day after day, justifying the value of a premature baby's life in terms of the cost of needed care.

"I just can't do it anymore," she finally said in her flat midwestern voice.

The thing I could not name became crystal clear. It was despair.

As we spoke, Harriet absentmindedly fingered an object she had taken off one of my shelves, a tiny dried starfish someone had brought me from the beach. Over time I have learned that no one in this sort of conversation does anything at random. Still listening, I watched her hands, noticing how delicately she handled this tiny object, from time to time holding it in the palm of one hand and gently placing the other over it.

Toward the close of our session, I pointed out to her what she had been doing with her hands. She looked down, surprised. "Does this little starfish have something to do with what we've been talking about?" I asked. Puzzled, she said she didn't know. "How do you feel about it?" I asked her. Without hesitation she replied, "It matters."

"Then why not take it with you," I offered. "Bring it back next time. Perhaps the reason it matters will come to you."

She slipped it into her breast pocket and stood. "Back in a week," she said and left the office.

As the day went on and I met with one person after another, the incident slipped to the back of my mind. But it was not over. In the final hour of the day, as I sat making notes and reflecting on those who had spent time with me, there was a knock on the door. Opening it, I was surprised to find Harriet. "Do you have a little more time?" she asked.

Sitting once again in the chair opposite, she looked at me. "I remembered," she said simply and laid the tiny starfish down between us. Then she began to tell me a story about an old man who is walking along a beach at low tide, picking up starfish drying in the sun and gently throwing them back into the ocean. He has been doing this for some time when a jogger overtakes him and asks what he is doing. The old man explains that the starfish will die in the sun, and so he is throwing them back into the ocean. Astounded, the younger man begins to laugh. "Why, old fellow, don't waste your time. Can't you see that there are hundreds and hundreds of starfish on this beach? And thousands of beaches in this world? And another low tide tomorrow? What makes you think that you can make a difference?" And still laughing, he runs on down the beach.

The old man looks after him for a long while. Then he walks on and before long he passes another starfish. Stooping, he picks it up and looks at it thoughtfully. Then gently, he throws it back into the ocean. "Made a difference to that one," he says to himself.

With tears in her eyes Harriet told me that she had somehow forgotten that every phone call, every letter, every form that she fills out matters. "I was so caught up in the insanities of the system that I did not remember that my work is not about changing a world I cannot change. It's about touching the lives that touch mine in a way that makes a difference. I used to do this in one way; now I do it in another. But I am touching those lives just the same."

Sometimes when a life of service has taken us to the fringes of human experience, what we find there is so overwhelming that our hearts can break. One might think that compared to the size of the problem what we do means nothing. But this is simply not the case. When it comes down to it, no matter how great or how small the need, we can only bless one life at a time.

Once in a medical meeting, someone asked another pediatrician, director of the adolescent clinic in one of New York City's inner city hospitals, how she could continue this work year after year when the kids she saw had so many social problems that nothing she did made a difference. "Why no," she replied with conviction. "With kids like these, *everything* I do makes a difference."

THE BOTTOM LINE

PAUL HAS HAD Crohn's disease for most of his life. At seventeen, he had the build and appearance of a thirteen-year-old. But he did not feel like a thirteen-year-old inside. He had been treated for years with drugs that had slowed his growth and maturation in hopes of controlling his disease, but the disease had progressed even so. He continued to lose weight, and pain was a daily reality. It had become obvious to all those around him that the time had come to consider surgery. But it was not obvious to Paul.

His previous doctor, a surgeon, had described the surgery to him in great detail. It involved the removal of the diseased portion of his large intestine and the creation of a colostomy, an opening on the surface of his abdomen through which the remainder of his intestine could empty. When presented with this option, Paul had left the doctor's office and refused to return.

He had come to see me only to please his parents. At first he would not even discuss the possibility of the operation, saying only, "It's too ugly, no one will love me, I can't live that way." Finally he was willing to tell me what he had been told about it. Taking a pencil and paper, he offered me an explanation of the surgical procedure complete with drawings that would have put the understanding of a fourth-year surgical resident to shame. "Paul," I said, "you will be asleep when all that happens. What will it be like after you wake up? What is it like to live with this?" He looked at me blankly. "Why, I guess I have no idea," he said.

I told him that often men found the care of a colostomy no more difficult or time consuming than many of the other ways they routinely cared for their bodies. "It takes a lot less time and skill than shaving," I told him. He was unimpressed. "Would you like to meet some of these guys, Paul?" I asked, hoping that he would say yes. There was a pause, and then he offered me an adolescent's shrug. "I guess," he said.

Through a national self-help group, I was able to locate three high-school boys in our area who had had colostomies and were willing to meet with Paul and talk with him. I encouraged him to phone them to see how it was for them. Reluctantly, he agreed. "But I will never have this surgery, Rachel," he told me, "no matter what they say."

"At least then you will know, Paul," I told him. "You owe yourself that."

As it turned out, he had been very surprised. All these young men looked their age and, as a result of the surgery, were far more active than he was. They played football, went dancing, and were able to attend school regularly. One was into computers, another had his own band. Despite himself, Paul had been impressed. When he shared his feelings about the operation, all three had told him that they had felt the same way at first and sometimes they still did, but often things did not happen the way that you feared that they would. Sure, some people were put off, but others did not mind at all. Two of the young men had steady girlfriends who found no difficulty in accepting them the way they were. He had even spoken with one of these girls.

All three boys had been willing to show him what a colostomy looked like, and one had even shown him how he cared for it himself. It had seemed simple enough to Paul. As he described these meetings, I was deeply touched by the generosity of these very young men toward a total stranger, and their compassion.

After speaking with these others, Paul had realized that he could manage to live with this surgery, something that had not seemed possible to him before. After several days of careful thought, he came back to discuss whether he would choose to go ahead or not. "I am going to do this, Rachel," he said. I told him I thought it was a wise decision but certainly not an easy one. He nodded. "What caused you to change your mind, Paul?" I asked. He looked at me and smiled. "Even with all those diagrams, I did not get it before," he told me with a grin. "For Chrissakes, those guys are well."

In my experience, no one ever really chooses surgery or chemotherapy. People only choose life and then welcome whatever means are offered to them in order to have it. Yet this choice is not always presented clearly, and that can make all the difference. Often the people who in the end clarify what is at stake and free us to make our decisions and live with them are not physicians.

I recall vividly the night before one of my own early surgeries, an eight-hour affair that would alter my body permanently. I was twenty-seven and unmarried at the time. Late in the evening a pleasant elderly woman, a technical aide, had come to my hospital room to shave my abdomen in preparation for the procedure. As she went about this humble task with great skill, she had asked me about the next day's surgery. Filled with resentment, self-pity, and a sense of victimhood, I told her what was planned and burst into tears. She had seemed quite surprised. "How would *YOU* feel if they were going to do this to *YOU* tomorrow?" I asked her angrily. She had taken my question literally and had thought it over. Then, patting me gently, she had said, "If I needed it to live, I would be glad for the help." Her answer had changed everything.

CRAZY CLEAN

CINDY'S HUSBAND DESCRIBED her to me as "crazy clean." Like her mother before her, her house was spotless; every metal surface shone, every drawer was precisely organized. This despite the fact that she lived with three small children and a big bear of a husband. She had an unerring eye for the slightest disorder. One of her young daughters told me that her mom could spot a Cheerio on the kitchen floor from the next room and would not be satisfied until the offender had confessed and picked it up.

Cancer changed all that. Her chemotherapy made her so weak that she could barely get from her bed to the bathroom. She did not have the strength to cook, and the entire neighborhood had invaded her perfectly organized kitchen and fed her family. Kind hands unfamiliar with the household rules washed, folded, and put away laundry in all the wrong places. Her perfect walls were covered with dozens of pictures made by the classmates of her three children, each with a prayer for her recovery, each stuck on with a piece of Scotch tape. During the worst of it, her husband brought home a kitten who shed everywhere but whose purring warmth comforted her through the dark hours of the night when she was so sick she could not sleep.

Now, she says with a laugh, she would never want to be the way she had been before she had cancer. "I drove my family crazy. I even resented my guests because they disturbed the order of things. I'd been that way for years."

She told me of a recent visit to her sister, a daughter of the same mother. "We were sitting together in the kitchen drinking tea and talking, and I happened to look into her living room. She has one of these carpets that shows every footprint. It had been vacuumed so perfectly that every fiber was pointing in the same direction. At one time, this would have given me a deep sense of satisfaction. Now it just looked sad and lonely, untouched by life." She began to chuckle softly. "There is so much more to life than a perfectly clean kitchen floor, Rachel," she told me.

The marks life leaves on everything it touches transform perfection into wholeness. Older, wiser cultures choose to claim this wholeness in the things that they create. In Japan, Zen gardeners purposefully leave a fat dandelion in the midst of the exquisite, ritually precise patterns of the meditation garden. In Iran, even the most skilled of rug weavers include an intentional error, the "Persian Flaw," in the magnificence of a Tabriz or Qashqa'i carpet. In Puritan America, master quilt makers deliberately left a drop of their own blood on every quilt they made; and Native Americans wove a broken bead, the "spirit bead," into every beaded masterpiece. Nothing that has a soul is perfect. When life weaves a spirit bead into your very fabric, you may stumble upon a wholeness greater than you had dreamed possible before.

There is often more wisdom to be found at the edges of life than in its middle. Life-threatening illness may shuffle our values like a deck of cards. Sometimes a card that has been on the bottom of the deck for most of our lives turns out to be the top card, the thing that really matters. Having watched people sort their cards and play their hands in the presence of death for many years, I would say that rarely is the top card perfection, or possessions, or even pride. Most often the top card is love.

INTEGRITY

BLESSING THE LIFE in someone usually requires a deep respect for their uniqueness, an openness to allowing them to uncover who they are rather than shaping them into who we want or need them to be. We cannot strengthen someone and violate their integrity at the same time. Innately, blessing life confers a greater freedom on those we bless.

The first thing that Richard told me about himself was that his intelligence tested in the high genius range. Laughing, I asked him why that mattered and unknowingly became the first adult person he was able to trust.

Richard's intelligence had shown itself at a very early age. He had taught himself to read at eighteen months and by three had read the *Encyclopedia Britannica*. He could remember much of it still. Both his parents were professionals; his mother was a judge and his father had an international reputation for research. Before his birth, they had enrolled him in one of our country's most outstanding private schools, and at three a place for him had been reserved at Oxford.

Richard's intelligence became his parents' prized possession. It was something they felt could not be entrusted to ordinary teachers in ordinary schools. When most children were attending preschool, he was taught at home by a select group of tutors, meticulously supervised by his parents. At the end of every day, he was examined by both of them on what he had learned. He does not remember playing with other children or ever reading a children's book. At twelve, he had run away from home and had not been heard from for four years.

No one knew how he had lived during this time. A few months before we met, he had been arrested for vagrancy in a state halfway across the country. He had refused to return to his parents' home or even to see them. Because he was underage, he had been made a ward of the court and was placed in a foster home. His father had contacted me and asked me to treat him. Declining to come in for a meeting, he had told me that he and his wife felt that their son had betrayed them but that he was still their son.

Richard sat back in his chair, looked at me, and waited. Looking back at him, I was struck by a sort of feral quality, as if he were unused to being in a room, in a house. Being in relationship to him seemed so beyond the ordinary that you paid it a different sort of attention. He reminded me somehow of the foxes I fed at night from my back deck. They would appear out of nowhere and just as suddenly vanish like smoke. Like them, he belonged only to himself. He had needed to escape from everything that society expected of him in order to be free. But this had left him voiceless, and drifting.

"What do you want to do now?" I asked him.

"I do not know," he said.

"Then we will wait," I told him.

The courts had placed Richard in an ordinary high school. The academic work offered him no challenge at all, but being among his peers for the first time presented great difficulty. At seventeen, he had never played sports or had a friend his own age. At first, Richard made many mistakes and slowly he learned from them. In the beginning he was withdrawn and silent, but others left him alone and he began to emerge and grow. Academically brilliant, and profoundly kind, he was a natural teacher and started to tutor those who were having trouble.

He discovered things that surprised him. He could sink a basketball from midcourt on four out of five tries. And he could take photographs. His first efforts in photography class were so extraordinary that his teacher had submitted them to a juried show. He had won a place in the exhibit, the youngest person ever to do so. The following year in an open competition, he had won a place as an apprentice to a nationally known photographer. In this world his IQ was as irrelevant as his social security number, and he was accepted because of the artistic integrity of his work. Slowly he began to build a reputation of his own for his unusual way of seeing the ordinary. He never lived with his parents again.

I saw Richard for five years. Several years after his last session, he mailed me a story along with an invitation to a showing of some of his photographs. The story is based on a tale attributed to Rabbi Nachman of Bratslev, or sometimes to the Sufis. I no longer have his letter, but as I remember it, the story goes like this:

Once upon a time there was a kingdom of great abundance. The fields grew crops twice the size of normal fruits and vegetables, the cows gave cream instead of milk, and the people were productive and happy. The pride of this kingdom was the young prince, the only child of the king and queen. The hopes of everyone were pinned on this stellar young man, and when he walked in the street the people murmured to one another, "How perfect he is in every way. What a perfect king he will make someday." The prince spent almost all his time studying with those who were teaching him how to be the perfect king.

All went well in the kingdom until one day the prince could not be found. Courtiers searched the palace. "The prince is missing" flew from lip to lip, and people everywhere were in despair. The distraught king and queen ran through the thousand rooms of the palace calling the prince's name. There was no answer. Eventually a little serving maid, sweeping the Great Hall, happened to look under the banquet table and saw the prince there. He was stark naked. "Sire," she gasped in alarm, "what are you doing under there. Where are your clothes?"

"I am a chicken," the prince told her. "I do not need any clothes." Upon hearing this, she ran shrieking to the king and queen, saying that she had found the prince and he had gone mad.

The entire castle gathered in the Hall to see this tragedy for themselves. People tried to persuade the prince to come out from under the table, or even to put on his clothes, but he refused, saying only that he was a chicken. They tried to tempt him out from under the table with the finest of foods, but he would not eat. "I am a chicken," he told them. Eventually the little serving maid scattered a handful of corn under the table which the prince ate gratefully.

The kingdom was in chaos. The king sent out a call for wise men to come to heal the prince's madness, and many responded. One by one, they spoke to the prince, trying to convince him that he was not a chicken, and one by one they left defeated. "I am a chicken," the prince told them all.

At last, the supply of wise men was exhausted, and the king did not know where else to turn. One day, an old farm woman asked for an audience with the king. "I will cure your son," she told him. The king looked dubious. "Are you a wise woman?" he asked her. "No," she said.

"A scholar?"

"No," she said.

"Then how will you cure my son?"

"I will cure your son because I understand chickens."

What is the harm? the king thought. *We have tried everything else.* And so he commanded a page to show the old woman into the Great Hall.

As soon as she entered the Hall, the old woman removed all her clothes, crept under the table, and sat down next to the prince. The prince looked at her and said nothing. In a little while, a servant came and scattered a few handfuls of corn, and when the prince began to eat, the old woman also pecked at the corn. They sat together in silence for some time longer. Finally the prince said to the old woman, "Who are you?"

"And you?" she replied. "Who are you?"

"I am a chicken," said the prince.

"Ah," said the old woman, "I am a chicken, too."

The prince thought about this for several days. Gradually he began to talk to the old woman about the things that are important to chickens, things that are different from the things important to men. She understood as only another chicken could understand. They spoke not about the world as it is but about the world as it could be. They became friends.

After several weeks, the old woman called to one of the serving girls and told her to bring some clothes. When the clothes arrived, she dressed herself. The prince was horrified. "You have betrayed me!" he shouted. "You told me you were a chicken!"

"But I *am* a chicken," said the old woman. "I can wear clothes and still be a chicken." The prince thought about this for some time. Then he turned to the pile of clothing and dressed himself also. They continued their conversations as before and ate corn together as before.

After a few days more, the old woman called to one of the serving girls and told her to bring a fine meal and set it on the table. When the meal arrived she crawled out from under the table and, sitting in a chair, began to eat. The prince was appalled. "You have lied to me!" he shouted. "You told me you were a chicken!" "But I am a chicken," said the old woman. "I can sit at a table and eat and still be a chicken." The prince thought about this for some time. Then he, too, crawled out from under the table and joined the old woman. They ate in silence for some time. Then the prince began to laugh. For all we know, he is laughing still.

The story has a very happy ending. The prince went on to become the greatest king the kingdom had ever known. Under his rule, freedom grew in the kingdom much the way that peaches and potatoes had grown in the past. Each person became free to be the person that they were meant to be, and the people who had once been productive and happy became wise.

The king was thrilled with the old woman's success. He called her to him and offered her any reward she wanted if she would tell him how she had convinced the prince that he was not a chicken. But she shook her head and left his presence empty-handed.

I was deeply moved by the story and called Richard to tell him how much it had meant to me. "Does it have a name?" I asked him. "I don't know if it does really," he said. "But I think it is about us." I was both amused and touched by being compared to this old farm woman. My own efforts are rarely so deliberate and resourceful. But if I share anything in common with her, it is a deep respect for the unique shape of the life in each of us and a belief in the importance of becoming free to live coherently with it. I had seen and supported Richard's integrity much as she had supported the prince. Perhaps in the end we are all chickens.

THE PATH

WHEN I WAS remodeling my home, I was torn between two ways of creating access to my front door. One way involved building a flight of steps from the street that opened onto a path leading directly to my door. From the moment you set foot on the first step, you could see the front door and know exactly where you were going.

The other way was quite different. You come through a gate and climb a short flight of steps to a small landing. Just beyond this landing is a tree of great beauty. As you climb, all you can see is this tree. When you reach the landing, you discover it joins a small deck bordered by a rose garden and passing through this find another flight of steps, quite steep, leading off to the right. The top step is well above your eye level, and climbing, you see nothing until you reach a deck at the top, where looking to your right you discover a breathtaking sixty-mile view of San Francisco Bay. Crossing this deck brings you to three gradual steps leading off to the left. Climbing these you unexpectedly find the little meadow which is my backyard, and rising from it, the exquisite profile of Mount Tamalpais, the highest mountain in our county. Only then can you see my front door, which is now only a few steps away. You have been moving toward it steadily, without knowing, all along.

In struggling to make this decision I consulted two architects, both of whom told me that one of the basic principles of the architecture of front entrances is that people need to see where they are going from the start. They agreed that the uncertainty of the second approach would create unease in any guest coming to the house for the first time. Despite the uniformity of this expert advice, I ultimately chose the second way.

Thinking about it now, it seems to me that knowing where we are going encourages us to stop seeing and hearing and allows us to fall asleep. In fact, when I find myself on such a direct path, a part of me rushes ahead to the front door the moment I see it. As I hurry to overtake this part, I usually do not really see anything that I pass.

Not knowing where you are going creates more than uncertainty; it fosters a sense of aliveness, an appreciation of the particulars around you. It wakes you up much in the same way that illness does. I chose the second way.

In fact, perhaps we only think we know where we are going as all the while we are really going somewhere quite different. I have done many things in order to achieve a valued goal only to discover in time that the real goal my choices have led me toward is something else entirely. Something I could not even have known existed when I first set foot upon the path. The purpose underlying life often wears the mask of whatever has our attention at the time. The very reason that we were born, our greatest blessing, or our way to serve may come into our lives looking like a new car, a chance to travel, or a cup of the finest coffee.

The truth is that we are always moving toward mystery and so we are far closer to what is real when we do not see our destination clearly.

A MATTER OF LIFE AND DEATH

ONE NIGHT WHEN I was sixteen years old, I went to sleep in my dormitory room at Cornell in upstate New York and awoke six months later in a hospital bed in New York City. My disease had declared itself for the first time in the most dramatic way possible. I had suffered a massive intestinal bleeding, which had put me into a long coma. My life as a well person had ended, and my life as a chronically ill person with Crohn's disease had begun. It was then that I first came to know my mother.

As a professional woman, my mother had always worked long hours. Often I saw her only when she arrived home after dark to finish my bath, read me a story, or kiss me goodnight. I remember her as a somewhat shadowy figure on the periphery of my childhood who smelled good and cared for me on the weekends.

But during the six months that I was in a coma, life changed for us both. I was an only child of older parents, and both my parents had been overprotective. My father's fear was fed by the words of my physicians. They told him that if I recovered from this coma, I would live as an invalid, severely limited by a disease that they could not understand or control. I would undergo many major surgeries. I could not be expected to live past the age of forty. Returning to college was, of course, out of the question. Respectful of their expertise and frightened for my life, my father had accepted every word.

But this was not my idea of my future. I wanted to be a doctor passionately, and as a spoiled only child I was accustomed to having my own way. My father and I had several stormy confrontations, and I remember the last of these well. I was lying in a hospital bed with my father on my left and my mother on my right. My father dominated the conversation, repeating the words of the doctors yet again. When I angrily told him that I would return to school no matter what the doctors said, he as angrily replied that he would not give me the money for my tuition. And then my mother spoke up for the first time.

Accomplished professional woman though she was, she had been born in Russia and had been subservient to the will of her husband in all personal matters much as her mother had been before her. I do not remember her ever questioning one of my father's decisions or making a family decision of her own. But these were different times. "I will pay your tuition," she said quietly. My father was aghast. "And where will you find the money to do that?" he challenged her. She went on as if he had not spoken. "I have had a secret bank account for many years," she told me in the same even tone of voice. "You can have it all."

My mother was a superbly trained public health nurse. Twenty-four hours later, she had signed me out of the hospital against medical advice and flown with me in a small plane back to college. It was her first airplane ride. She lived with me there for the next six months, taking me to my classes, sometimes pushing my wheelchair when I was too weak to walk, caring for me until I could manage for myself. Then she left me there and went home.

It was a difficult two years, as I was still sick and very weak. I could not eat ordinary food and was twenty-five or thirty pounds below my normal weight. The powerful drugs I needed to take to control my symptoms had radically changed my appearance. Just living pushed me to my limits and sometimes beyond. Often I was filled with self-pity, but there was no one to depend on but myself. Slowly I found a strength I had not known I had and a way to live this new life and go on.

Years later, I spoke with my mother about this difficult time and how important it had been. I reminded her of our daily phone calls and thanked her for her support and her belief. I wondered why she had let go of her only child at a time when most parents would have rushed in to protect and pamper, help and fix. It had been dangerous. Hadn't she been afraid?

"I was terrified for you," she told me, "but I was even more frightened for your dreams. If they died, this disease would have claimed you." And so she had given me the chance to try, to see if I could become a doctor. It had seemed to her that if others had chosen my life for me, I might have been stopped there, frozen and bitter, always wondering if I could have done it. "There are so many ways to die, Rachel," she told me.

My eyes filled with tears. I had simply not known. "And if I had failed, Mom?" I asked her. "If you had failed, you would have found out for yourself what was real. Then perhaps in time you could accept it and dream again."

Befriending the life in others is sometimes a complex matter. There are times when we offer our strength and protection, but these are usually only temporary measures. The greatest blessing we offer others may be the belief we have in their struggle for freedom, the courage to support and accompany them as they determine for themselves the strength that will become their refuge and the foundation of their lives. I think it is especially important to believe in someone at a time when they cannot yet believe in themselves. Then your belief will become their lifeline.

THE MIRROR

I THINK I must have been Janet's last resort. A librarian, she would soon be forty, and had always lived alone. Charitably speaking, Janet could be described as very, very plain. Within the first twenty minutes of our initial session together, she had shown me pictures of her family. Her sisters and her mother were truly beautiful women.

As she spoke, I looked at her from a woman's perspective. Her clothes were not becoming to her, she wore no jewelry or makeup, her hair was pulled back with a rubber band into a ponytail at the nape of her neck. Her finest feature was her eyes. Clear and gray, they were now filled with tears.

Life is not easy for a very plain woman. From early childhood, she had felt ashamed of her looks and painfully shy. The response of others to her simply confirmed her sense of wrongness. In school, children had made fun of her appearance. As a teenager, her peers had avoided her. Her family, while loyal, were often apologetic about the way she looked. Many years before, she had simply given up. In her entire life she had never had an intimate relationship. She felt at ease only in her home or in the library. "Librarians are invisible," she told me. She spent her days at work and her evenings in front of the TV. She had lived this way for a long time.

But sometimes things just add up, and as her fortieth birthday drew closer Janet became profoundly depressed. I began to meet with her every week, uncertain whether or not she might become suicidal. I offered her a place of acceptance and caring, but in the end it was not me, but my patients, who healed her.

As she sat in my waiting room week after week, she began to respond to the others she saw there. The people in my waiting room often have no hair, or have lost a part of their bodies, or are very sick. Many are as young as Janet. She had never met people like them before, and she was surprised that she felt so comfortable with them. Shy though she was, after a while she began to talk with some of them. She had noticed that others often came with them, people who drove and shopped and helped. After thinking about this for a while, she hesitantly told me that if some of my patients had no one or if their families needed an extra hand, perhaps she could be of help.

Which is how Janet met Will. Will was a devastatingly handsome thirty-two-year-old man who had become HIV positive about a year after his partner was diagnosed with AIDS. Will had nursed him through his long, progressive illness and ultimate death. Slowly, he too had become sick and had needed help.

At first, Janet drove Will to doctors' appointments much as she drove several others. But most of the others had some family, and Will was alone. As time went on, she began to shop for him and then to cook extra food at home, freeze it, and take it to him for dinner. They became friends. As things became worse, his parents had flown here several times, and I had met them and done a few sessions with them and Will. They were older people and it had been hard for them at first, but they were a close family and had been able to support Will in ways that really mattered. Janet had met them, too, and liked them. Like Will, they were kind people.

Within a year, Will became very ill. His parents had wanted him to come home to them, but he had refused. He had lived in California for many years and he wanted to stay here. He had applied for hospice care but discovered he was not eligible, as there was no one living with him who could act as his caregiver. Many of his closest friends had already died of AIDS, and he had no one to turn to for help. Janet had told me about this in one of her own sessions. We sat and looked at each other for a while. Then we began a dialogue of few words and long silences.

"It's a lot of responsibility," I said.

"Yes, it is," she responded.

"I am used to my own ways of doing things and my own place," she said.

"Yes, you are," I responded.

"And I have a full-time job," she said.

"Yes, you do," I responded.

"And he is going to die," I said.

Her eyes filled with tears. "Yes, he is, Rachel," she said softly.

After a few more days of thought, Janet had moved in.

Will died in the spring. When I heard, I called Janet. Her phone message told me that she had gone out of town. I was concerned for her and wondered if she would be able to handle things. Her depression had lifted over the past months, but I knew that Will's death would be a great blow.

A few weeks later when she came to see me, she told me she had been visiting with Will's parents and had attended his funeral. As she talked about the events that had led to his death, I looked at her, trying to figure out why she looked so different to me. With a shock, I realized that she was wearing lipstick. When I commented on this, she looked away from me for a moment. It seemed to me that she blushed.

Still looking away, she told me about something that had happened shortly before Will died. He had been very weak and mostly bedridden for some time. That morning he had not been doing well, and so she called him from the library several times during the day. The hospice social worker and the nurse visited daily and often a neighbor would look in, but as the day went on she worried about his being at home alone until she finished work.

Coming home, she had run up the stairs, her arms full of groceries. She opened the door, calling his name loudly so that he could hear her in his bedroom. But Will was not in his bedroom. Fully dressed in a jacket, shirt, and tie, he was sitting in the living room waiting for her. His clothes, still elegant, looked as if they had been bought for a much, much larger man, but his hair was carefully combed and he had shaved. The effort involved was hard for her even to imagine.

Stunned, she asked him why he had gotten dressed. He had looked at her for a long moment. Then he eased off the couch, and, getting down on one knee, he had asked her to marry him. She had put the groceries down then and helped him up. Hugging him for the first time, she had told him how very important he was to her.

I looked at her in silence. Still blushing, she met my eye. "In my heart I did marry him, you know," she told me. "He will be here with me always."

WHO SERVES?

In 1984 I was invited to England to lecture to professional groups about the use of guided imagery with people who are ill. At that time, few people in these audiences had ever heard of the mind/body connection or recognized its potential power.

One of these talks was a grand rounds at Queens Hospital in England. I had actually been asked to give two talks, identical in nature and back to back, one for the hospital's physicians and one for the nurses. At this time in England, these groups did not sit down to learn together. Just prior to the second talk, the nursing sister who had organized it asked me if I would mind if a member of the public were admitted to the audience.

I marveled for a moment at how closely defined the professional role was here and how clearly the lines were drawn between those who could serve and those who could not. Misreading my hesitation, she hurried to say it was the former janitor of the hospital who had recently retired and now visited patients as a volunteer. She realized that it wasn't quite appropriate, but she had told him that she would ask me. Amused, I said that he would be most welcome. She raised her eyebrows, surprised and slightly embarrassed by my lack of conventional professional boundaries.

My talk was greeted with considerable skepticism. At the close of the brief question-and-answer period that followed, one of the head nursing sisters stood, thanked me for my time, and commented that while this new approach seemed reasonable for Americans, there in England, it was really not possible to enter the personal life of a patient in this way unless one were a psychiatrist. Heads nodded in agreement all over the auditorium. Confronted by the entire British way of life, I had nothing more to offer, and she then announced that any and all would be welcome to join me and the nursing administration at tea.

A surprising number of people came, wanting to talk a little more. Seeing a small elderly man in a tweed jacket in the crowd, the same sister brought him forward to be introduced. It was the retired janitor.

Diffidently, he told me that he had wanted to talk with me about some things that had come up during his visits with hospitalized patients. Most of the people he visited were elderly, and he had been touched by how sad they were and how drab and cheerless a place the hospital seemed despite the best efforts of the staff. Thinking to cheer people up, he had begun to bring some posters and fine-art prints from his own personal collection and lend them to people to put on the walls of their rooms.

One day, he was showing a picture of a picnic to an elderly lady who had been hospitalized for several weeks, a print of Seurat's *Sunday Afternoon on the Island of La Grande Jatte.* She had sighed and said how lovely it would be to actually be there. It had seemed quite natural to suggest to her that they close their eyes for a few minutes and pretend that they were. After a moment, she had begun to talk about what it was like to be there. Birds were singing. She could smell the grass and hear the little river that flowed nearby. All this had amazed him, but she seemed so much more relaxed afterward and so pleased with the whole thing that he offered to do it with her again the following day.

His success encouraged him to try this with others, who seemed to get as much out of it and so he had been doing this sort of thing for many months. "Some people have even told me that they visit their picture at night when I am gone and that it is a great comfort to them," he said. "One man believes that his headaches have gone away. Odd thing."

I looked into his warm gray eyes and told him how nice it must be to have him visit. Then I looked across the top of his head and met the eyes of the head sister. She looked shocked.

BEYOND THE AMERICAN WAY

DEATH IS CERTAINLY not a part of the American way of life. Commenting on this, Woody Allen once said, "In America, death is seen as optional." Many of us are caught up in a fierce struggle with life, forcing our wishes upon it and shaping it according to the American Dream. In a culture where few are even willing to grow old, it is not surprising that death is sometimes viewed as if it were a social problem. Once when I asked a patient in the last stages of cancer how she felt about dying, she told me that she felt "embarrassed."

Another of my patients told me that she was afraid that she would not be able to die a good death. When I asked her what she meant by this, she said, "I worry that I will not be able to do things properly," much as at another time she might have had anxiety about a dinner party going awry. And perhaps this is our cultural fallback: If death is not preventable, perhaps it can be made socially acceptable.

There is a growing belief that there is a right way to die, a death according to plan, where every good-bye is completed, every promise fulfilled, every conflict resolved, and everyone discovers in the end that they were loved. Occasionally things do work out this way, but life is rarely this tidy. Life is passionate and mysterious. It has its own ways of working things out, and everything of great value does not come gift wrapped. There are times when death is brutal, and even ugly, but all death has profound meaning. Over time each person who is genuinely touched by a death will find that meaning for themselves in their own way, even those who have been disappointed in themselves or feel they have failed someone else.

Sometimes these deeper meanings are very accessible. A friend once told me after the lingering death of her mother that she was surprised to find that she had learned something of great importance. "She showed me what it is like to die, Rachel," my friend said, "and I am not afraid." Other times, the gift of meaning is not as easily seen.

At a crowded party, a woman in her thirties, upon hearing what I do, told me how much she resented all this talk of death as something meaningful. Her husband had died young of cancer three or four years before, and she still was unable to think of it without anger. As the cocktail hour swirled around us, she told me that it had been terrible. As therapy after therapy had failed, he had become increasingly withdrawn and rejecting, lashing out at everyone and rebuffing the efforts of all those around him to be of help or comfort.

He had blamed everyone for his suffering and the lack of fulfillment in his life. He had spoken bitterly about the choices he had made and reproached his friends and family for allowing him to make them. Despite all those around him, eventually he had died alone, surrounded by abused people that he had wounded deeply. She had cried and cried about it. The pain was less now, but even after all this time she could not find any sense of meaning in his death and she could not forgive him.

No one shares a story like this in such a setting unless they are in pain. My heart went out to her. I asked her what she had learned personally about death from this terrible experience. She paused and looked at me for a long moment. Then with great passion she said, "I do not want to die this way."

"Yes," I said, "so how do you need to live?" She looked at me, puzzled. "How do you need to live to be sure that you do not die this way?" I asked again.

As we continued to look at each other it seemed to me that she looked past me for a moment, making eye contact with something intensely personal. Then she reached out and touched my hand and turned away into the crowd.

Some months later, I received a note from her telling me that my question had caused her to think about her timidity and her fears. There were many things that she had left undone. She wanted to open her heart to certain people. She had not done it because she feared rejection. She had been asked to do several things at work that felt quite wrong to her. She had not refused to do these things or left her job as she feared she would be unable to find other work. She had a considerable artistic gift and had dreamt of studying and becoming a painter. She had not done this either because she was afraid to fail at it.

She knew that she was not living in a way that was true to herself but had not known where to find the courage to do things differently. My question had changed that. "I am not going to die the way my husband died," she told me. "Once is enough."

The first meaning of all death is loss. But meaning is dynamic. Over time, new meanings may evolve that are far less universal and more our own. It is important to revisit our wounds to see what new meanings may have grown there. If we become frozen in anger and pain, it may be many years before we recognize what these are.

THE EMPEROR'S NEW CLOTHES

IT TOOK TIMMY more than a year to die of leukemia. Five years old, bewildered by pain and weakness, toward the end he stopped talking and would just hold fast to one of his parents' hands night and day. After he died, his mother and father were inconsolable. A concerned friend suggested they consider going to a nearby mental-health service center that had a spiritual orientation and ran bereavement groups. She would call ahead and make the arrangements.

Not knowing how else to help themselves, they had gone to the center. Almost on the threshold, they were greeted by a woman, hands outstretched, who asked if they were David and Debra. When they nodded, she introduced herself as the bereavement group leader and told them she had heard about Timmy's death. "If you can see it in a spiritual way, this loss will be one of the most beautiful experiences of your lives."

Debra is a quick and blunt lady. As her husband stood there openmouthed, she stared at this woman and said, "Are you *CRAZY?*" and taking her stunned husband by the hand, she turned and left.

Befriending life often requires accepting and experiencing loss. There is no question that great loss may have a deeper meaning and may indeed transform those touched by its terrible grace. But it is foolish to think that spiritual growth will somehow *remove* loss, much in the same way that an aspirin removes pain. Spiritual awakening does not change life; it changes suffering. The Zen Buddhists say, "Before enlightenment, chop wood, carry water. After enlightenment, chop wood, carry water." The loss is the same. Only the meaning changes. As its meaning evolves, the suffering may become less but the loss will last forever.

I remember the memorial service that was offered for Timmy, a gathering of a few hundred shocked and grieving people. The Quaker minister who spoke to us was only slightly older than Timmy's parents, and was himself the father of a little boy. He did not tell us that this was a beautiful experience. Instead he pointed to the pain in the room, encouraging each of us to allow it to touch us in our own way and to know that we are not alone in being touched.

The pain would help us to love our children. It would remind us to love each another. He told us that Timmy was not replaceable. Nothing important ever is. He reminded us that the life in every person is unique. And then he pointed to the Mystery. Why should a little boy suffer and die? He asked us to listen for the questions that we now had in our hearts because Timmy had died. Does God exist? Does life have a purpose? Does love go on forever? Does it matter?

He encouraged us to hold those questions close and to follow them. To begin a dialogue with the world about them. To measure the events of all of our lives against them. These questions would help us to move closer to life, to know life more intimately. Looking out over the hushed gathering, his own eyes filled with tears, he wondered aloud if perhaps that was the wisdom.

As I sat there grieving, an odd question laid its hand on my shoulder. It was not the sort of question that could support a Ph.D. thesis or become the focus of scientific research. Such questions must be capable of answers. It was my grandfather's sort of question, the kind that is in itself a source of strength. *Is it possible that there may be an unknowable purpose to life itself?* At that moment there was a great silence around this question. There is a great silence around it still. Yet having it has enabled me to work with people with cancer year after year and love life, even so.

FORGIVENESS

A YOUNG HOSPICE nurse came to talk out her feelings about a death that troubled her deeply. A few months earlier, she had admitted a young man to the in-service unit late on a Friday afternoon. Edward was very ill with AIDS and had come to the hospice at the urging of his neighbors, who were concerned that he was not receiving adequate care at home. He had Kaposi's sarcoma, a blood vessel tumor suffered by people with AIDS, and there were several dark purple tumor masses disfiguring his face. Despite this, he seemed beautiful to her, and she had been powerfully drawn to him. "He was a beautiful soul, Rachel," she told me, her eyes filling with tears.

After she had finished her paperwork, she spent a few hours just sitting and talking with him. She told me that this had been a very special time for them both. In the course of these few hours, they had spoken of many things, including death. She had asked him what he feared the most about it. He had paused and then told her that he feared dying alone. On learning the nature of his illness, his family had simply disowned him and did not wish to be contacted even in the event of his death.

Having been raised in foster care herself, she had been deeply touched by Edward's story. Taking his hand, she had promised him that she would be there when he died. I looked at her. She flushed and said that it had been a foolish and unprofessional thing to say.

She had never promised a patient such a thing before, but at the moment it had seemed absolutely true. She could not say why.

It was close to midnight when she left, and she had been off duty for the rest of the weekend. She had thought of Edward several times and had looked forward to seeing him again on Monday. But on Monday morning, she discovered that he had signed himself out of the hospice the night before. Puzzled, she asked one of the social workers to look in on him during her home-visit rounds. The social worker discovered that Edward had died at home sometime during the night. In his bedroom she had found a note with Cynthia's name and the hospice's phone number on it.

As Cynthia spoke of this, her voice shook. The note had been wrapped around a beautiful Victorian silver mirror with Edward's initials engraved on it. He had written, "You have seen me and I am grateful." She began to cry softly. "He was very sick, but I never thought he would die this soon. If only I had been there, he would not have left the hospice." She had been very troubled by this thought and by the feeling that she had betrayed her promise to him.

About a week or so after he died, Cynthia began to have a series of vivid dreams. They were always the same. She would be walking along a road with a great many other people. Suddenly she would see Edward coming toward her in the crowd, staring at her intently. The moment she recognized him, she would look away, filled with guilt and unable to meet his eyes. Deeply distressed, she would wake up.

She had this same dream for several nights in a row, and then she began to catch glimpses of him during the day, in supermarkets, in the subway, and once even in the background on the television news. At first she thought this was her imagination, but it was happening more and more frequently. She looked at me, frightened. "I think he is haunting me. He is reproaching me for what happened. What do I do?" And then she began to sob.

I moved closer and took her hand. "Cynthia," I said, "perhaps there is something more to know." She looked at me in distress. "In these dreams, have you ever actually looked at Edward?" I asked her. She shook her head. "I can't," she said. "I just can't."

"It may be helpful. Are you willing to try if I am here with you?" We sat together for a few moments in silence and then she nodded. "If you close your eyes, can you see him?" I asked her. Slowly she closed her eyes and took a few deep breaths. I sat holding her hand and waiting.

After a few moments, she nodded again. "What is happening?" I asked her. "He is right here, staring at me," she said. "He seems to be trying to tell me something, but I do not know what it is." She tightened her hold on my hand. "Ask him why he is still here," I suggested. We sat in silence for a few minutes. "I don't know what he wants," she told me. "He won't speak to me."

"How does he look to you, Cynthia?" There were a few seconds of silence and then, without warning, Cynthia began to cry. When she could speak again, she said, "It's his face. He has come to show me his face. Rachel, his skin is perfect. All those tumors on his face are gone."

I continued holding her hand tightly. "Oh, Rachel," she said, "his face is shining." We sat together in silence for another few minutes. It was very still and peaceful in the room. Slowly Cynthia opened her eyes. "He's gone," she told me and let go of my hand. She never saw him or dreamt of him again.

Sometimes I think death may be a reclaiming of wholeness, not just for the dying but for the rest of us as well. The esoteric schools often speak of death as a form of service and say that the state of consciousness in which we die may heal some great rift between matter and spirit. This may be so, but certainly the way people die often serves those who live on, offering us the opportunity to know the importance of our love, and the blessings of our relationships, no matter how short our time together has been.

THE GIFT OF THE MAGI

THERE ARE WAYS of giving to people that may take from them as much as is given, ways that diminish a person's belief in themselves and even their trust of life. Sometimes after someone has been rescued by a highly technical intervention, they may feel vulnerable and dependent upon it for their lives. Such people, though restored to a greater physical health, may live from then on as invalids.

Bob was one of the first people in our area to have a pacemaker implanted in his heart. Before his surgery, he had been a pirate of a man, pushing himself to the limit, enjoying his family, his friends, his work, his food, and his drink. Gradually these limits moved closer and closer in, but his attitude toward them was still the same. When he was so ill that he could only walk a block, he would walk that block and not one half-step less.

His surgery had been difficult but so highly successful that he was presented to grand rounds. His cardiac function had been restored beyond anyone's wildest hope, and his doctors were delighted.

But his own response to all of this was puzzling. His joy of life, always so infectious, seemed gone. Although he was now capable of running two miles, he rarely left the house. He insisted that he never be left alone and felt anxious unless someone was within range of his voice. Several times a night, he would awaken and take his pulse. He resisted the efforts of his family to draw him out.

Once, when he had refused to stay alone in the car while his wife did fifteen minutes of shopping, she had confronted him, asking him what he was afraid of. He had told her that he was afraid that the battery in his pacemaker would fail. The mechanism that now occupied the center of his body had come to occupy the center of his life.

I worked with Bob for two years. Gradually he came to some greater acceptance of his pacemaker, but he never fully regained what he had lost. His first words to me were too strong for him to move past. Showing me the thirty-inch scar that ran through the mat of hair on his chest, he had told me, "I see this and I feel as if I am broken and have been repaired. Before, I felt sick but I was whole."

But we are all different and my own mother's response to her heart disease was, of course, another thing entirely. In the last part of her life, her heart condition became severe, and she would collapse unexpectedly in a cardiac arrest. In the year before she died, this happened several times in our home.

I remember one of these terrible occasions in particular, seeing her fall to the living-room floor without a pulse, resuscitating her with the help of the 911 paramedics, and putting her to bed only to find her walking toward the door an hour later in her hat and gloves. "Where are you going, Mom?" I gasped. She gave me her best smile. "To church. Bingo is at two," she said. And she left.

She was under the care of one of my friends, who is a brilliant cardiologist. With great skill, he undertook the medical management of her heart with a carefully and ingeniously designed regimen of new and powerful cardiac drugs. She took four different medications in the morning and five or six at night.

From the beginning, he had suggested that I leave things in his hands and simply be my mother's daughter. It was good advice, and I was able to follow it for about a week. Resolutely, I would pass the copy of the *Physician's Desk Reference* on my office shelves several times each day. But, of course, my resolve faltered. After ten days I took the *PDR* down and began to read.

I was concerned to discover that some of the drugs my mother was taking completely disabled the sensitive feedback mechanisms that enabled the normal heart to function. In effect, my mother's heart was being completely controlled by her doctor's choice of drugs. And furthermore, according to the *PDR,* several of the newer drugs were unforgiving and had to be taken at precisely the right time in order to help and not harm the patient. One of them, a dilator of the coronary arteries, would reverse its effect if even a single dose was missed, causing the coronary arteries to constrict and precipitate a heart attack.

I was horrified. At eighty-five, my mother was, to say the least, absentminded. What if she forgot to take a pill or became confused and took two? What then?

Because of her age and her illness, I had brought my mother from New York to California to live with me. She kept her many bottles of heart medications in a little drawer in our kitchen next to the kitchen sink. Twice a day, she would open this drawer and lay out a dose of several drugs. She had been doing this alone for a few weeks, but that was before I read the *PDR*.

The next morning at 8 A.M. I was standing next to her as she prepared to take her morning dose. "Remember the blue one, Mom," I said in the most casual way that I could manage. "And two orange ones." That evening, I was there again, as she measured out the second set of pills. "Half of a green one," I murmured, "and only one yellow one."

This went on for a few weeks until one morning, just after I had again commented on the blue pill, my mother turned to face me. Drawing herself up to her full height, she looked me in the eye. "Rachel," she said, "do you know that I will die when it is my time? Not one second before and not one second after. And when that happens, you will probably tell yourself some sort of a story: 'It was because she forgot the yellow one or because she took two blue ones.' But that will not be the real reason at all."

Extending a palmful of pills toward me, she asked, "You don't think that these things can outwit God, do you?" But I had. For a long, long minute I looked at my mother's old arthritic hand, filled with brightly colored pills of many shapes and sizes. Then I looked into her eyes. They were brimming with laughter and something deeper, perhaps compassion. She smiled at me in exactly the same way that she would smile at my father, just before she would declare "GIN!" and lay down her hand. Then something released me, and I began to laugh.

Many years afterward I heard a Tibetan lama address this same issue in a far different language. "We die, not because we are ill but because we are complete," he told his dharma class. "Illness is the occasion of our dying, but not the cause."

COMPLETION

I REMEMBER READING once in a book on developmental psychology that only a parent can confer adulthood. At the time I did not really understand what this meant. I think now that I do. There is a validation that can only come from those who have given us our life, who have known us entire, from our very beginnings. Even in great age, the power of a parent to grant such validation is undiminished. Such power verges on the mystical.

My mother's brand of femininity was distinctly her own, as were her ideas about adulthood. Everyone in her family was a service professional, and the unspoken sine qua non of maturity was the courage to move society forward. Professionally, she herself was a maverick. As one of the early Henry Street nurses, she had been intimately involved at the start of Public Health Nursing in the United States.

Her major interest had been well baby care, and she pioneered in recognizing and respecting the innate feminine wisdom of mothers. At the time, such thinking was radical and viewed with suspicion by pediatricians, a profession so proud of its new science and technology that at mid-century almost seventy-five percent of American babies were bottle fed. My mother's outspokenness had caused her to be viewed with suspicion as well.

I believe I know the very moment that I became an adult, when my relationship to my mother as a child was complete. It happened in a public place, in the presence of a large number of people. Yet it was a completely personal moment witnessed by none of them.

I had been one of two women and several men invited to speak at a conference entitled "The Power of Imagination," a pioneering day-long meeting on mind/body health. It was 1984, when such ideas were very new and poorly accepted by the medical profession. Of the thousand people in the audience, only a few were physicians.

At the time, my mother was elderly and very ill. Two days before the conference, a friend asked me if I planned to invite her. Surprised, I responded that I had not thought about it as she had no interest in mind/body health. My friend, who is Japanese and has a finer sense of such things than I, responded, "But of course not, Rachel. She has an interest in you."

When I thought it over, I realized that my mother had never actually heard me speak publicly. I thought about the difficulty of getting her to the auditorium and what might happen if, sitting alone in this large audience, she had one of her frequent "heart spells" as I was speaking. It was a daunting thought, and I was tempted to dismiss my friend's suggestion out of hand. Still, a simple fairness suggested that my assumption of her lack of interest might not be completely accurate, and so I asked her if she wanted to come. She accepted with alacrity.

We went to the hall two hours early. At that time, my mother's heart was failing and she could not walk very far without resting. It took a while to get her seated in the empty auditorium. I settled her in the middle of the tenth row. As the auditorium filled and I sat on the stage with the others, I saw her reach into her purse for her nitroglycerin tablets. My heart sank.

When it was my turn to speak, I described the difference between curing and healing and the new technique of guided imagery that could further people's own ability to heal. I shared my belief that a medicine that did not recognize this innate power in people failed them in a crucial way. These were radical ideas for the time, and I told story after story from my practice in support of them. As the hour drew to a close, I ventured a look at my mother. She was listening intently. She seemed to be all right. I was relieved.

When I finished speaking, there was complete silence. I had expected this as only the previous week many of the physicians at the Kaiser San Francisco Hospital, offended by these same ideas, had walked out of the grand rounds I had given there well before the end of the hour. But this was not an audience of physicians. Suddenly people began to applaud and slowly many even stood up. I was stunned.

Only one person in the tenth row remained seated. Her arms were crossed and there was a very tiny smile on her face. As we continued to look at each other, her eyes narrowed and she nodded slowly, twice. No other acknowledgment I have ever received has equaled it. I draw strength from it still. Five months later, she was dead.

CELEBRATION

THE PEOPLE WHO come to the Commonweal retreats all have a personal relationship with cancer. Some were diagnosed a few weeks ago; others have survived their diagnosis by many years. Some are living with cancer and others dying of it. We make room for them all.

At seventy-three, Irving was in the final stages of pancreatic cancer when he spent a week at Commonweal. He was deeply depressed, and it seemed to take most of his strength just to get through the day. During the daily morning discussion group he would sit, drawn into himself, saying nothing and crying silently. He refused all invitations to participate in the discussion, and so he was simply included as a member of the circle along with his grief.

One of the opportunities for self-discovery the retreat offers people is the chance to do some sandtray work. The sandtray room has shelves on every wall, each holding a great number of small objects, some symbolic, others literal, which encompass the complexity and scope of both inner and outer life. In this Jungian technique people are invited to choose whatever objects they are attracted to, place them into a shallow box filled with sand that stands on a table in the center of the room, and then talk about their personal significance. The objects are chosen intuitively, and often their meaning becomes clear only after people begin to talk about the arrangement they have made in the sand.

Our wisdom is often carried deep within us, and sandtray gives this part of everyone a visible voice. In this simple process, people often uncover insights about the purpose, importance, patterns, and beauty of their lives and sometimes find a direction for their healing.

Irving had refused to participate in so many of the other retreat activities that it was not surprising when he said that he did not want to do a sandtray. One by one, the others had their sandtray sessions and frequently shared their insights in the morning group. On the third morning I asked Irving if he would come to the sandtray room with me just so that he would know what the others were talking about.

The sandtray room fascinates most people: the hundreds and hundreds of small things create a world of imagination and color. It is a magical place, and people are often drawn into it. Irving was captured by it in spite of himself. He began to walk slowly through the room, absorbed by the things on the shelves. I sat down at the table on one side of the box of sand and just waited.

Within a few minutes he had taken an object off the shelves, a large crystal paperweight in the shape of a diamond. Holding this against his chest with both hands, he continued to walk from shelf to shelf in complete silence. Whenever he passed through the sun pouring in the window or stood under one of the lights, the paperweight would send a spray of tiny rainbows across the white walls of the room and the ceiling. He seemed completely unaware of this. After several minutes he turned and looked at me.

I nodded toward the paperweight. "Would you like to put that in the sand?" I asked. He stepped forward and placed it in the exact center of the box and, sitting down opposite me, began to bury it in the sand. When it was no longer visible, he sat there looking at the spot where it had been for a long time. I was surprised at how silent and empty the room had become. It reminded me of the first moment after someone dies when you find yourself suddenly alone.

Next to the sandtray stood a glass filled with candles, each a foot or so long and no bigger around than a soda straw. Noticing the glass, Irving began to take candles from it and place them in the sand in a circle around the buried paperweight. He seemed intent on getting them each the same distance apart and tilted slightly outward.

At last he seemed satisfied with their placement and sat back in his chair to contemplate them. There were twelve of them. We contemplated them together. After a while, I offered him a box of kitchen matches. For the first time, he smiled. Slowly and very deliberately he lit one candle after the other, and when all were lit he began to sing very softly to himself. I leaned forward in order to hear him. He was singing "Happy Birthday."

I had no idea what any of this meant, but I began to sing with him. Happy birthday to you, happy birthday, dear Irving. At the end of the singing, he closed his eyes, and an expression of deep peace came over his face. We sat together in this way for several minutes. Then Irving stood and I stood too. As we left the room together, I looked back over my shoulder at the burning candles. They looked like a crown of light.

Throughout the remainder of the retreat, Irving maintained his silence in the morning group, but he was no longer crying. The peace he had found in the sandtray room was still with him, and he sat among us as radiant as a Buddha. The group accepted this as completely as it had accepted his tears.

A few weeks after the end of the retreat, a member of Irving's family called us to tell us that Irving had died. She thanked us for all we had done for him and told us of the profound change that had happened. He had gone home and told his family and friends that he was dying and spent time with each of them telling them what they had meant to him and receiving their love in return. This intimate sharing had not been possible before because Irving had never been willing to talk about his death. "Whatever you did, we are so grateful," they told us. I was puzzled. Prior to their phone call I would have said that we had not done anything much.

There were many things that happened during the week which may have been of help to Irving. Sometimes simply being accepted as you are and cared about by others can affect people in very profound ways. Many years later when I spoke about Irving during a workshop on Presence, a participant who was a Jungian analyst told me that Irving's sandtray was a classic example of the mandala of the Self, a symbolic affirmation of the integrity and immortality of the soul. But I am not a Jungian and I had not known this. Neither had Irving, but he had recognized the innate truth of it just the same.

Perhaps we do not die all at once. In my experience, the ego that has covered over our deepest wisdom does not suddenly release us at the moment when the breath stops. Rather, our habitual ways of being become more and more fragile and begin to crumble around us over weeks or even days; and the buddha seed that they have covered over becomes clearer, stronger, more available. Dying may be a time of intense learning, as painful and as transforming as labor, and in the end we may give birth to ourselves.

If something does endure and go on when we die it is our accumulated wisdom, which marks the place on the trajectory of our lifetimes where we will begin again. For some, the greatest gathering of such wisdom may occur in the days before death. In *The Death of Ivan Ilych,* Tolstoy exquisitely describes step by step the last weeks in the life of a bourgeois civil servant of little or no spiritual bent, who experiences at the moment of his death a true compassion for all living beings, so deep that many might never approach it even through a lifetime of meditation and spiritual practice.

The final step in the healing of suffering may be wisdom. Perhaps no suffering really heals completely until the wisdom of its experience has been found and appreciated. We do not return from the journey into pain and illness to the same house that we left. We have become more and the house we will live in will be more as well, for however long we may inhabit it.

After twenty years of accompanying people as they deal with cancer, I would say that the experience of suffering and the wisdom we may find there will be completely our own. Often it will help us to live better. Sometimes it may help us to die better as well.

VI.

RESTORING THE WORLD

THE VIEW FROM the edge of life is different and often much clearer than the way that most of us see things. Life-threatening illness may cause people to question what they have accepted as unchanging. Values that have been passed down in a family for generations may be recognized as inadequate; lifelong beliefs about personal capacities or what is important may prove to be mistaken. When life is stripped down to its very essentials, it is surprising how simple things become. Fewer and fewer things matter and those that matter, matter a great deal more. As a doctor to people with cancer, I have walked the beach at the edge of life picking up this wisdom like shells.

One of my patients who survived three major surgeries in five weeks described himself as "born again." When I asked him about this, he told me that his experience had challenged all of his ideas about life. Everything he had thought true had turned out to be merely belief and had not withstood the terrible events of recent weeks. He was stripped of all that he knew and left only with the unshakable conviction that life itself was holy. This insight in its singularity and simplicity had sustained him better than the multiple, complex system of beliefs and values that had been the foundation of his life up until this time. It upheld him like stone and upholds him still because it has been tested by fire. At the depths of the most unimaginable vulnerability he has discovered that we live not by choice but by grace. And that life itself is a blessing.

Some of those who have had a near-death experience, who have actually set foot over that edge and then returned, have had an additional insight. Their experience has revealed to them that every life serves a single purpose. We are here to grow in wisdom and to learn to love better. Despite the countless and diverse ways we live our lives, every life is a spiritual path, and all life has a spiritual agenda.

Such ideas have the power to change the way you see yourself and the world.

In the sixteenth century the great Kabbalistic rabbi Isaac Luria offered a profoundly beautiful cosmology of the world, a sort of mystical version of the Big Bang theory. In the beginning there is the Ein Sof, pure Being without manifestation, the Infinite, Absolute Source of the world. The world as we know it begins with the Or Ein Sof, an emanation of light from the Source. Rabbi Luria explains the fragmented nature of this world by postulating an accident of cosmic proportions: the vessel holding the Or Ein Sof shattered and broke open, and the light of God was scattered throughout the universe into an infinite number of holy sparks. These countless sparks of holiness are hidden deep in everyone and everything.

Like many other mystical cosmologies, this Creation myth is based on an idea of service. The purpose of human life is to uncover these sparks of light and restore the world to its original wholeness. Everyone and everything we encounter is a shell or container for a hidden spark of holiness. It is up to us to help free the hidden holiness in everything and everyone.

We restore the holiness of the world through our lovingkindness and compassion. Everyone participates. It is a collective task. Every act of lovingkindness, no matter how great or small, repairs the world. All those ever born have shared this collective work since the beginning of time. This myth suggests that the human race is a single Karass dedicated to this holy purpose.

The name Kabbalah uses for this collective work is Tikkun

Olam, we repair and restore the world. Everything in life presents us with this opportunity. It invests all our struggle with a deeper meaning and deepens all our joy.

In talking of a particularly dark time in her life, a friend once told me that in the depths of her alcoholism a thought had occurred to her and proved a turning point. What if her struggle to find a way to live beyond her addiction had a deeper meaning? She had been living in darkness for many years. What if she was the only person in the world who could redeem the goodness in this particular piece of darkness? This task might be hers alone. In some larger, more mysterious sense it might be her life's service. This thought had lifted her sense of guilt and shame and dignified her struggle. It had given her a power she had not been able to find elsewhere. She wonders now if everyone's struggle to overcome whatever diminishes them and live whole has this same meaning.

Tikkun Olam points to the value of every life. My grandfather explained this to me when I was very small. "We need to remember to bless the life around us and within us, Neshume-le," he would tell me. "When we bless others, we free the goodness in them and in ourselves. When we bless life, we restore the world." My parents, as socialists, believed in working for the common good. But my grandfather taught me that we bless life because it is holy and because we are holy as well.

It often seems that the problems in the world are large and overwhelming and there are limits to what we can accomplish as a single person or even as a single group. It can be profoundly disheartening. But Tikkun Olam means that we each make a difference and we can heal the world.

Service is the work of the soul. We might view moments of genuine service as a movement toward the soul, a return to what is most genuine and real in each of us. In the trajectory of a lifetime, this turning toward our goodness happens not once but many times. Some of these turnings are small and some are large. All are important. Much in life distracts us from our true nature, captures the Self in bonds of greed, desire, numbness, and unconsciousness. But every act of service is an evidence that the soul is stronger than all that and can draw us toward it despite all.

Perhaps our greatest service is simply to find ways to strengthen and live closer to our goodness. This is far from easy. It requires an everyday attention, an awareness of all that diminishes us, distracts us, and causes us to forget who we are. But every act of service bears witness to the possibility of freedom for us all. And every time anyone becomes more transparent to the light in them, they will restore the light in the world.

LINEAGE

SERVICE IS NOT the attribute of any one religion any more than holiness is. Many of those who serve life have no formal religion, while others follow any one of the many religious traditions on the face of this earth. All are a blessing to life.

When my mother was about sixty, one of her nephews was ordained as a priest. Her four brothers had all married Christian women; and I was raised among a half dozen first cousins who were devoutly Catholic, among them the children of my aunt Mary who was a former nun. I have many memories of visiting my cousins at the Maryknoll convent in upper New York State where they spent the summers, playing baseball with them and the younger sisters and novitiates.

I also remember accompanying my mother to my cousin's ordination shortly after I graduated from medical school. The High Mass and the ritual, which went on for more than two hours, were entirely in Latin. At one point in the service my cousin and the other young men with him genuflected and lay completely prone on the floor before the cross on the high altar.

I stole looks at my mother. The granddaughter, grandniece, and daughter of Orthodox rabbis, she had been raised in a ghetto in Russia. At times during her adolescence, her face had been blackened and her hair cut short to make her unattractive to the young Cossack soldiers. She had escaped Russia with her family as a girl just before the first of the pogroms and had witnessed and even personally encountered many forms of anti-Semitic treatment in her lifetime. Her face was unreadable. I found myself wondering what could possibly be going through her mind.

Later, as we left the church, I asked her what she had thought of the whole thing. She had smiled with genuine pleasure. "Isn't it wonderful that in this day and age a young man would choose to dedicate his life to serving God?" she told me. "My father would have been so proud." We walked on a few steps in silence and then she looked at me. "And you, too," she said. "It must be in our blood." I looked at her, puzzled. But she had no more to say.

Now that I am almost as old as she was then, I think I understand. There are many ways to befriend the movement toward wholeness in others. All of them are holy.

BEYOND WORDS

"HOW HARD IT is to be young," Father O'Shea told me. I laughed and asked him what he meant. Eyes twinkling, he told me of the first patient he had been called to see as a hospital chaplain. Very young and desperate to be of service, he had gone to visit a woman who was facing major surgery the following morning. She was lying in her bed, tense with anxiety. He had no sooner pulled up a chair when she told him, "Father, I feel certain that I am going to die tomorrow."

Nothing in his training had prepared him for this, and he had sat there with absolutely no idea of how to respond. To cover his confusion, he had reached out and taken her hand. She had begun to talk then. Still holding her hand and barely listening, he had reached back in his mind for some of the great words of comfort from his tradition, the words of Merton, of Teresa D'Avila, of Jesus. He had them all with him when he had entered the room but somehow now they were gone.

The woman continued to talk and even to cry a little, and his heart went out to her in her fear. At last she closed her eyes, and he had taken this opportunity to ask God for help, for the words that he needed. But he had found no words at all. Eventually she had simply fallen asleep and he had left, vanquished, convinced that he was not cut out to be a priest. He had spent the rest of the day and most of the night in an agonized assessment of his shortcomings and his calling. He had been too ashamed to visit her again.

But a few weeks later he had received a note from her, thanking him for all he had done for her during his visit, and most especially for all the wonderful things he had told her, the words of comfort and wisdom. She would never forget them. And then she quoted some of what she had heard him say, at length.

Father O'Shea began to laugh, and I did, too. "It was so long ago," he chuckled. "Thank goodness we can never be that young again." He paused for a moment to wipe his eyes. "You know, Rachel," he told me. "Over these years I have learned that when I pray to be able to be of service to someone, sometimes God says 'Yes' and sometimes God says 'No,' but quite often God says, 'Step aside, Patrick. I'll do it myself.'"

THE FINAL PATIENT

I FIRST MET Delia in the emergency room when the police arrested her. Two hours before, she had brought her three-week-old son, Teejay, to the hospital because of a fever. The resident doctor who was called to see him that evening was struck by his small size and noted several bruises on his skin. Teejay was the child of a very young unmarried mother on welfare. The resident made a presumptive diagnosis of child abuse, and, keeping Delia and her son in the emergency room under the pretext of waiting for tests, he had called the authorities.

I became involved because, as attending physician, I was responsible for all pediatric emergency care for the month. By the time I arrived at the emergency room, Teejay had been scheduled for admission to the hospital under a protective order. The police and I met in the doorway of his examining room, and I insisted on examining the baby myself before they took his mother away. Reluctantly, they agreed.

Delia was fourteen when she discovered that she was pregnant and left high school. There in the examining room she looked at me in despair. She was holding her baby tightly in her arms. I asked her if she would undress him for me and watched her as she handled him. Her hands were covered with tattoos. They were gentle and tender. She laid him naked on the examining table and covered him with his little woolen blanket. Teejay was tiny and thin. He appeared to be dehydrated. Concerned, I began to question his mother about his care. Hesitantly she told me how hungrily he fed and how he often vomited up everything he swallowed. She mentioned how long and hard he cried and how difficult he was to comfort.

I looked at the resident leaning against the wall with his arms crossed in front of him. "Have you considered pyloric stenosis?" I asked him, suggesting the possibility of a thickening of the intestine at the exit of the stomach, a common cause of persistent vomiting and failure to thrive in the newborn period. But he had not. I examined the baby's tiny belly with one finger. Just below his breast bone in the area of the pylorus was a little mass the size of an olive, the classic sign of stenosis.

"What makes you think that this infant is abused?" I asked him. "Well, he's three weeks and doesn't even weigh what he weighed at birth," he answered with some irritation. "And he's covered with bruises." Stepping forward, he turned Teejay onto his stomach. Over both his shoulders and at the base of his spine were several flat, bluish discolorations. They were the typical birthmarks seen in seventy to eighty percent of darker-skinned newborn infants.

X rays confirmed a diagnosis of pyloric stenosis. After the police had been sent away and Teejay had been admitted and scheduled for surgery, I sat down and spoke with his mother, apologizing to her for what had happened. "It's okay, Doctor," she told me. "It's okay. They doan' listen. I tole them I never hurt my baby but they doan' hear. They never hears." It made my heart ache.

I followed Teejay and his mother for the next year and a half in my own practice. When I left pediatrics in 1976, he was the last patient I ever saw. In the hours before his final visit, I cleaned out my desk and sent the boxes from my office off with the movers, all the while questioning if I was doing the right thing by throwing away my career as a pediatrician to follow a dream of a different sort of medicine. Over the years I had been a pediatrician, I had been involved in the lives of thousands of children. Would I ever care for children again? I was not at all sure that I would.

The nurse called to tell me that Teejay and Delia were waiting, and, with a heavy heart, I went to see them. Teejay had become a delicious and loving toddler. He shrieked and put up his arms to be hugged as soon as he saw me. As I examined him, I was again overwhelmed by doubt. I loved my little patients. How could I not be a pediatrician? I had trained for this work for almost half of my life and I had no idea what would happen next or even where I would go.

Afterward as we talked, Delia, knowing that it was my last day of work, kindly asked how I was feeling. We had spoken often over the last few months about my leaving. She had supported my belief that medicine needed to change, that ways could be found to care for people's hearts and souls as well as their bodies, to empower people in their own healing. Back then I had been certain I was making the right choice, but now that the moment had actually come, I felt very afraid. "Delia," I told her, "perhaps Teejay will be my last patient."

At the thought of not seeing the children, tears filled my eyes. Very gently Delia reached across and laid her hand on mine. She reminded me of the terrible night on which we had met. How no one had heard her, no one had believed her. Her baby had almost been taken away. "This hospital is sick," she told me, "can't see, can't hear, ain't got no heart, no soul. They all that way. Maybe you doan' see lotsa little baby patients anymore, but you is still a doctor. Only you just got one big patient now."

She looked away from me for a few moments. "I be praying for you," she told me softly. "You works for The Man, He take care of you. Doan' worry. He take you where you need to go." And, taking the little gold cross from around her neck, she reached out and put it around mine.

MYSTERY

THE FIRST TIME I heard the word *Mystery* I did not understand what it meant. As an avid reader of mystery stories, I had the idea that something is a mystery only because its solution has not yet been found. But mystery is different from Mystery. By its very nature Mystery cannot be solved, can never be known. It can only be lived.

We have not been raised to cultivate a sense of Mystery. We may even see the unknown as an insult to our competence, a personal failing. Seen this way, the unknown becomes a challenge to action. But Mystery does not require action; Mystery requires our attention. Mystery requires that we listen and become open. When we meet with the unknown in this way, we can be touched by a wisdom that can transform our lives.

Mystery has great power. In the many years I have worked with people with cancer, I have seen Mystery comfort people when nothing else can comfort them and offer hope when nothing else offers hope. I have seen Mystery heal fear that is otherwise unhealable. For years I have watched people in their confrontation with the unknown recover awe, wonder, joy, and aliveness. They have remembered that life is holy, and they have reminded me as well. In losing our sense of Mystery, we have become a nation of burned-out people. People who wonder do not burn out.

Everything and everyone has a dimension of the unknown. Mystery helps us to see ourselves and others from the largest possible perspective, as a unique and possibly endless process that may go on over lifetimes. To be living is to be unfinished. Nothing and no one is complete. The world and everything in it is *alive.*

A sense of Mystery can take us beyond disappointment and judgment to a place of expectancy. It opens in us an attitude of listening and respect. If everyone has in them the dimension of the unknown, possibility is present at all times. Wisdom is possible at all times. The Mystery in anyone may speak to them and heal them in the grocery store. It may speak to us and heal us too. Knowing this enables us to listen to life from the place in us that is Mystery also. Mystery requires that we relinquish an endless search for answers and become willing to not understand. That we be open to witness. Those who witness life may eventually know far more than anyone can understand.

Perhaps real wisdom lies in not seeking answers at all. Any answer we find will not be true for long. An answer is a place where we can fall asleep as life moves past us to its next question. After all these years I have begun to wonder if the secret of living well is not in having all the answers but in pursuing unanswerable questions in good company.

A QUESTION OF STYLE

NOT ONLY CAN we witness Mystery; in some profound way we are Mystery. Our lives may not be bounded by our history and may go on for longer than we dare dream. If Life itself is not fully defined by science, perhaps we too may be more than science would have us believe.

When Ahiro came to see me, he was in the final stages of prostate cancer. He had come to prepare himself to die. He was Japanese, a beautiful man who had lived with integrity and a certain elegance. His life had been his family and his work. From the beginning, he had a clear agenda for our meetings and took charge of them. He told me that he wanted to invite those who had blessed his life to come to our sessions, one at a time, in order to thank them for all they had given him.

Such an agenda is not all that unusual at this time in someone's life, but some of those he planned to invite took me by surprise. I had thought that he would invite his wife, his children and some close friends, but among these beloved people were several of his professional competitors. Listening to some of his stories about them, I would have even said his enemies. But he felt a deep respect for them and believed they had spurred him to a level of professional excellence he could not have achieved without them. He wanted to thank them, too.

And so we began. About halfway through this agenda, as we were discussing the meeting we had just had with one of his sons,

Ahiro suddenly paused in mid-sentence and looked at me. "Rachel," he said, "I am an educated man. I must believe that death is the end. And you, as an educated woman, surely you believe that death is the end also. Don't you?" Caught unaware, I looked back at him. He was leaning toward me, smiling, but his eyes were very serious. For the first time I wondered if our meetings had a deeper agenda than I had realized.

"I used to think that death is the end," I answered slowly, "but now I simply do not know. Death seems to me to be the ultimate mystery that gives life its meaning and even its value. I do not know if death is the end." He sat back in surprise. "Why, surely you do not believe in a heaven with little angels flying about?" He looked at me and raised an elegant eyebrow. "Do you?"

"I don't know," I told him. There was a pause. Something shifted in his eyes, and I had the distinct sense that we had engaged each other on some level I could barely appreciate. Then he smiled at me and let the matter drop.

We continued to meet week by week with those on his list. But now in every one of our sessions, he would raise this topic, often when I least expected it, as if by catching me unaware he might find out what I really believed about death. I shared stories and experiences. He shared from his extensive reading. I began to look forward to these discussions. They were wide-ranging and very animated, quite often funny and sometimes profound. Each time, after listening to his carefully reasoned arguments in support of the finality of death, I would tell him, "I still don't know." I think he found it frustrating. And intriguing.

During our next-to-last meeting, he again raised this issue. Hearing my "I don't know" once again, he began to laugh. "Rachel," he said, "I am an educated man. I *must* believe that death is the end. But just in case it isn't, I will come back as a great white crane and give you some sort of sign that I have lost this argument."

And then this tall and elegant man stood. Putting both hands behind him and folding one leg up, he tilted his head in an exquisite gesture so that for a heart-stopping moment he became a great white bird. We both laughed aloud in delight.

"Something about showing up as a great white crane is a little obvious," I told him. "Do you remember that duck on the Groucho Marx show that used to drop down on a string whenever a guest inadvertently said the mystery word?"

"Yes," he said chuckling, "it's really not my style. I am more of a minimalist."

"Perhaps you will find another way," I told him. He looked at me for a considered moment. "I will do something that you will recognize," he said, suddenly serious.

Only a few months later, this remarkable man died. Shortly afterward I was in the TransAmerica building, a large pyramid-shaped structure in the downtown business district of San Francisco, waiting for an elevator to take me to an appointment. The building is tall and so the elevators are quite slow. This gives everyone a few minutes to themselves. In this brief time, I found myself thinking of Ahiro and how much I missed being able to talk with him. I remembered some of the many extraordinary things I had discovered about him and what a delightful man he had been.

At last one of the elevators arrived. It was empty. And so with my heart and mind filled with memories of this relationship, I stepped in. The doors closed, and the elevator started upward so abruptly that I was thrown slightly off balance. I glanced down hurriedly to regain my footing and there, lying on the floor of the elevator, was a single, large, perfect white feather.

In my mind, I continue my discussions with Ahiro. As always, he has presented the issue in a way that I did not expect, and he has certainly raised the level of the dialogue. I still do not know if there is a life after death, but perhaps that is not really the point.

The important thing is that Mystery does happen and offers us the opportunity to wonder together and reclaim a sense of awe and aliveness. The feathers that fall into all our lives offer neither proof nor certainty. They are just reminders to stay awake and listen, because the mystery at the heart of life may speak to you at any time.

ON THE CUTTING EDGE

"CAN YOU COME and give us a grand rounds?" my old professor said in an early-morning phone call. "Any topic you like, as long as it is cutting edge." I began to laugh. "On the cutting edge of medicine or on the cutting edge of life?" I asked him. "Either," he replied. So I gave a grand rounds about Medicine and Mystery.

Of the fifty doctors present, most were young: third-year residents or physicians newly in practice, highly trained and breathtakingly competent. A few were middle-aged, experienced practitioners or graying and respected teachers. After a brief discussion on the nature of Mystery, I asked them all to take a moment and remember some experience in their professional lives that they could not easily explain, a time when something occurred that changed them or caused them to wonder. I suggested they take a few moments to make some notes about this experience. After a surprised silence, everyone found pen and paper and began to write.

For the next two hours we shared these stories. Many had never been told before. Close to the end of the rounds, an older physician told us about his sister's death many years ago. He had been twenty and studying to be an engineer when his sister, who was two years younger, had lost her struggle with leukemia. As his sister became sicker, their parents had asked him to come home from school to be with the family. He had been given the job of reading to his sister.

The story he told us happened a day or so before his sister died.

He had been sitting with her in her bedroom, reading. His sister lay in her bed with her eyes closed, breathing with effort. As he read he would glance up occasionally to find that his sister had not moved. He was not even sure if she was awake but he continued to read, as he did not know what else to do.

He had been reading aloud for about an hour when he felt his sister's hand on his arm. Glancing over, he saw that his sister's eyes were open and shining with excitement. She was staring at a blank wall. "Sam," his sister said, "look! There's someone here! Someone has come! Can you see him, Sam?"

So he had closed the book and looked very carefully at the wall. "I could not see a thing," he told us. But he could *feel* it. There was something in the room, a presence, deeply loving and infinitely kind. He had never experienced such a thing before. He felt his heart drawn to it as if it were claimed. Deeply moved, he took his sister's hand. A few seconds passed and then he had simply known that he was to become a doctor. After his sister died, he had gone back to school, changed his major, and gone on to study medicine. The group sat quietly waiting for more. But the doctor had nothing more to say.

After the rounds, he came up to talk a bit. Sensing that there was more to his story, I asked him about it. Yes, he told me, what had happened was a little different, and he had felt uncomfortable speaking about it in front of the others.

"It's not that I knew that I was supposed to become a doctor," he told me. "What I knew was that I *was* a doctor. I had always been a doctor. That I had been born with a doctor's soul in me. Whatever it was that came for my sister had come for me, too. It felt like a sort of a healing, a coming back to my true self." He stood looking thoughtful. "Perhaps it was that sort of thing for us both," he said.

Several days afterward, I met one of the resident doctors in the corridor who wanted to talk about the rounds a little more. During the discussion it had seemed to him that the familiar lecture hall, with its windowless gray walls, gray chairs, and gray carpet, had become another sort of place entirely. He had been surprised that there were so many stories of Mystery among a random group of physicians. What did I think that this meant? He had been wondering about it.

Some questions had come up for him afterward. He looked away, slightly embarrassed, but he continued on. Did I think that the practice of medicine could be a practice, like meditation or prayer? Did it bring you into a closer relationship with the Unknown?

I looked at his tired young face struggling with this new way of seeing his work. People brushed by us in the corridor, hurrying as always. I thought of compassion, harmlessness, altruism, service, and covenant, the qualities inherent in the Hippocratic oath. They seemed to me to define a profoundly spiritual way of life. "Yes, I do," I told him. "Mystery once occupied the same central place in medicine that science occupies now," I told him. "Perhaps it still does."

Science has cast a deep shadow over our ideas about life. We may even have allowed science to define life for us, but life is larger than science. Life is process, and process has Mystery woven into it.

Things happen that science can't explain, important things that cannot be measured but can be observed, witnessed, known. These things are not replicable. They are impervious to even the best-designed research.

All life has in it the dimension of the Unknown; it is a thing forever unfolding. It seems important to consider the possibility that science may have defined life too small. If we define life too small, we will define ourselves too small as well.

MARY

MARY'S SON HAD come home for a week's vacation from college, feeling tired and looking pale, his usual vitality gone. Concerned, she had taken him to a physician, who had diagnosed a rare form of cancer. It was untreatable.

When she heard the diagnosis, Mary had left the doctor's office and gone home. Her son was now back at school. She had walked up her front steps, flung open the door of her house, and howled at the top of her voice. Still screaming her outrage, she had gone from room to room, flinging open windows, shaking her fists in the air, and shouting. Mary's home was in a conventional neighborhood where many of the families were Irish Catholic. Her husband, concerned as always about what the neighbors would think, followed after her, closing windows as she opened them and trying to calm her to no avail. She continued to howl, and he, overwhelmed and frightened, had called the family therapist they had been seeing as a couple. The therapist had called back almost immediately, and her husband had rushed with the phone to the bedroom where Mary stood shouting before the open window. "Mary, Mary," he had said, "the therapist is on the phone." With this she had rounded on him and screamed, "The therapist? The therapist? *YOU* talk to the therapist, Harry. I'll talk to God!"

It took all of Mary's enormous passion, will, and vitality to get through the next fourteen months. Together with her four daughters, she had taken her son to anyone who might offer help. They had tried everything known, but the cancer had raged through his body until finally, a shadow of himself, he had died in her arms. He was twenty years old. All of her love as a mother had not been able to save him. She felt that the life in her had gone with him. She was numb for many months. Inconsolable.

About two years after his death, she had gone with her brother to a Catholic church that she had never visited before. Unable to pray, she had wandered through the nave, stopping before a statue of the Virgin. Suddenly the pain that had been frozen in her heart all those months found words. "How could you do it, Mary?" she asked aloud. "How could you surrender your son? How could you find a way to live after he died? Where is there any hope of comfort?" Tears rolling down her face, she had told the Virgin that she had been good: a good person, a good mother. There was nothing more that she could have done.

"Why?" she demanded. "Why?" What possible reason could there be for someone this full of life, this new, this shining, to suffer and die? She knew beyond doubt that she would never, never get over this loss. Still crying, she told the Virgin how young her boy had been, how he still sometimes forgot to eat and how he did not know how to wash his clothes properly. "He needed a mother, Mary," she said in tears. "He needs a mother there, too. I do not understand, but I give him into your care." Turning away, she had left the church.

A day or two later, as she was driving to work, she was surprised to find herself humming an old hymn under her breath, a hymn about comfort. She often finds herself humming it. And very gradually, over time, she has found more room to breathe.

I was stunned by the power of her story, awed by the depth of her love for her son and the agony of his loss. I could not speak. Mary looked at me and smiled. "And the Mystery, Rachel?" she said. "The Mystery is that it is possible to be comforted."

Recently, Mary wrote to tell me that two of her daughters are pregnant. This spring, one of them will have her first grandchild, a little boy.

AFTER DARK

I CAME AWAKE wondering how many times the phone had rung before I heard it. Fumbling in the darkness, I got it to my ear. "Rachel?" the voice said, apologetic and frightened. "I'm so sorry, but Jerry has thrown up everything he has eaten tonight. I didn't know what to do."

Jerry, a hospice patient, was in the very last stages of esophageal cancer, and his intestine was almost completely blocked by tumor. The voice on the phone was his wife, calling in the dark from their kitchen. "It's normal for him to be doing this now, Lee, but how frightening it must have been for you both." She sighed. "I felt helpless. Is there anything I need to do?"

"Is he in any pain?" I asked.

"No," she said.

"Is he able to drink liquids?"

"Yes," she replied.

"It may be time for him to stop eating, Lee. Why not make him a cup of tea, and if he feels hungry, one of those protein drinks in your blender."

We spoke for a while about a liquid diet, and she asked me if there was anything else she might do. "It sounds like it's been a hard day. Maybe you want to read to him for a while or just sing to him a little. I think it might help you both. And call again if you need to." And we bid each other good night.

The women who call at night are always speaking from the heart. In the beginning when I was a pediatrician, the women would call about the children. But my scope has broadened. Now the women call about their partners, their parents, their sisters, their friends. Their voices are sometimes weary, sometimes sad, almost always anxious. They are looking for someone to wait with them.

I find that most of what I do when someone is dying is to reassure those who are caring for them that something they have never seen or experienced before is normal. Many of my colleagues in this work have found themselves doing this, too. One of them, complaining of being awakened three times in the night by people essentially asking "Is this normal?" wondered aloud if this was a good use of his extensive medical training. But I think that it is. Fear is the friction in all transitions. Our experience has made us familiar with unfamiliar ground. What better use for this knowing than to ease fear?

This was not always the case. When I was much younger and proud to be an expert, I, too, thought that this role was not a good use of my expertise. It felt like I was not doing something important. I hadn't understood the power of knowing life at times like these.

The family of one of my patients who died at home wrote to say what it had meant to be able to call when they felt anxious or afraid. They had called many times. "So much was strange to us. We would get caught up in worry of whether we were doing this thing right or if something we observed but didn't understand would have some hidden meaning and become awful and agonizing for Jim. We would get so worried that we were failing Jim in some way that we would freeze up. But over and over you kept telling us that what was happening was normal and that we were doing fine. Jim died peacefully in our home yesterday. My daughters were there and my granddaughters, too. Because you made it normal, we were able to make it holy."

According to the Kabbalah, all things can be made holy. Buried in the mundane and even the most difficult is a spark of God that invests life and all of life's experiences.

The light in the world is rarely obvious on the surface of things. Perhaps at the most profound level of service we find ourselves able to help others uncover this, to find in the most challenging and painful of experiences a blessing and a source of strength. In doing so we may bring about the fundamental injunction that begins the world, LET THERE BE LIGHT, and create for ourselves and others a place of refuge in the darkness.

THE THIRTY-SIX

REMEMBERING COMPASSION TAKES time, and sometimes the most profound learnings are not a part of a curriculum but are come upon by chance or even grace, the way that Glory found the pinecone. She brought it with her to the afternoon class; a large cone, split down the middle and attached to a Y-shaped branch. I stared at it in fascination, resting there in her lap, and hoped that she would say something about it. If you squinted your eyes, it was exactly the size and shape of a human heart.

Glory is a young family practitioner who practices in a small rural town. Her patients range from the newborn to the very old, and her practice has afforded her a profound window on life. I met her at one of the physicians' retreats I teach on detoxifying death. During the first evening's discussion, she had said that she would find her own death a relief; in fact, life being as it is, she couldn't imagine why anyone would struggle to live if there was a way to leave with honor. She had felt this way for as long as she could remember.

It was an unusual thing for a physician to say, and the group who listened were surprised. She did not seem suicidal or even depressed, merely matter-of-fact. As she spoke, I found myself wondering what lay behind her words. I had some ideas, but, as it turned out, I couldn't have been more wrong.

When she began to talk about the pinecone, all this became

clearer. In a voice that we could barely hear, she told us that she had found it on the path as she was coming in to lunch and had known instantly that it was hers. She looked at it lying there in her lap. "It's my heart," she told us. "It's broken. Split in half."

She began to tell us about a vast sadness that she had experienced all her life, a personal sense of the suffering in the world that goes on and on. She had felt this suffering even as a child. It had broken her heart, made her unwilling to live any longer than she had to. Yet brokenhearted though she was, people seemed to seek her out at times of pain and despair. It was hard for her to understand why this was.

As a young person and later as a doctor, she had been there for them, had comforted and stood with them. They had thought her heart was whole, had trusted in it. She touched the pinecone in her lap. "I have hidden this all of my life, Rachel," she said, speaking to me from across the room. We all sat in silence for a few minutes: there was nothing anyone could say.

Our retreat center has a labyrinth exactly the dimensions of the one in the cathedral at Chartres in France. The Chartres labyrinth is a walking meditation that has roots in the fourteenth century, a path enclosed in a circle inscribed on the floor. The path inside the circle is long and convoluted and eventually leads into the center; it is more than a third of a mile into the center of the circle and out again. The following afternoon, during the period of meditation, Glory decided to walk this path alone.

At the beginning, she had clasped her hands behind her back and started walking slowly and deliberately, looking down, trying to keep her balance on the narrow path. She had been walking step by step by step for about ten minutes or so and was becoming a little bored when she began to experience an urge to hold her hands out, palms up. She fought this impulse for a while, telling herself it was irrational. Finally, she had surrendered to it, and walked on with her hands held out before her.

Within a minute or two she had the distinct impression that her pinecone was resting on her upturned palms. She knew she had left it on the bed in her room, but with her eyes on the floor she could feel the weight of it quite clearly in her hands. She felt as if she was being told to offer it to others, just as it was. It was a strange and puzzling thought, but it somehow seemed the right thing to do.

She walked on in this way for several more minutes and at last came to a place in the labyrinth close to the circumference of the circle where the path unexpectedly turns sharply to the right. As you turn, you discover that you have reached the end of the path and a few more steps will take you to the center of the circle.

Turning to the right, Glory suddenly felt the pinecone in her hands move as if it had become her own living heart. Deeply shaken, she looked up for the first time and found an unmistakable Presence in the center of the labyrinth, waiting for her. For just the briefest moment she could see Him quite clearly. His heart was open, a place of refuge for all who suffer. It had been broken open by the suffering in the world in the same way hers had been.

Suddenly she understood why others had come to her for refuge since her childhood. The suffering she was able to feel had made her trustworthy. She stumbled the last few steps into the center of the labyrinth, knelt down, and for the first time since she was a child, she wept.

In a talk about compassion, a former teacher of mine once said that practice prepares the mind, but suffering prepares the heart. Perhaps the final step in the healing of all wounds is the discovery of the capacity for compassion, an intuitive knowing that no one is singled out in their suffering, that all living beings are vulnerable to loss, attachment, and limitation. It is only in the presence of compassion that we can show our wounds without diminishing our wholeness.

The Dalai Lama has said that "compassion occurs only between equals." For those who have compassion, woundedness is not a place of judgment but a place of genuine meeting.

FINDING SAFETY

BILL WAS AN internationally known architect. Of the many award-winning buildings he had designed and built I have only seen a picture of one. It stands on a hilltop above a vineyard in northern California. Made of iron pipe with a wooden platform as floor and open walls, it is topped by an iron cross. The most minimal of structures. It is also one of the most powerful statements imaginable of the capacity of a building to enclose space in a way that allows us to see it as sacred. Shortly after he built it, Bill and his wife had been married in it.

But I did not know Bill through his work. I knew him through the integrity with which he fought for his life and ultimately met with his death.

A life is made up of many stories. Bill told this story to his wife, Mary, and me late one afternoon as we sat on either side of his hospital bed in the little study of his home. At the time he was desperately sick with prostate cancer and waiting to find out if his latest tests would show that there was further treatment available for him. It did not seem likely. The house was still, and as we sat together I could feel the weight of his wife's anxiety and Bill's as well. This struggle had gone on for a long time. I felt a longing for a place of ease and safety, just a few moments of respite. I imagine that we all did.

As he lay in bed between us struggling to breathe, I asked Bill if he could remember a place where he had felt safe. Without hesitation, he began to describe his childhood home, the fields and the woods, the sound of the birds at sunrise, and then he remembered a story.

The story is Bill's oldest memory. It happened in rural New Jersey more than fifty years ago, when he was four or five years old and living in a house reached by a dirt road that ran alongside a small river.

Often in spring the river would flood. Once, soon after a flood, Bill was walking along the road and found a rainbow trout, washed up from the river, struggling to live in a drainage ditch beside the road. Small as he was, he was horrified. As he described it, it seemed to him that there was something very wrong about this beautiful fish, trapped and struggling in too small, too shallow, too muddy a place. He was just a little boy and it was a big fish, but somehow he managed to get it up into his arms. He carried it across the road and waded out into the river a little ways and put it back. Deeply moved, I asked him what he remembered most clearly about this. He said he remembered the moment when the fish between his hands realized it was once again part of the river.

There are many meanings in every story. On one level, this is a beautiful childhood memory shared by a very sick man. On another, it is a story about a man whose compassion goes back to his very beginnings. But I think there may be deeper readings still.

Certain practices run through all the branches of Buddhism. One of these is a practice done to celebrate enlightenment and the promise of freedom. At such times in China, Japan, Nepal, and Korea, live fish are bought at the market, taken to bodies of running water, and set free. These fish symbolize the possibility of a return to the Source and to that great freedom which is our true refuge and our home.

There is also a Buddhist teaching concerning the death of a

teacher, one who has accumulated the power to free others and help them to live well. The death of such a one is called "taking on the Rainbow Body," and it is believed that the physical body of such men and women somehow becomes a rainbow of light.

Bill was not a Buddhist. He did not know any of this intellectually. He was an architect, a vintner, a fly fisherman, a sailor, a friend, a husband, and a father. But there was in him, as there is in us all, something that went deeper than all these things, an unconscious part that was very old. If you were quiet and listened, sometimes, without Bill's knowing, it would speak to you directly.

And so, as we were waiting together, anxious and fearful, hoping to find that further treatment was available, I think that this part of him told the three of us this story. Perhaps it spoke to us so that we would understand where Bill truly was in his life. Or even more important, so that we would know that, despite appearances, all was well.

Over many years of listening to people with cancer, their dreams, their poems, their stories, I have come across many images for the soul, some conscious and many unconscious. I think the rainbow trout is one of the most beautiful.

THE WAY IT IS

THE BUDDHISTS SAY that one of the signs of true enlightenment is the experience of a vast, immutable joy that underlies the personal joys and sorrows of this life. The Cosmic Giggle suggests that for those in the know, the essential nature of life is such goodness that the only possible response is joy. Perhaps Joy is one of God's commandments. Certainly it weaves like a bright ribbon through the teachings of many of the world's religions. In the cracks between the many rituals and prayers, the Cosmic Giggle emerges and overtakes even the most solemn, the most holy.

One of the great American dancers of our time, Anna Halprin, told me a memory from her childhood. Her own beloved grandfather was a Hasid, a member of a sect of Judaism that takes joy as the means to worship and experience God. Hasids approach God through the ecstatic, through dance and song. She told me that her grandfather was the holiest man she had known. "Rachel," she said, "he had twinkling eyes and a long snowy white beard. As a small child, I thought that he was God."

Every Saturday she would run to the synagogue and climb the stairs to the women's section. Sitting there behind the screen, she would look down on the worship service and watch the men dance. "In among them was my grandfather, his arms in the air, feet stamping the ground, his black silk coat and snowy white beard shining and his face radiant with joy. And so I knew very young that God danced."

My own grandpa was far more solemn in his celebration of the holy. I remember him dancing only once, in his own synagogue, on the holiday of Simchas Torah. This is the day of celebration for the gift of Torah, the five books of Moses whose wisdom enables people to know how to live close to God. Every synagogue has several Torahs, great scrolls written out by hand on lamb or goatskin parchment in the most ancient form of Hebrew and rolled onto two poles topped with silver handles.

A Torah scroll can last for centuries. When it has worn out and can no longer be restored, a Torah scroll is buried as if it were a person. The Torah scrolls are the holiest objects in a synagogue and are kept behind a curtain in the holiest part of the synagogue, the ark behind the altar.

Each Saturday, during the service a scroll is brought out and unrolled so that a portion of it can be read aloud. The reading of the Torah is continuous and seamless. When the Torah has been completely read, it is immediately begun again. Simchas Torah marks this ending and beginning.

On this holiday the Torah scrolls are taken from the ark, and the men of the congregation dance down the aisles of the synagogue holding them in their arms in celebration of the covenant with God and the joy of living rightly. The very last letter of the last word in the Torah and the very first letter of the first word in the Torah, taken together, form the Hebrew word for the heart. As the men dance past, people reach out to touch the Torah scrolls in their arms and then put their fingertips to their lips in a kiss.

My parents were young socialists who did not favor this sort of thing, and so my grandfather had bribed my nana, who adored him, to bring me to the synagogue for this celebration. It was the first and only time I had ever been to his synagogue. I was four years old.

The Torahs in my grandfather's synagogue had been brought from Russia and were generations old. The scrolls had covers of velvet beautifully hand embroidered in gold, and all the silver scroll handles were covered with little silver bells. The biggest Torah scroll was even taller than I was and the smallest, so tiny, that even I could carry it.

I have to this day a memory as clear as a photograph of my grandfather, as the rabbi, carrying the largest Torah scroll of all, dancing down the aisle toward me, his face lit with joy. I had scrambled up and stood upon my seat in order to better see what was happening. My grandfather, suddenly seeing me there among the others, filled with excitement in my new pink dress, my hair in little pigtails with beautiful pink bows, had passed the great Torah to another man, swept me up into his arms and danced with me through the synagogue.

I remember the little silver bells on the Torah handles ringing and everyone laughing as the men danced all around us with their arms wrapped around the books of wisdom. God seemed very close just then.

The bright ribbon of joy can be found in many of the Torah's stories as well. My grandfather often told me these stories as if they had happened to the women involved and not to the men, and so I had many images of heroic and very human women who lived long ago and had a deeply personal relationship with God. These women were far from perfect: sometimes they lied, sometimes they stole things that were not theirs, sometimes they disobeyed or were jealous, but they all loved God and He loved them dearly in return. "They are the Mothers of our people, Neshume-le," my grandfather told me.

I remember his story of Sarah, perhaps because my own mother had this same name and perhaps because it was filled with a certain rebellion. Sarah was married to a man called Abraham, who had served God faithfully for many years.

One evening when she and her husband were very old, she was preparing dinner in their tent while Abraham sat outside the door enjoying the last rays of the sun. Suddenly God appeared to Abraham and expressed His appreciation for Abraham's years of faithful service. As a reward, God offered to fulfill one of the wishes of Abraham's heart. Abraham was overwhelmed. Somehow he managed to stammer out that what he wanted most was to have a son. "Done!" said God.

Inside the tent, Sarah, overhearing this male conversation, began to laugh softly to herself. What did God think, that she, at a hundred years of age, would bear her husband a son? Hearing her laughter, God asked sternly, "Who laughed?"

"No one," answered Sarah hastily. "It was only the fat in the fire." Of course, God being who He is, nine months later Sarah gave birth to a little boy. The Bible tells us that she named him "Yitzak," or Isaac. It comes from the word for "laughter" in Hebrew. Through him will come the great line of teachers and wise men that will culminate in the Messiah.

"Why does she call him Laughter, Grandpa?" I asked in bewilderment. "Is it because she laughed when God told her that he would be born?"

"Perhaps, Neshume-le," he said smiling at me tenderly. "Or perhaps it is because Joy is every child's real name."

THE PRESENCE OF GOD

My grandfather and I had many discussions about the teachings and principles of Judaism, but I can remember only one disagreement. It had to do with the nature of the "minyan." The idea of the minyan is central to the spiritual life of Jewish people. While anyone can pray at any time, before an official prayer service can be held there must be at least ten men present. This group of ten men is called a minyan.

"Why, Grandpa?" I asked, puzzled. Patiently he explained the law to me. It is believed that whenever ten adult men are gathered together in the name of God, God Himself is actually present in the room with them. "Immanent," my grandfather said. Any room then became consecrated ground, a holy place where the sacraments of the religion could be performed. After five thousand years of persecution and homelessness, nothing could be taken for granted. Holy ground had to be portable.

I was fascinated by this. My grandfather told me that this law was so important that often men were called from their homes to come to the synagogue because there were fewer than ten men present to pray for the dead, inscribe a baby into the book of life, or conduct one of the many rituals that acknowledged that life is holy and bound people to God. Once or twice in Russia, he had even gone out into the streets and collared a passing Jew, a total stranger, to complete the circle of ten. One did not refuse such an invitation, said my grandfather. It was considered to be a duty.

"But why only men, Grandpa?" I asked. He hesitated. "The law says ten men," he responded slowly. I waited for a further explanation, but he said nothing.

"Isn't God present when ten women gather together?" I asked. Thinking back on it, I imagine this to have been a difficult moment for him.

"The law says nothing about this, Neshume-le. It has always been ten men, since the beginning."

I was astounded. "If something is old, does it have to be true?"

"Certainly not," he responded.

"Well, then I think that God is there in the room when ten women gather, too," I stated flatly.

He nodded. "This is not what the law says," he told me.

We had never disagreed about anything before and I was shaken, but my grandfather seemed quite comfortable with the distance between our beliefs. We never discussed the matter again, and I thought that he had forgotten it.

A few years later, he became very sick. In the months before he died, I was allowed to visit with him only briefly so as not to tire him. I was almost seven years old and terribly proud of my reading, and so I would read to him from one of his books or we would simply sit quietly together. Sometimes I would hold his hand while he slept. Once after a nap he opened his eyes and looked at me lovingly for a long while. "You are a minyan, all by yourself, Neshume-le," he told me.

THE FRICTION IN THE SYSTEM

THIRTY YEARS AGO, when the *Concorde* began to fly between the United States and Europe, it was the focus of a great deal of media attention. At Mach 2—1,350 miles per hour—one could cross the Atlantic for the first time in less than four hours. No one had ever flown a commercial plane this fast before.

Several prominent media people were invited to fly on the first few maiden flights. To make the occasion even more special, these VIP passengers were given a tour that included a visit to the cockpit and a brief lecture.

One of these passengers was surprised to discover that no one actually kept the plane on course. Because of its phenomenal speed and the slowness of human reaction time, the course was actually maintained by two computers. The first computer took a course reading every few seconds and, if the plane was off course, instantaneously fed this information to the second, which would make the needed correction and confirm the new course.

After a brief visit to the cockpit, he returned to his seat aware that something had caught his attention but unsure of what it was. For the next hour or so, he puzzled over it without being able to identify it. Finally, he asked a member of the crew if he might see the cockpit once more.

Once there, he realized almost immediately that it was not something that he had seen but something that he had heard. As the computers fed course readings and corrections back and forth between them, they made a certain sound. What he had noticed was that this sound was almost continuous. Turning to his tour guide, he remarked on this and asked what percentage of the time the plane was off course. The crew member smiled. "About ninety-nine percent of the time, sir," he replied.

"And we will land in Paris at 9:03 P.M.?" said the VIP, marveling. "Yes, sir," the crewman replied. "Plus or minus sixty seconds or so."

This story was told to me and I have no idea of whether or not it is true, but it certainly raises an interesting thought. Perhaps it is not only a slow reaction time that would cause problems if the course was tracked by human beings. People put far more friction than this into their own feedback systems. How passionately many of us want to be right. It is not hard to imagine a human being telling another that he was wrong every few seconds and getting the defensive response "No, I'm not." You would miss Paris by many miles. You might even miss Europe. Even more important, a human being, being wrong 99 percent of the time, might lose heart.

Might it be possible to focus ourselves on the purpose we wish to serve in the same way that the *Concorde* is focused on its destination and navigate a trajectory in just this same way? Once we stopped demanding of ourselves that we be on course all the time, we might begin to look at our mistakes differently, giving them an impeccable attention and a frictionless response. They will not prevent us from reaching our dreams nearly so much as wanting to be right will.

Those who have the courage to offer us honesty, to be our navigators, might even come to be seen as worthy of a certain gratitude as collaborators in helping us reach our destination. "You are off course," they might tell us. "Why, THANK you," we might reply.

Serving anything worthwhile is a commitment to a direction over time and may require us to relinquish many moment-to-moment attachments, to let go of pride, approval, recognition, or even success. This is true whether we be parents, researchers, educators, artists, or heads of state. Serving life may require a faithfulness to purpose that lasts over a lifetime. It is less a work of the ego than a choice of the soul.

THE REWARD

My parents, young socialists, had firmly instructed my grandfather, who was a Kabbalist and an Orthodox rabbi, that he was not to speak to me about God and other such superstitions. They might just as well have told him not to breathe. So the whole of my religious education was covert, which of course made it far more effective than the ordinary Sunday school approach. For many years I thought that it was proper to talk about God only in a whisper.

Concerned that I was too young to fully keep his secret, my grandfather never revealed the source of his wonderful stories nor that most of the people in them were Jewish. This gave the Books of Moses a sort of universal human quality, which seems to me to be quite genuine.

Many of my grandfather's stories were family stories, that is, they were about God teaching His children how the world works. As a child myself, this really interested me. What the stories taught me seemed to be a part of all the other things I was learning about how the world worked: cross only on the green, say thank you, the big one is a quarter and the brown one is a penny, and the like.

As they tried to figure things out for themselves, the people in Grandfather's stories spoke to God directly and often. I loved when God responded in mysterious ways, and my grandfather and I would talk about what He could possibly have meant.

One of the most interesting of these discussions was about

Moses and the Promised Land. I was learning about rewards in kindergarten and had a nice collection of little pieces of paper, each with a gold or a silver star pasted on it. I loved these stars and worked very, very hard for them. I knew exactly what I had to do to get a silver star and what further effort would get me a gold. It was all predictable.

But Moses never got to the Promised Land, and I just couldn't understand it. Each week, I showed my grandfather my stars, and we would count them together. Once, while we were doing this, I asked him why, after all that he had done, God had not given Moses his reward. "Well, Neshume-le," he said, "what makes you think this?" I was puzzled. In the story he had told me, after all his hard work Moses only got to *see* the Promised Land and to watch the others go there. Everyone else had been given their dream. It didn't seem fair to me.

When I told this to my grandfather, he smiled. "But Moses did get his dream," he said. "Moses was a leader, Neshume-le, and a leader always has a different dream from the others."

He reminded me of mitzvot, those human actions that help move things in the direction in which God is trying to move them. When a person does such an action, they become God's hands in the world. "There are many mitzvot, but the greatest mitzvah of all is said to be the freeing of captives," he told me. "Moses's dream was for his people to be free. And so his reward was that he got to see that happen. Because he was a leader, his dream was different from the dreams of the people, Neshume-le. A real leader has the same dream that God has."

THE REAL STORY

WHEN I WAS small, my extended family felt that my parents' lack of religious practice was scandalous. One year I was invited to a Seder at the home of one of my relatives who felt that I should be exposed to the ways of my religion.

The Seder is the elaborate ritual dinner that celebrates the holiday of Passover. My first Seder was not a good experience. The prayers and readings of the Passover story were in Hebrew, a language I did not understand. It went on for many hours, and no one was allowed to eat until the last amen. I had been expected to sit patiently without explanations through all of this. By the time the chicken soup was served, it was nine o'clock and I was in tears.

"I'm never going there again," I told my grandfather. "I hate Passover. I hate that stupid story."

"Ah, Neshume-le," he said with a sigh, and then he told me his own version of the Passover story. It goes like this:

Thousands and thousands of years ago the Jewish people were slaves in Egypt. Like slaves everywhere, they suffered greatly and they had a dream of freedom. Their leader, Moses, spoke to God about this dream and the terrible suffering and God encouraged him to go to Pharaoh, the king of Egypt, and tell him to let the Jewish people go. Not surprisingly, Pharaoh refused.

Discouraged, Moses went back to God for help. Faced with the hardness of Pharaoh's heart, God sends suffering, in the form of a plague on the land of Egypt. "Suffering has great power to soften the heart," said my grandfather. But the Pharaoh still refused to free his slaves.

God sends another plague. And another. But the Pharaoh had hardened his heart to both the suffering of the Jews and the suffering of the Egyptians. He makes promises to Moses and goes back on them. Finally God sends the angel of death to take the first-born son of every Egyptian family. This is too much even for the hard heart of the Pharaoh, and he tells Moses that the Jews are free to go.

"Is that the end of the story, Grandpa?" I asked. "No," he said gently, "actually it is only the beginning." I was pleased. The Seder had been so long that I was certain that the story was longer than this. "What happened next?" I asked. He smiled at my impatience. "Well, Moses brings the news of their freedom to the rest," he told me. "Are they very happy, Grandpa?"

"No, Neshume-le, they are not. They told Moses that they did not want to go. They asked many questions. Where are we going? Who will feed us? Where will we sleep? Moses was deeply surprised. He could not answer any of these questions and he did not know what to do. How could he tell God that after all that He had done to make freedom possible, the people did not want to go?"

I was surprised, too. "But they were suffering, Grandpa. Why didn't they want to go?" My grandfather looked sad. "They knew how to suffer," he told me. "They had done it for a long time and they were used to it. They did not know how to be free.

"But when Moses went back to God to tell Him what had happened, God was not surprised at all. He said to Moses, 'Tell the people that I, Myself, will lead them out of Egypt to the Promised Land.' Now," my grandfather said, "this is a very rare thing. Usually God sends others, a Seraph or an Archangel or a Messenger to carry out His Will. But this He will do Himself. Moses tells this to the people and very begrudgingly they leave their homes and go out into the desert. There is no food there, there is no water. And they live there for forty years."

I was shocked. "But what about the Promised Land, Grandpa? Wasn't it true?"

"Yes, it was true, Neshume-le, but the choice people have to make is never between slavery and freedom. We will always have to choose between slavery and the unknown."

"But how can they live without food and water?" I asked in distress.

"They have God, Neshume-le," my grandfather said softly. "Every morning God rains Manna down from heaven and the people eat it. By noon it has evaporated. Every night they shelter beneath the great wing of His presence. Day after day they worry and doubt and day after day God is there. After forty years, even the most doubting of them had learned that God can be trusted. And then they come to the Promised Land."

I sat for awhile thinking of this story, my mind full of pictures. One of them was an image of a long ragged line of people, moving out from the land where they had lived for generations into the darkness and emptiness of the desert, with all their bundles of belongings, their dogs and their cats and their crying children. And at the head of this procession of complaining, worrying, and doubting people is God Himself, in the form of a Pillar of Fire.

"Why does God come Himself, Grandpa?"

"Ah, Neshume-le, many people have puzzled over this question and have thought many different things. What I think is that the struggle toward freedom is too important for God to leave to others. And this is so because only the people who become free can serve God's holy purposes and restore the world. Only those who are not enslaved by something else can follow the goodness in them."

It was almost twenty-five years before I went to another Seder. This time, the service was in English. We all participated by reading parts of the Seder ritual assigned to us by our host. The part I was asked to read contained an obscure command from God. It states that in each generation it is a parent's obligation to tell their children the Passover story and specifies how this is to be done. "And thou shall relate it to thy children in that day, saying, 'This is done on account of that which the Lord did unto me, when I came forth out of Egypt.' "

This phrase is repeated two or three times over in the ritual. Each time I read it aloud, I wondered what it could mean. Why should God insist that something that happened thousands of years ago be personalized in this way? But reading it aloud for the third time, I suddenly realized the truth in it. The story my grandfather had told me did not happen thousands of years in the past. It is happening now. It is the story of every patient I have ever treated, every person I have ever known. It is my own story.

The slavery that keeps us from following our goodness is an inner slavery. We are trapped by ideas of worthlessness and lack of self-esteem, by desire or greed or ignorance. Enslaved by notions of victimhood or entitlement. It is a story about the fear of change, about clinging to places and behaviors that are small and hurtful because letting go of them will mean facing something unknown. I heard again my grandfather's words: "The choice is never between slavery and freedom; we must always choose between slavery and the unknown."

Freedom is as frightening now as it was thousands of years ago. It will always require a willingness to sacrifice what is most familiar for what is most true. To be free we may need to act from integrity, on trust, sometimes for a long time. Few of us will reach our promised land in a day. But perhaps the most important part of the story is that God does not delegate this task. Whenever anyone moves toward freedom, God Himself is there.

It has been said that sometimes we need a story more than food in order to live. For generation after generation in the ritual of the Seder, first the soul is fed by this story. Then we eat the chicken soup.

Few of us are truly free. Money, fame, power, sexuality, admiration, youth; whatever we are attached to will enslave us, and often we serve these masters unaware. Many of the things that enslave us will limit our ability to live fully and deeply. They will cause us to suffer needlessly. The promised land may be many things to many people. For some it is perfect health and for others freedom from hunger or fear, or discrimination, or injustice. But perhaps on the deepest level the promised land is the same for us all, the capacity to know and live by the innate goodness in us, to serve and belong to one another and to life.

ACKNOWLEDGMENTS

THIS BOOK HAS been blessed by many people. May your blessings come back to you a hundredfold.

Blessings to Amy Hertz, my editor, for being simply the best and somehow the first to know what any book is really about. To Esther Newberg for being the only Esther Newberg in the world and the gold standard of integrity. To the unsinkable Susan Petersen Kennedy for the vision and courage that have made Riverhead a place of sanctuary from all that is not genuine in the culture and a place of service for us all.

Blessings to Dean Ornish for the purity of his belief, his lovingkindness and the goodness of his heart, and to Molly Blackwell Ornish for the blessing of her love. To Marion Weber, my unique and visionary colleague, for the great blessing of her friendship and the generosity of her wisdom, to Sukie Miller without whom none of it would ever have happened, and Michael Lerner, whose friendship and colleagueship are simply beyond compare. To Waz Thomas and Jenipher Stowell for listening for hours at all hours and blessing every story, and to Yola Jurzykowski, the dearest, most loyal heart in this world.

Blessings to the good people at Commonweal for their patience, their compassion, and their support, to Michael Rafferty, Mark Rafferty, Mimi Mindel, David and Nadine Parker, Carolyn Brown, Marni Rosen, and Taylor Brooks. Blessings also to Mary Wade and

Iseult Caulfield for their humor, their grace, and their steady hand on the tiller, and to Sharyle Patton for the lightness of her being.

Blessings to Laurance Rockefeller for having become so transparent to the light in him and sharing it with such generosity and for his courageous companionship on this adventure.

Double blessings to Rob Lehman and the board and staff of the Fetzer Institute for their support and partnership, to Charles Halperin, Andrea Kydd, and the Nathan Cummings Foundation for their generosity and belief, to the Project on Death in America for the grace of their collaboration, to Wink Franklin and the board and staff of the Institute for Noetic Sciences for their enduring colleagueship over all these years, and to the MACH Foundation and Yola Jurzykowski for the gift of absolute trust.

A blessing to all those who so generously shared their wisdom and their love on the phone: Charles Terry, Betsy MacGregor, Jon Kabat-Zinn, Jack Kornfield, John Tarrant, Noelle Oxenhandler, Rabbi Zalman Schacter, Rebbitzen Eve Schacter, Barry Barkin, the Baal Shem Barucha, Joan Borysenko, Rabbi Elaine Zecker, and David Eisenberg, and a special blessing to Stephen Mitchell for reading every word and making it kosher.

A bright blessing to you, Brendan O'Regan, who blessed us all so lavishly. We miss you. And to Don Vivekan Flint, whose life blesses us still.

Blessings to all the physicians who have come to the CME programs of the Institute for the Study of Health and Illness at Commonweal and to the medical students at the University of California, San Francisco, School of Medicine. You have restored my belief in medicine and my hope for the future. You are a light in this world.

A loving blessing to those who share the same grandfather: Margaret Rose Walker, Helen Rachel Dignam, Herbert Deleon Pierson, David Joseph Pierson, Rebecca Ziskind and the late A. Arthur Gottlieb; and to those who call him great-grandfather: Nicole Walker Harvila, Michelle Walker Wenske, Edward Vincent Walker, Mindy Gottlieb Davidson, Joanne Meredith Gottlieb, Rebecca Alice Pierson, David Christopher Pierson, David Herbert Pierson, and Natalie Raven Dignam Montijo; and a special blessing to those little ones who call him great-great-grandfather: Melissa Beth Davidson, Karen Leslie Davidson, Isabella Grace Montijo, Wren Anastasia Montijo, and Sophia Rose Wenske.

Blessings and thanks to my assistant Corrie McCluskey for her easy laugh and her strength, for her drop-dead competence and for being there always to research the Web, set up a lecture, or find just the right vitamins at the market. Many blessings to Nina Stradtner who blesses my space and to Josh Dunham Wood who builds it so beautiful, a loving blessing to Jackie Berg for tracking every last one of my numbers and for being my friend, and to Mama Berg for having been such a blessing to us all.

A heartfelt blessing to everyone who read *Kitchen Table Wisdom* and wrote to say that it mattered. It was simply not possible to write back to each one of you, but I read every one of your letters and was upheld and strengthened by them. I hold you all in my heart.

A blessing to everyone whose story adds light to this book and makes it shine; you will know who you are even though I have hidden you in your story, given you another name or another profession or another form of cancer or combined your story with another. Your generous sharing has blessed my life and will, I hope, bless the lives of many others.

And last, a blessing to my beloved grandfather, Rabbi Meyer Ziskind, who knew me before I knew myself and loved me enough to last a lifetime.

PERMISSIONS

Some material in the following chapters is adapted from other sources.

Introduction to Part I

"Build altars in the places . . ." Exodus 20:24. Scripture quotation is taken from the *Holy Bible,* New Living Translation, copyright 1996. Used by permission of Tyndale House Publishers, Inc., Wheaton, Illinois, 60189. All rights reserved.

Rod McIver, interview with Lenore Lefer in *Heron Dance,* issue 23. Richmond, Vermont, 1999. Used by permission.

"The Shell Game"

Rachel Naomi Remen, foreword in *Meditations on Diabetes: Strengthening Your Spirit in All Seasons* by Catherine Feste. Used by permission of the American Diabetes Association, Alexandria, Virginia, 1999.

"Knowing the Heart"

"Days pass and the years vanish . . ." from *Gates of Prayer: The New Union Prayer Book,* copyright © by the Central Conference of American Rabbis and used by permission.

"From the Heart"

LaVera Crawley, "Literature and the Irony of Medical Science," in *Teaching Literature and Medicine.* Anne Hunsaker Hawkins and Marilyn Chandler McEntyre, eds. New York: Modern Language Association of America, 2000. Used by permission.

"Call Home"

Rachel Naomi Remen, foreword in *Stand Like Mountain* by Brian Luke Seaward, published by Health Communication, Inc., Deerfield Beach, Florida: 1997. Used by permission.

Introduction to Part IV

Elaine Weiss, *Surviving Domestic Violence: Voices of Women Who Broke Free,* Agreka Books, University of Utah Press, copyright 2000. Used by permission.